Mrs. Golda Meir, Israel's first Envoy to the Soviet Union, surrounded by thousands of Russian Jews after her first visit to the Moscow synagogue. (September, 1948.)

MOSCOW AND JERUSALEM

MOSCOW AND JERUSALEM

**TWENTY YEARS OF RELATIONS BETWEEN
ISRAEL AND THE SOVIET UNION**

AVIGDOR DAGAN

with an introduction by

ABBA EBAN

ABELARD-SCHUMAN

LONDON   NEW YORK   TORONTO

LONDON	NEW YORK	TORONTO
Abelard-Schuman	Abelard-Schuman	Abelard-Schuman
Limited	Limited	Canada Limited
8 King St. WC2	257 Park Ave. So.	228 Yorkland Blvd.

An Intext Publisher

Printed in the United States of America

ACKNOWLEDGEMENTS

I wish to express my great gratitude to Foreign Minister Abba Eban for kindly introducing my book, and to thank him and Ambassador Gideon Rafael, Director General of the Israel Foreign Ministry for giving me the possibility of writing it by enabling me to use the Ministry's archives.

I would also like to thank my colleagues Ambassadors Gershon Avner, Shmuel Benzur, Katriel Katz and Max Nurock, who have read the manuscript and offered valuable advice on a number of points. I am further grateful to my friends Mr. Eytan Benzur and Mr. Moshe Carmil who have assisted me in procuring required material and information.

The pictures used in this book originate from the photo archives of the Israel Government Press Office and of the Tel Aviv newspaper Maariv. The picture of Mrs. Golda Meir surrounded by masses of Russian Jews in front of the Moscow synagogue, was reprinted from the album "Golda" published by A. Lewin-Epstein (Tel Aviv, 1969).

A.D.

ACKNOWLEDGMENTS

CONTENTS

branch on which it is sitting / Moscow spreading
false accusations against Israel

INTRODUCTION

This study fills a gap in the modern historiography of the Middle East. It surveys Soviet-Israeli relations from 1947 onwards on the basis of documents hitherto unpublished. More important is its clear outline of the structure, methods and basic aims of Soviet policy in the Middle East. While keeping strictly within the confines of Moscow's relations with Israel, the author throws light on Soviet policy in the area and helps the reader to draw conclusions about fundamental features of Soviet policy.

One of the lessons that the free world may learn from the story of Soviet-Israeli relations is that Soviet political thought in this context has had no basis in principle. The line has veered with each new evaluation of the usefulness of Israel on the one hand, and the Arab States on the other, to Soviet global interests. The invasion of Czechoslovakia in August 1968 has taught us that not even a Communist ally is safe from sudden reversals in Moscow's policy. In the early fifties, this fact was not sufficiently known. It was something of a shock when the Soviet statesmen who, a few years earlier, were among the first to champion the right of the Jewish people to independence and to criticize the Arab attack upon Israel, began to lend political aid to the aggressors whom they had so uncompromisingly denounced. It was perhaps less of a shock that, after their Arab wards provoked and lost the Six-Day War of June 1967, Soviet spokesmen fell so low as to speak of Jews as Nazis, and to impute to Israel the genocide of which Israel was very nearly the victim.

The Six-Day War was to a large extent a product and outcome of Soviet policy. For fifteen consecutive years, the Soviet Union barred the Security Council from censuring a single act of Arab hostility towards Israel. Denial of free passage through the Suez Canal and the Straits of Tiran; hindrance of the development of water resources; murder of Israeli citizens on Israeli soil by Arab saboteurs; patronage of terrorist infiltration by Arab Governments; declared and continuous threats of destruction—all these were systematically and automatically shielded by Soviet veto. For twelve years, since 1955, the Soviet Union had launched and sustained a vast program of arms to the Arab States, equipping their arsenals with a proliferation of lethal weapons thought likely to accomplish the declared Arab aim of wiping out Israel. Throughout that time, the Soviet Union uttered no public word about the duty of Arab States to respect Israel's sovereignty and security. Instead, the political, military and economic backing which it extended to Egypt, Syria and other Arab countries actively encouraged the anti-Israeli policy of the Arabs. Unbalanced and biased Soviet propaganda fanned Arab enmity towards Israel, inevitably igniting the fires of war. We have the authority of the former Egyptian Minister of War for the fact that his Government was alarmed by panicky information from Moscow about Israel's intentions. It was a Soviet falsehood concerning "heavy concentrations of Israeli forces on the Syrian border" that gave Egypt the cue to mass its army in Sinai, to expel the international force, and to blockade the Straits of Tiran, which was an act of aggression even by Soviet criteria. Had the Soviet Union fairly distributed its friendship among the peoples of the Middle East, had it desisted from exploiting regional disputes and tensions to further its own ends in the inter-bloc conflict, had it exerted its influence on the Arab world to bring about explicit Arab recognition of Israel's sovereignty and right to security, the Middle East would not have been pushed to the brink of explosion and beyond.

Is the Soviet Union truly interested in permanent peace and stability in the Middle East? The chronicle of Soviet-Israeli relations, as this book describes it in detail, unhappily yields no affirmative answer. The story ends with the rupture of diplomatic relations on June 10, 1967. The subsequent Security Council meetings, disfigured by venomous Soviet outbursts against Israel in a vain attempt to sway the Council into branding Israel as aggressor and compelling it to withdraw unconditionally to the lines of June 4, prove that there has been no real change since then in Soviet postures or plans. The loss of more than a billion dollars' worth of Soviet arms in the Arab debacle of 1967 seems to have pointed out no moral in Moscow. It is hardly symptomatic of reorientation of Soviet policy towards thoughts of an honest and balanced peace that the volume of new Soviet weapons poured into the Arab States has not only made good that enormous deficit but even exceeds it. Arms used by Arab terrorists—murdering and wrecking, with Moscow's indulgence—are almost all of Soviet make. Soviet propaganda still spreads the baseless charge of Israeli "aggression," a slander rejected outright by public opinion throughout the world and specifically by United Nations organs in which Israel's adversaries enjoy a vast numerical advantage. The Soviet Union is rendering a disservice to its Arab friends when it clamors that there is a Security Council resolution calling for the withdrawal of Israeli forces to Armistice lines as of June 4, 1967. There is no such resolution. What has been resolved upon is a policy that looks to the establishment of peace by agreement and, as the first aim, the fixing of recognized and secure borders, an aim to which all other considerations and principles are secondary and contingent.

To this radically new direction of United Nations thinking, Moscow still affects blindness. Even in the so-called "Peace Plan" submitted by it at the beginning of 1969, the enunciation of its policy was again this: "The situation which existed in the region in May 1967 will be renewed." It is not concern for Arab friends but its own global ambitions that prompt the Soviet Union in its efforts to request a renewal of the nightmarish anarchy which not Israel alone but every man of goodwill in the world is determined to end.

Soviet Middle East policy is an extention of Czarist expansionism. The attitude to Israel in 1947 and thereafter was temporary. It became evident that Arab nationalism was more likely than Israel to be a tool of Soviet policy in its global ambitions. In order that this tool might be wielded to maximum profit, Soviet endorsement of the anti-Israeli activities of the Arab States was escalated to dimensions almost without parallel in the history of the nexus between Big Powers and little nations. As recently as February 27, 1969, the absolute identification of Soviet policy with the anti-Israeli operations of the Arab States was climaxed by the Soviet Government—as officially broadcast by the TASS news agency, not only giving its full and explicit backing to Arab terrorism but even presenting that terrorism as justified in international law. Nothing could be more harmful to the chances of progress towards peace.

This book is a sober arraignment. It puts much of the blame for the endless unrest in the Middle East squarely on Moscow's doorstep. Yet it also shows, obliquely, how differently Israeli-Soviet relations could have developed and can still develop; and what boons a change in Soviet policy might bring to all the peoples of the Middle East. Soviet policy, if transformed, could become a stimulus to universal security and peace. Israel has left nothing in its power undone to coexist peacefully with the Soviet Union in a many-faceted cooperation, animated by the spirit of international solidarity which typifies Israel's links with other countries. Is it too much to hope that the Soviet Union will now give testimony of goodwill towards Israel and of a selfless concern for the true welfare of the Middle East by halting the tide of armaments, abandoning hostile propaganda and summoning the Arab States to join hands with Israel in a future of peace?

Abba Eban

* * * * * *

MOSCOW AND JERUSALEM

PART
I

1947-1957

I

1947
The Soviet surprise

There was a big question mark at the very beginning of the relations between Israel and the Soviet Union. Why did Moscow support the establishment of the Jewish State? The question is not less puzzling than the question of exactly why and when the Soviets changed their minds and adopted a hostile rather than a friendly attitude toward the State of Israel which they had helped to create.

Andrei Gromyko, Soviet Representative, in a speech delivered in the General Assembly of the United Nations on May 14, 1947, was in complete contradiction to the explicitly anti-Zionist attitude which both Communist ideologists and practical politicians had expressed repeatedly and consistently over several decades. The only other known instance of Communist authorities abandoning the rigid anti-Zionist line was a short-lived resolution of the Supreme Soviet in August 1919, which stipulated that "inasmuch as the Zionist party has not been designated as counterrevolutionary in previous decrees, and since the cultural-educational activities of the Zionist party do not go contrary to the decisions of the Soviet Government, no

Soviet organization is to place obstacles in the way of that party's aforesaid activities." Before and after that resolution—which, while not specifically revoked, was ignored in practice only a few months later—the Soviets showed only hostility toward Zionism.

Gromyko's speech, therefore, came as a great surprise. From conversations the author had at the time with some leading Communists in Czechoslovakia, both Jews and non-Jews,[1] he gained the impression that the Soviet decision to support the establishment of a Jewish State in Palestine was a surprise for them as well. At the time, he was given a dual explanation of the Soviet step:

1. The Jewish tragedy during World War II was so overwhelming that "something had to be done" for the surviving Jews.
2. The decision took into consideration the opinions of Communist parties outside the Soviet Union which, in a number of countries, were advocating a Popular Front and which had to think of general public opinion in those countries and particularly of the ideas of potential allies among the progressive elements.

The same explanation is offered also in most of the literature about the period. Other reasons given for the Soviet decision are:

3. Moscow was disappointed with the Arab nationalist movement which, during the war, was pro-German.
4. Above all, in Soviet eyes most Arab Governments in the years immediately after the war were pro-British, while the Jews in Palestine, engaged in a bitter struggle against Britain's Mandatory Power, were regarded as a potential ally in the fight against the West.

---

1. Among them were Vlado Clementis, later Minister of Foreign Affairs, executed during the Slánský trial, and Eduard Goldstuecker, later Czechoslovakia's first, and so far only, Minister to Israel. Goldstuecker, as Rector of the University of Prague and President of the Czech Writers' Association, played an important role during the "Czech Spring" in 1968. He lives now in exile in England.

Some of these reasons may be partly correct, but none of the authors who have tackled the problem seems to be entirely satisfied with them. At least one—W.Z. Laqueur, in *The Soviet Union and the Middle East*—gives clear expression to his doubts by adding that "the Palestine problem was for the Soviet Union a secondary issue to which nobody in Moscow attached much importance" and that "there is, in fact, some doubt whether the decision to support the establishment of a Jewish State was taken at top level; in view of subsequent developments, it is at least possible that this course of action was recommended by some Foreign Ministry advisers and approved by Stalin in a fit of absentmindedness."

It is difficult to take seriously the suggestion that this was how things worked in Moscow in Stalin's time or at any later stage. The theory presenting the matter as a chance decision is even less credible than the theory of "expiation of Gentile conscience." The Palestine problem in itself may have been a "secondary issue" for Moscow, but it must not be viewed in isolation. In the wider context of Soviet postwar policy it could not have been entirely unimportant.

We know today that the Soviet Union, in the first years following the end of World War II, overestimated its chances of penetrating into the Mediterranean area. The basis for the assessment, which later proved wrong, can be easily understood in the light of the situation in 1946 and 1947. France and Italy had Communist parties of a strength unparalleled in the history of the Communist movement in the West. In Greece, the Communist guerrillas were as yet undefeated. At the time Gromyko was delivering his speech, Yugoslavia was still firmly in the Soviet bloc and the break with Tito was more than a year away. It is worth remembering that at the Paris Peace Conference in April 1946, Molotov demanded that the Soviets be given a sole trusteeship over Libya. (A month later, in May, the Russians changed their demand and asked that Libya be restored to Italy under a United Nations trusteeship. It can be assumed that the change was motivated by the desire not only to eliminate the influence of the Western Powers but also to strengthen the

Italian Communists, who could then claim that Libya was in fact returned to Italy—thanks to the Communist Soviet Union.)

On the eastern shores of the Mediterranean, there were—at least in Russian eyes—the pro-British Arab regimes on the one hand and, on the other, the Jews craving for a state of their own and fighting the British to achieve this aim. We know that, at least during the year prior to Gromyko's speech, discussions were taking place concerning the probable developments in the Arab League countries. The Soviet Orientalist Lutski, in his book on the Arab League (*Liga Arabskikh Gosudarstev*), argued that progressive elements in the Arab world had a good chance of gaining the upper hand because of the weakness of the reactionary leaders of the League. However, in another book published almost simultaneously (*Arabski Vostok v Mezhdunarodnykh Otnosheniakh*), another Russian Middle East expert, P. V. Milogradov, found the feudal rulers of Arab countries still powerful, recalled their Fascist ties, and was not at all optimistic about the chances of turning the Arab League into a progressive political body.

By the spring of 1947, the view prevailed that a change of heart in the ruling circles of the Arab countries was unlikely and that the Arab League was just "a tool of British imperialism." (This view remained prevalent in Soviet publications at least till 1950. Only later—for instance, in L. Petrov's article in *Trud*, April 15, 1950—does the League become a toy in the hands of American, instead of British, imperialists.) These factors, as far as can be ascertained without access to Soviet archives, constituted the probable basis for Moscow's decision to support the establishment of Israel. The decisive factors may be summarized as follows:

1. Soviet *Drang nach Westen* and hope to penetrate into the Mediterranean area.
2. The Soviet's belief in the necessity to eliminate Great Britain, the strongest Western Power at that time, from the area.
3. The Soviet's negative assessment of the usefulness of the Arab countries in this effort, and the erroneous evaluation of the Jews'

readiness to fight, after the establishment of the State of Israel, for anything but the interests of the new state.

The decision, therefore, was based on a cool evaluation of the factors that Moscow at the time believed would best further its power interests and for the attainment of which it was ready to forget, at least temporarily, past ideological objections to Zionism. The decision did not rest on any pro-Jewish sentiments.

II

Explanation of Soviet support for the establishment of the State of Israel

Such sentiments never existed. What brought the Soviet Union to the support of the State of Israel were not Russian sympathies but Moscow's assessment that there was a coincidence of interests which the Soviets could use to foster their own aims. Again one can quote Lutski—this time from his book, *Anglijskij Amerikanskij Imperializm na Blizhnem Vostoke*—who described the Soviet Union as "the only true friend of Jewish national independence." But the explanation he gave for this sweeping statement—that the United States merely pretended to support the State of Israel while in fact trying to truncate the state through secret arrangements with Britain, sabotaging the United Nations resolution on Palestine, and finally extending only *de facto* recognition to Israel—made it rather obvious that this main intention was anti-American and anti-Western, not pro-Israeli.

Even Gromyko's speech of May 14, 1947, in which he stressed that both Arabs and Jews "have historical roots in Palestine" and stated that it would be unjust "to deny the right of the Jewish people to realize [their] aspirations to establish their own state," was prefaced by a strong attack on Britain. He accused the British of changing Palestine into an armed camp, a police state which was not concerned with improving the material conditions and raising the cultural level of the population. However justified the accusations may have been, one cannot escape the impression that from the Soviet point of view, the part of the speech stressing the "bankruptcy" of the British Mandatory Administration was not less important than the recognition of the right of the Jewish people to a state of their own. Neither should it be forgotten that Gromyko underlined the point that he advocated the establishment of a Jewish state— "only if relations between the Jewish and Arab populations of Palestine indeed proved to be so bad that it would be impossible to reconcile them and to ensure the peaceful coexistence of the Arabs and Jews." In other words, he made it clear that the Soviet Union would, in fact, prefer the establishment of a binational state. All this is mentioned not to minimize in any way the importance of the speech but to bring into focus the real concern of Moscow: the elimination of British and Western influence in another part of the Mediterranean and Middle Eastern area.

The idea of a bi-national state was soon relinquished entirely, but all other points in Gromyko's speech were consistently developed in Soviet contributions to the discussions that followed.

On October 13, 1947, the Soviet delegate, Semen Tsarapkin, declared that "relations between Arabs and Jews had reached such a state of tension that it had become impossible to reconcile their points of view on the solution of the problem." He repeated in the Ad Hoc Committee that it would be unjust to deny to the Jewish people the right to create a state of their own. "Every people—and that includes the Jewish people—has full right to demand that their fate should not depend on the mercy or the goodwill of a particular state. Members of the United Nations could help the Jewish people by acting in accordance with the principles of the Charter, which called for guaranteeing to every people their right to independence and self-determination."

In the final debate on the Ad Hoc Committee's recommendations on November 26, 1947, Gromyko spoke again. His speech again contained strong attacks and charges against Britain, as well as criticism of the speeches made by representatives of Arab countries. Gromyko asserted that "the solution of the Palestine problem based on a partition of Palestine into two separate states will be of profound historical significance, because this decision will meet the legitimate demands of the Jewish people." He emphasized, however, that the partition plan was not directed against the Arabs. On the contrary, "this decision corresponds to the fundamental national interests . . . of the Arabs as well as of the Jews." Rejecting Arab speakers' "attempts to cast aspersion on the foreign policy of the Government of the Soviet Union," Gromyko declared:

> The Government and the peoples of the Soviet Union have entertained and still entertain a feeling of sympathy for the national aspirations of the nations of the Arab East. The U.S.S.R.'s attitude towards the efforts of these peoples to rid themselves of the last fetters of colonial dependence is one of understanding and sympathy. Therefore, we do not identify with the vital national interests of the Arabs the clumsy statements made by some of the representatives of Arab States about the foreign policy of the Soviet Union. . . . We draw a distinction between these statements . . . and the basic and permanent interests of the Arab people.

Then he made the following prophetic statement:

> The Soviet delegation is convinced that Arabs and Arab States will still, on more than one occasion, be looking towards Moscow and expecting the U.S.S.R. to help them in the struggle for their lawful interests. . . .

This statement would seem to support the somewhat Machiavellian thought, later expressed by certain political analysts, that the Russians, in fact, supported the establishment of the Jewish State merely to force the Arabs to "look towards Moscow." The idea is not borne out by Russian behavior at the time, but of course it can be neither proved nor disproved.

One more delicate point should be mentioned here. Gromyko delivered his speech only one day after *Pravda* asserted that "the time was coming when the people of the Iranian province of Azerbeijan, bordering the Soviet Union, would regain their freedom." If there was need for further demonstrating the necessity of seeing the Soviet decision in the wider context of Moscow's increased interest in the Mediterranean and Middle Eastern area at the time, here it was.

III

1948
Full Soviet support of Israel during its War of Liberation

Whatever the real reasons behind the Soviet decision to support the establishment of the Jewish State may have been, there is no doubt that the positive attitude toward Israel, adopted in 1947, remained unchanged throughout the following year. A long series of quotations from speeches by Soviet (and Soviet bloc) representatives, delivered in 1948, proves the coinciding interests of the Soviet Union and Israel at the time.

In March 1948, when the Americans, apparently having had second thoughts, tried to change the Assembly decision of November 29, 1947, and to substitute a temporary United Nations trusteeship for the partition plan, Gromyko, on March 30, accused the United States of being "concerned not with the just settlement of the question of the future of Palestine and the relations between Arabs and Jews, but with its own oil interests and military-strategic positions in the Near East." He claimed that the establishment of a trusteeship "would harm the peoples of Palestine—the Arabs and the Jews—whose legitimate rights have already been sufficiently violated in the past, particularly during the period of the administration of Palestine under the Mandate," and insisted on the implementation of the partition resolution which the Soviet Union had accepted "precisely because this decision corresponds to the interests of both peoples inhabiting Palestine, each of which has the right to create an independent State."

In meetings of the First Committee in April and May 1948, Gromyko (on April 20), the Byelorussian delegate, Kaminski (on April 21), and the Ukrainian representative, Vasili Tarassenko (on April 22), made a concerted attack against "politically bankrupt Britain" and against United States efforts to "wreck the decision on the partition of Palestine." On April 23, the Soviet delegate, Aleksandr Panyushkin, reiterating that the decision of November 29, 1947, "met the deep-rooted national interests of the Arabs and Jewish peoples of Palestine," laid the blame for the situation in Palestine on "the United Kingdom, whose policy was calculated to kindle national hatred between Arabs and Jews." He spoke of "Arab bands" which had penetrated into Palestine with the connivance of Britain. "Arab and Jewish blood is being spilled in Palestine in order to satisfy the interests of the United Kingdom and the United States." The Soviet delegate, Semen Tsarapkin, on May 3 qualified the willingness of the Arab States to examine the question of trusteeship as "merely a political maneuver on the part of certain circles in the Arab States [whose] aim was to rid themselves of the resolution of November 29, so as to satisfy some territorial and political claims later." On May 4, ten days before the actual proclamation of Israel's independence, Gromyko declared that "a Jewish State is in existence, in spite of attempts by certain countries to impede the implementation of partition." On the very day of Israel's Proclamation of Independence, when the Special Assembly session was discussing the American proposal to appoint a United Nations mediator, Gromyko used the fact of "the existence of one of the two States provided for in the General Assembly's resolution, the Jewish State," as an argument against the appointment.

In the Security Council debates of 1948, the Soviet delegation consistently followed the line adopted in May 1947. On April 16, Gromyko strongly opposed several paragraphs of the truce resolution which, in the opinion of the Soviet Union—and also of the representatives of the Jewish Agency for Palestine—were "directed against the interests of one of the parties." Among other things, he opposed the paragraph which would have stopped Jewish immigration to Palestine "since [such] a resolution by the Security Council would not only fail to meet the lawful and incontestable interests of the Jews but would, on the contrary, be prejudicial to their interests and aggravate their position." At the same time he demanded—as a "minimum requirement"—"the prohibition of all further entry into Palestine of armed bands or detachments from outside. . . . We cannot admit that it is right to speak of a truce while leaving on the territory of Palestine foreign bands which have invaded the country with weapons in their hands in order to fight against the other party." In the meetings of April 23 and May 12, Gromyko and Tarassenko continued to oppose technical points of the truce resolution which would have been detrimental to Jewish interests and fought against the American proposal of a United Nations trusteeship which aimed to supplant the partition resolution.

After the armed attack on Israel by the Arab States, Gromyko, on May 18, condemned the Arab countries "which are prepared to accept any decision, if only they can thwart the possibility of the creation of an Arab State in Palestine together with the creation of a Jewish State." On May 20, Tarassenko attacked Britain as being directly responsible for the war in Palestine, or at least "for the actions of Transjordan's armed forces in the State of Israel [which are] manifestly illegal and manifestly aimed at a breach of peace in Palestine. . . . The United Kingdom bears the responsibility because it has inspired the actions of the Transjordanian armed forces. These forces are in fact armed forces of the United Kingdom . . . commanded by British officers, maintained by British money, closely connected with Britain and subject to British High Command. . . . The United Kingdom Government is doing all it can to thwart the possibility of putting an end to the disorders in Palestine." On May 21, Gromyko continued the attack on Britain, coupling it this time, however, with strong criticism of the Arab States:

The Soviet delegation cannot but express surprise at the position adopted by the Arab States in the Palestine question, and particularly at the fact that those States—or some of them, at least—have resorted to such action as sending their troops to Palestine and carrying out military operations aimed at the suppression of the national liberation movement in Palestine. . . . We can only wonder at the course taken by the Arab States, which have not yet achieved their own full liberation from foreign influence, and some of which have not even real national independence.

On May 27, Tarassenko repeated that the armed struggle in Palestine was taking place "as a result of the unlawful invasion by a number of States of the territory of Palestine, which does not form part of the territory of any of the States whose armed forces have invaded it." On May 28, he again attacked Britain in these words:

It is no exaggeration to say that the United Kingdom resolution is designed to stifle the State of Israel and the Jewish people in Palestine. The United Kingdom resolution would induce the Security Council to adopt a form of nonintervention [while] we have recently heard one of the parties state repeatedly that it considers it has an imprescriptible right to carry out armed intervention in the internal affairs of Palestine, to destroy the State of Israel by force of arms and to bombard the peaceful cities of Israel under the pretext of restoring order.

He further criticized the British draft resolution for making it possible for the Arabs to renew fighting in a few weeks, while during that period the balance of forces "will have changed unjustly and to the advantage of the invaders." The resolution, in Tarassenko's words, "proposes that the Security Council should set the seal of legality on the blockade of the State of Israel." In the same speech, he also said:

We do not know of a single case of invasion of the territory of another State by the armed forces of Israel, except in self-defense, where they had to beat off attacks by the armed forces of other

States on Israeli territory. That was self-defense in the full sense of
the word. . . .

Jewish immigration cannot constitute a threat to the security of the
Arab States. It is insignificant in comparison with the population of
the Arab countries. There would be no point in banning Jewish
immigration on the basis of such considerations, apart from the fact
that the Security Council would be in danger of encroaching upon
the sovereign rights of a State, contrary to the provisions of the
Charter of the United Nations.

Again Gromyko, on May 29:

What is happening in Palestine can only be described as military
operations organized by a group of States against the new Jewish
State. . . . The States whose forces have invaded Palestine have
ignored the Security Council's resolution. This is not the first time
that the Arab States, which organized the invasion of Palestine,
have ignored a decision of the Security Council or the General
Assembly. The Soviet delegation deems it essential that the Council
should state its opinion more clearly and more firmly with regard
to this attitude of the Arab States towards the decisions of the
Security Council.

On July 7, Gromyko criticized Count Folke Bernadotte, U.N.
mediator in the Arab-Israeli dispute, for trying to override
United Nations decisions:

The Mediator proposes the creation of a union comprising the
Jewish State and Transjordan. . . . The Mediator's proposals . . .
provide for a redrawing of the Jewish State's boundaries, with the
aim of cutting down the territory of that State and transferring the
cut-off portions to Transjordan, together with the part of Palestine
earmarked for the Arab State. This in itself reveals the origin and
aim of the Mediator's proposals. The authors of these proposals are
prepared to hand over the whole of the territory allotted to the Arab
State, to Transjordan, which is governed by a puppet king in the pay
of the British Treasury, although Transjordan is not entitled to one
single inch of that territory. . . . World public opinion has already

condemned the action of certain Arab circles that attacked the Jewish State and occupied the territory allotted to the Arab State in Palestine.

On July 8, after news of renewed fighting had reached the Security Council, Gromyko characterized the renewal of hostilities as "an adventure by certain Arab circles in Palestine, whose aim it is to wreck the United Nations decision at all costs, and whose actions are encouraged by certain States." On July 13, he criticized the Mediator for his suggestion to arrange a plebiscite in Palestine and described the proposal as being contrary to the General Assembly's decision on Palestine. On July 14, he enlarged on his criticism of Count Bernadotte, condemning him for "absolutely ignoring the fact that a resolution on the future of Palestine already existed" and asserting that his "new proposals added fuel to the flames and went a long way to encourage those who started the fighting in Palestine." In the same speech, he said:

> During the truce there were various quite inadmissible acts of provocation on the part of the British puppet, King Abdullah. . . . Open preparations for a renewal of fighting were carried out by the Arabs, who dispatched their troops to invade Palestinian territory and made no bones about informing the whole world that it was their firm intention to prevent the creation of independent Arab and Jewish States in Palestine.

On July 15, it was the Ukrainian delegate, Dmitri Manuilski, President of the Security Council at the time, who continued the attack on the Mediator, condemning, in particular, the plebiscite proposal. "He cannot but be aware that the adoption of such a proposal would mean the liquidation of the State of Israel." Manuilski at the same time lashed out at Britain which, "despite the termination of the Mandate, does not want to lose Palestine, [but] wishes to maintain its domination over that country through Arab instrumentality, through puppets, either the Transjordanian King Abdullah or any other similar candidate." Finally Manuilski criticized American policy on Palestine as torn between two tendencies, one taking into account the "compact Jewish population, a group which warmly supports the establishment of a State of Israel in Palestine," the other trying to secure the interests of American oil companies. "Clearly a victory of the second tendency in the settlement of the Palestine question would not portend any good for the State of Israel."

Also on July 15, the Soviet delegate, Yakub Malik, spoke against the British objection to the use of the term "Provisional Government of Israel" in the American draft resolution. (This was after American and Soviet recognition of Israel but before the State had been recognized by Britain.) In the same meeting, Malik took exception to the American proposal on the demilitarization of Jerusalem.

On July 27, Manuilski and Malik reacted to the British request that the Security Council deal with the case of the five members of the staff of the Jerusalem Electric Corporation who were kidnapped by I.Z.L. men[2] as "virtually amounting to interference in the domestic affairs of the State of Israel."

On August 18, Malik, then President of the Security Council, spoke on the problem of refugees. Some passages in his speech are not without interest even today:

It is remarkable that the representative of the United Kingdom laid such great emphasis on the Arabs' so-called fear of Jewish immigration into Palestine. His remarks were so worded as to convey the impression that he was determined to develop that fear among the Arabs, instead of helping to dissipate it. . . . Who is responsible for the fact that half a million people are subjected to privation, suffering and all the hardships common to refugees? . . .

Responsibility . . . lies in the first place with the Government of the United Kingdom and with the British military authorities in the

---

2. I.Z.L. is the abbreviation of Irgun Zwai Leumi (National Military Organization), military branch of the right-wing New Zionist (Revisionist) Organization active during the British Mandate.

Near East. A large share of the responsibility rests also with certain influential circles in the United States of America who, in the interests of the U.S. oil companies, have sought to secure the revision of the General Assembly decision on Palestine of November 29, 1947. . . . The only way to ensure the settlement of the Palestine problem and the restoration of half a million Arab refugees to their peaceful labor and habits [Malik did not speak of restoration to their former homes] is to implement the resolution on Palestine which the General Assembly adopted on November 29, 1947.

The pro-Israeli—and, of course, at the same time, anti-British and anti-American—line of Soviet policy continued. There is, however, good reason to interrupt the quotations from the speeches of Soviet representatives in United Nations discussions. In August 1948, a Soviet legation was opened in Tel Aviv, and at the beginning of September, Golda Meir, Israel's first Minister to the Soviet Union, and her staff arrived in Moscow. From then on, the United Nations ceased to be the only forum of Israeli-Soviet contacts and dialogue.

IV

1948
Establishment of diplomatic missions in Moscow and Tel Aviv
Israeli and Soviet Jewry
Ehrenburg's article in *Pravda* September 21
Moscow's line: Israel *yes*, Zionism *no*
Support of Israel continued

Golda Meir arrived in Moscow on September 6, 1948. The next day she was received by Foreign Minister Molotov. In her cable describing the meeting, she reported that he "expressed his confidence in the strength of our State and its Government and that we shall overcome." The presentation of credentials in the Kremlin on September 10 passed in a "friendly atmosphere." On September 15, Mrs. Meir visited the Deputy Minister of Foreign Affairs, Valerian Zorin, and spoke about Negev frontiers, the refugee question and Jerusalem. "Zorin promised that their line will not be changed and that they will help in every justified claim." Two days later, the first business talks with Soviet authorities (about supplying wheat and barley to Israel) opened with promising prospects.

Everything seemed to go well on the government-to-government level. Then, on September 21, the notorious article by Ilya Ehrenburg appeared in *Pravda*. There is little doubt about what motivated the article. It came after "touching scenes" occurred during the first visit of the Israelis to the Moscow synagogue (on September 11), where they were called to the Reading of the Law, Rattner, the military attaché, in uniform; after the Israelis' visit to the Jewish Theater on September 16, with "enormous

excitement around us," and after the question of Jewish immi-
gration from the Soviet Union to Israel was raised in Mrs.
Meir's first meeting with the head of the Foreign Ministry's
Middle Eastern Department (and also on September 16[3]).
Obviously, the Russians decided to let the Israelis—and the
Soviet Jews—know that they drew a line between their support
of the State of Israel and the solution of their own Jewish
question. Israel *yes*, Zionism *no*. That was the tenor of Ehrenburg's article. Soviet Jews were not to have any contact with
Jews outside the Soviet Union. There would be no immigration
to Israel from Communist countries.

On Rosh Hashanah (the Jewish New Year), October 6, 1948,
tens of thousands of Jews welcomed the Minister of Israel and
her staff in front of the synagogue, and spontaneously formed
a procession which accompanied the Israelis to the highway
on their departure. The following month the Yiddish review
Einigkeit, which had dared, at least indirectly, to criticize
Ehrenburg's article, was suppressed, the Jewish Anti-Fascist
Committee was liquidated and its leaders were arrested.

It has often been said that this marked the end of the "friendship" between Israel and the Soviet Union. This view is not
difficult to rebut. It is true that the enthusiasm of the Russian
Jews for the young State of Israel most probably came as a
shock to the Soviet authorities. They may have been honest in
their surprise at the fact that Jews, who had the good fortune
of living in the great Communist State in which "a Jewish
question did not exist," should be looking to Israel as their real
homeland. For over thirty years, Russia had not experienced a
spontaneous, not Party-inspired, demonstration of the kind
Moscow witnessed during Rosh Hashanah that year. Also unexpected and embarrassing to the Soviets was the fact that Israel
should have raised the question of immigration almost immediately after the establishment of diplomatic relations. But if they
felt they had to take definite action, the steps were directed, for

---

3. On September 16, 1948, the first applications for immigration to Israel
reached the Legation in Moscow.

the time being, not against Israel, but against the Zionist yearn-
ing of their own Jews. While it was clear to everyone in Israel
that the Jewish State could not abandon the three million Russian Jews, the Soviets may have been harboring the illusion that
friendly relations with Israel were compatible with a repressive
policy toward the Russian Jews.

True, there were warning signals. On September 24, Golda
Meir cabled that the Soviet press was stressing that the Soviet
Union was supporting Israel's struggle because "our opponents
[are] imperialists and our aim [is] real independence." Explaining the word "real," she added that in conversations with Foreign Office officials, they made it clear that "they are sure of our
anti-British attitude but not of our ability not to be dependent
on America." On December 2, Mordekhai Namir, then Coun-
selor at the Legation in Moscow,[4] reported his conversation
with Ehrenburg. "His friendly advice [was] to suppress all
efforts to attract [Soviet Jews] to Zionism and to *aliyah* [Jewish
immigration to Israel] if we do not want to bring upon ourselves
the wrath of the authorities as well as of the local Jews." On
December 16, *Novoye Vremya* mentioned, for the first time, the
lack of gratitude shown by Israel in the anti-Soviet attitude of
its press despite the consistent help which the Soviet Union was
giving the Jewish State.

However, the Soviet line remained unchanged in everything
concerning the relations between the two States. On November
9, Golda Meir attended the military parade during the October
Revolution celebrations, and was afterward invited, with other
Heads of Missions, to Molotov's house. She cabled that "in the
opinion of diplomats, the Israelis were the center of attention"
at the party. Over a glass of vodka, Mrs. Meir said to Molotov,
"If we only had a small part of the weapons that I saw at the
parade today!" And Molotov answered: "You will. We also had
to start from scratch."

That was in Moscow. There were no signs of change in the

---

4. Mordekhai Namir later became Secretary General of the Histadrut (Israel
Trade Unions Organization) and Mayor of Tel Aviv.

Soviet attitude at the United Nations either. Andrei Vyshinsky, head of the Soviet U.N. delegation, on September 25, 1948, continued with his criticism of the Security Council for having "failed to carry out its duty with respect to the Palestine question" by ignoring the General Assembly decision of November 29, 1947. On October 28, Malik stressed the importance of "changing the truce into a lasting official peace . . . by means of direct negotiations." On December 11, the Czechoslovak delegate, Houdek, made the following statement:

> Israel is a reality which has not been seriously challenged by the regrettable and uncompromising attitude of the Arab States. The actual existence of the Jewish State, therefore, must always be taken into consideration. In view of that fact, the Assembly is no longer entitled to make any territorial arrangements of a fundamental character, because that would signify an infringement of the sovereignty of the State of Israel. . . . Such an action on the part of the Assembly would represent a flagrant violation of the Charter, its purposes and principles, and more particularly of Art. 2, par. 7 thereof. No territorial changes or exchanges are therefore permissible unless mutually agreed upon by both parties.

At the same meeting, Vyshinsky spoke against British efforts of "taking from Israel the Negev territory which comprises approximately two-thirds of the State of Israel."

There certainly was nothing to indicate any change of heart on the part of the Soviet Union.

V

1949
First doubts and first warnings

Some indication of second thoughts, or at least of uncertainty and nervousness in Moscow, became noticeable at the beginning of 1949. In February of that year, the Soviet press carried the first news about Western preparation of a Middle East pact, quoting Italian reports of assumed Israeli participation. On February 13, the Soviet Ambassador in Washington, Panyushkin, invited Ambassador Elath to lunch and inquired if the rumor that Israel was about to join the Marshall Plan was true. He added (to quote Elath's report of the conversation) that the Soviets "had no intention to ask Israel to join their bloc, but their demand was that Israel should remain entirely independent from foreign influence and rule."

On March 14, Chargé d'Affaires Namir visited Vyshinsky to convey the congratulations of the Government of Israel on his appointment as Foreign Minister. He used the opportunity to assure Vyshinsky that "the Government and the people of Israel greatly appreciate and will never forget the great role the Soviet Union has played in our proud struggle for our rights," and to express the hope that, during his term of office, "the friendly relations between our two countries will continue and become even stronger." Vyshinsky showed no sign of doubt on this occasion. He answered:

We have a common interest. [The literal translation from Russian is: We have a work in common.] It was not by chance that the Soviet Union supported Israel's claim for independence. This attitude resulted from the basic principles of the policy of the Soviet Union in national questions. The Soviet Union supported your claims from the very beginning, when the situation was still very difficult. She did so and is doing so with both hands and wholeheartedly. We too hope that the friendly relations will continue as before and will be strengthened to the mutual good of our two countries.

The first proof that some uncertainty about Israel did in fact exist in the mind of the Soviet Government came on April 16, on the occasion of Golda Meir's farewell visit to Vyshinsky.[5] When she used the opportunity to convey to him the decision of the Government of Israel to remain neutral vis-à-vis the two blocs, Vyshinsky found it necessary to ask her to clarify whether this meant that Israel would not join an anti-Soviet alliance and would not give it military bases. He showed "complete satisfaction" when Golda Meir confirmed the correctness of this interpretation. To dissipate any lingering doubts, she added that the American loan Israel had received a few weeks earlier was granted without any political conditions—TASS had cabled from Tel Aviv on March 20, quoting Mikunis (Secretary General of the Israeli Communist Party [MAKI]), that the loan represented a fortification of imperialist positions and enabled the Anglo-Saxon Powers to exercise control over the economic sovereignty of Israel. She suggested an expansion of economic relations between Israel and the Soviet Union by a Soviet long-term credit.

There was another warning sign in Namir's conversation with Deputy Foreign Minister Zorin on May 5. Zorin went out of his way to sound friendly, and he expressed admiration for the way in which "Israel solved, in one year, all its main problems: pushed out the British, gained independence, inflicted military defeat on Arab armies, and forced them to sign armistice agreements." But when Namir remarked that there might still be

5. Mrs. Meir was recalled from Moscow in April 1949 to become Minister of Labor in Ben Gurion's Government.

difficult times ahead and that Israel might need the help of friends in future too, Zorin answered that Soviet "support will continue all the time that Israel will continue on the right political line."

Zorin did not specify what Moscow regarded as the "right political line" for Israel to follow, but it was becoming increasingly clear that the impression that Israel was inclining toward the West was gaining ground among the Soviet leadership. Moshe Sharett, Foreign Minister of Israel, did everything to dissipate this impression. In June, he decided to invite Gromyko to Israel, hoping that the visit—which certainly would not be to the West's liking—would serve as proof of Israel's neutrality. In October, Namir was instructed to inform the Soviet authorities that the reports, according to which the Israeli armed forces were to be organized on the American pattern, were lacking all basis.

All this was duly registered in Moscow, but the worm of doubt kept gnawing. The declaration of basic principles adopted by the Knesset (Israel's Parliament) in the spring (on March 9), in which Israel declared its "loyalty to the principles of the United Nations Charter and friendship with all freedom-loving States, and in particular with the United States and with the Soviet Union," was forgotten in the autumn. At the end of October, a report reached Israel of an unpublished interview between Vyshinsky and an Egyptian journalist. According to the report, Vyshinsky denied that the Soviet Union had refused to grant a loan to Israel for political reasons. Israel was, in the eyes of the Soviet Union, the only true democracy in the Near East. But he added: "We hope that Israel will refuse American demands for military bases. If it is proved that Israel is working for Anglo-American interests, then the Soviet Union will see in Israel a nondemocratic State that will not be able to enjoy the support of the Soviet Union." A few days later, on November 2, *Vechernaya Moskva* published a TASS cable from Tel Aviv, quoting *Kol Haam* (*Voice of the People*, organ of Israel's Communist Party), which attacked Ben Gurion for "openly joining [in a meeting of Mapai] the American camp of warmongers and the policy of cold war against the Soviet Union."

Very little of all this was evident in the United Nations debates of 1949. In the Security Council's discussion of Israel's application for United Nations membership on March 3, Malik reminded the Council that

As early as December 1948, at the Security Council meeting in Paris, the Soviet delegation . . . spoke in favor of Israel's admission, as it considered that there was already every reason for the Security Council to examine the application of the State of Israel and to reach a favorable decision on it . . . as it is well known that the Israeli Government is a peace-loving Government which loyally complied with the requirements of the United Nations and in particular with the Security Council's orders. . . .

A few other passages from the same speech, all of them pro-Israeli, are worth quoting:

Yesterday many members of the Council rejoiced and exulted at the conclusion of an agreement between Egypt and the State of Israel. The attitude and statements of the Egyptian representative show, however, that excessive optimism may be somewhat premature in this field.

Leave the Jewish people to themselves and they will be masters of the territory assigned to them. But that is, evidently, not to the liking of some international monopolies and aggressive circles, and they are trying to prevent its realization.

Statements have also been made on the Arab refugee question, but why should the State of Israel be blamed for the existence of that problem?

In the Ad Hoc Committee on the same issue, the Soviet delegate, Aleksandr Soldatov, on May 4, deplored

the efforts of certain delegations to postpone a decision, making [Israel's] admission conditional upon the internationalization of Jerusalem and solution of the refugee problem. There are grounds to believe that the unconditional admission of Israel could accelerate the solution of problems outstanding in the interest of peace and security in Palestine. Unconditional admission does not, however, absolve Israel from implementing the resolutions previously adopted by the Assembly . . . in the interest of reestablishing friendly and stable relations between Arabs and Jews.

On May 9, Malik repeated that admission of Israel should not be conditional upon any question arising from the discussion of the Palestine issue in the General Assembly.

In the Assembly debate on May 11, the Russians did not take the rostrum, but left it to the Polish delegate, Drohojewski, to speak for the entire Soviet bloc. Drohojewski's speech, while pro-Israeli in effect, contained the only warning undertone heard from the Soviet bloc in the United Nations that year. He began by saying that recent statements by Israel's President, Chaim Weizmann, with regard to the Holy Places and the future relations between Israel and its neighbors were to be noted with satisfaction. Poland also expected that the problem of Arab refugees would be settled in a just and equitable manner. Then he went on:

The period of sentimental interest in the fate of Israel has come to an end; an era of cooperation based on mutual interest is beginning. The Jewish people, advancing along peaceful and progressive lines, could rely on the assistance of Poland, the Soviet Republics and the People's Democracies of Europe. Israel will doubtless remember that those countries had been its true friends at the troubled time of its emergence. It was not long since the British Foreign Office had tried and failed to prevent the creation of Israel. United Kingdom and United States diplomacy had been ready to betray the new State before its birth. The United States Government's change of policy with regard to Israel had occurred for reasons of political expediency divorced from any sense of justice or faith in Israel's future. That should not be forgotten. . . . Neither should it be forgotten that Israel was deeply indebted to the working classes. Poland will watch the future of Israel with sympathetic interest.

This was clear language. However, for the time being there were no portents that the Soviets intended going beyond this warning. The line with respect to the Middle East problems before the United Nations did not change. In August, Tsarapkin called twice for direct negotiations as demanded by Israel. On August 8, he said in the Security Council while its President:

> Now that armistice agreements have been voluntarily concluded, the next [task] is . . . to draw up definite agreements . . . to provide for a final and permanent peace settlement for Palestine. . . . Some think that the final peace settlement should be left to the Concilia- tion Commission. . . . There are, however, very strong indications that this final peace settlement can be reached—and in our view must be reached—by direct negotiations between the parties, with- out outside influence or outside pressure. . . .

And two days later, on August 10, he repeated:

> All the decisions of the Security Council and of the General Assem- bly especially stress the principle that the parties should reach agreement and settle the questions between them independently and by direct negotiations. . . . Experience has shown that there is no need for a third party which would bring pressure to bear on the parties concerned.

On December 9, Tsarapkin still called King Abdullah of Transjordan a "British puppet and an obedient henchman of United Kingdom policy in the Middle East," and added: "In order to destroy the new State, the United Kingdom had pro- voked the intrusion of foreign elements in Palestine. Through the Arab Legion, the British had taken possession of an impor- tant piece of territory in Arab Palestine, including a sector of the City of Jerusalem."

The situation of Russian Jewry considerably deteriorated in 1949. During the High Holy Days there were again thousands of Jews in the street in front of the synagogue, but nobody dared to approach members of the Israeli Legation. Too many had been arrested the year before for showing in some way their pro-Israeli sentiments (though on Yom Kippur [the Day of Atonement, the highest Jewish holiday], prayer was recited "for the souls of our brothers, the sons of Israel, who fell on the battlefield on the soil of the Holy Country for its freedom and independence"). There were reports of thousands of Jewish families from the Ukraine being transferred forcibly to Birobidjan. In November of that year, the Jewish Theater was shut down.

Still, there was no fundamental change in the relations between the two States. Except for the question of Jerusalem, there was not a single issue directly concerning the Middle East in which the Soviet Union did not take Israel's side; and the General Assembly's December 1949 decision on Jerusalem was not even mentioned in the Soviet press. For the time being, the Soviets evidently chose only to remind Israel repeatedly of its indebtedness to the Soviet bloc, and to warn it that Soviet support was conditional upon Israel's not "working for Anglo-American interests." Israel tried hard to avoid any step that could be interpreted as serving the interests of the West in "the cold war." The Israeli delegation abstained whenever there was a clear-cut division of sides. Even in the vote of October 22 on observance of human rights and fundamental freedoms in Bulgaria, Hungary and Rumania, it remained silent though it was clear that abstention in this case would meet with strong opposition at home. It was only toward the end of the year that the Israeli delegation occasionally found itself on the other side of the aisle from the Soviet Union, though usually on questions not of vital importance for the Soviet Union. In most cases, the Arab States also voted against the Soviet bloc on these issues.

Then came the year 1950 and with it the crucial problem of Korea.

VI

1950
The Tripartite Declaration
Israel's stand on Korea
Moscow's change of line from full support to passive neutrality

The year 1950 did not start well for Israeli-Soviet relations. There was a series of small points of contention which, as they accumulated, did not conduce to clearing the air.

In January, the Israeli Communists organized demonstrations in Jerusalem, Tel Aviv and Haifa against the visit of former U.S. Secretary of the Treasury Henry Morgenthau, Jr., who, in their opinion, was coming to persuade the Government of Israel to accept the Marshall Plan and to join the anti-Soviet Middle East Pact. *Novoye Vremya* reported that the police suppressed the demonstrations with inhuman cruelty, and added that "so the 'socialist' and 'neutralist' Government of Israel confirmed its reactionary character and its subservience to the imperialists." In February, Tsarapkin, speaking to a member of the Israeli delegation in New York, remarked that the Government of Israel had lately been showing signs of leaning toward the West. He was particularly concerned about the Israeli vote of December 1, 1949, on the draft resolution on "Condemnation of the preparations for a new war." (Israel voted against the Soviet, and in favor of the Anglo-American draft resolution, but so did all the Arab States with the exception of Yemen, which abstained.) The same month, Soviet Minister Pavel Yershov

presented a note protesting against the alleged call-up of Soviet
citizens living in Israel and against interference in matters concerning Soviet property in Jerusalem. In March, there was an
attack in the *Literaturnaya Gazeta* on Moshe Sharett, calling
the Foreign Minister "a chatterbox and a servant of Acheson."
And in April, *Novoye Vremya* attacked Prime Minister Ben
Gurion for having smeared the Red Army in his speech in Ein
Harod on April 7. In fact, the press attacks became so numerous
that the Legation was instructed to protest to the Foreign Ministry in Moscow.

But not all the signs were black. On April 17, Malik informed
the Secretary General of the United Nations that, in view of the
opposition of the population of Jerusalem, both Arabs and Jews,
the Soviet Union was withdrawing its support of the resolution
on internationalization. On April 23, Deputy Minister of Foreign Affairs Lavrentyev assured Chargé d'Affaires Namir, "We
have never deviated from the path of our friendly relations [with
Israel], which have been existing all the time without any
change." On May 4, a report was received that Marshal Kli-
ment Voroshilov, addressing the Military Committee of the
Cominform, made a statement to the effect that Iran, Greece
and Yugoslavia had to be regarded as bases of aggression in the
Middle East; they were supported by Egypt, Syria and Iraq, but
the main military factor in the region, Israel, was trying to keep
neutral. Finally, as late as June 12, Malik, in a conversation
concerning the question of Jerusalem, assured Abba Eban, "We
shall do everything to help you." These and similar encouraging
points were still tipping the scale toward continued friendly
relations; but two important developments, appearing on the
scene almost simultaneously, seriously threatened a drastic
change. The first was the Tripartite Declaration of the United
States, Britain and France of May 25, and the second was the
outbreak of the war in Korea exactly a month later.

The Tripartite Declaration put Israel in a precarious situation
vis-à-vis Moscow. It was issued without previous consultation
with Israel (or with the Arab States). Having had no part in its
formulation, the Government of Israel did not regard itself

bound by the Declaration. Nevertheless, the statement was welcomed, in the words of Prime Minister Ben Gurion, "to the extent that it was designed to increase security and peace." The part of the Declaration that was most important from Israel's point of view was the statement that the Three Powers "recognize that the Arab States and Israel all need to maintain a certain level of armed forces for the purpose of assuring their internal security and their legitimate self-defense and to permit them to play a part in the defense of the area as a whole." On the one hand, the Government of Israel was hoping that this would mean the end of discrimination against Israel in the supply of arms from the West; on the other, it was clear that "playing a part in the defense of the area as a whole" could mean nothing else but defense against an attack on the area by the Soviet Union. There could hardly have been any doubt that this at least would be Moscow's interpretation, logical and justified in the context of the relations among the World Powers in 1950. There was no way out of the dilemma in which Israel found itself as a result of the Declaration. To denounce it would have meant practically closing the door to Western arms supplies, which were vital; subscribing to it would have amounted to an end of the still more or less friendly relations with the Soviet Union. To reject a declaration by which the three Western Powers undertook, "should they find that any of these States was preparing to violate frontiers of armistice lines . . . immediately [to] take action, both within and outside the United Nations, to prevent such violation," was, for a young state threatened on all sides by hostile neighbors, virtually impossible. It was equally impossible to persuade Moscow that Israel welcomed the Declaration for its own security and not because it was directed against the Soviet Union.

The seeds of doubts—well nurtured by the Israeli Communist Party—now germinated. The Soviet press, which, as we have seen, had even before then taken every opportunity to accuse Israel of leaning to the West, now started a campaign which virtually presented Israel as a Western base. Then came a far wider and more acute issue—the outbreak of the Korean War, which overshadowed the crisis created by the Three-Power Declaration and became the core of vilification.

The Korean question had been on the United Nations agenda since September 1947, when it was first submitted to the General Assembly by the United States. In November of the same year, the Assembly established a Temporary Commission on Korea. The Soviet bloc countries, however, did not take part in the vote and the Ukraine, which was to be one of the nine members, did not take its seat on the Commission. On June 25, 1950, the Secretary General of the United Nations was informed, both by the United States Government and by the Commission on Korea, that North Korean forces had invaded South Korea in strength that morning. An urgent Security Council meeting was called the same day. The Soviet Union, which had withdrawn its representative from the Council on January 13 (stating that it would not participate in the Council's work until "the representative of the Kuomintang group had been removed"), absented itself also from this meeting. On June 27, the Council, in the Soviet Union's absence, adopted a resolution defining the attack as a breach of peace, calling for immediate cessation of hostilities, demanding withdrawal of North Korean forces to the 38th Parallel, and asking for the assistance of United Nations members in carrying out the resolution. The resolution was carried unanimously; only Yugoslavia abstained. Egypt was not present at the vote, but explained later that its action was to be interpreted as an abstention. On June 29, the Secretary General transmitted the Council resolution to all member States of the United Nations, asking what assistance, if any, each would be ready to extend.

Moshe Sharett, on June 30, did no more than formally acknowledge receipt of the Secretary General's cable. On July 3, however, he informed the Secretary General that the Government of Israel, at an extraordinary meeting held the previous afternoon (with President Weizmann in the chair), adopted the following decision:

The Government of Israel opposes and condemns aggression wherever it may occur and from whatever quarter it may emanate. In fulfillment of its clear obligations under the Charter, Israel supports the Security Council in its efforts to put an end to the breach of peace in that area. The Government of Israel hopes that the United Nations will continue to align all the Great Powers in a common effort for safeguarding the peace of the world.

It may be of interest to quote also the replies received from the Arab States. Lebanon (on July 7) "affirmed its desire to support any action designed to strengthen world peace within the framework of the United Nations [and] will at all times refrain from rendering any assistance whatsoever to any aggressor." Syria (on July 8) replied in the same way but added that, "because of the obligations of fraternal solidarity existing between Arab countries, [the Government of Syria] takes the greatest interest in the problems that affect the other Arab States [and] in this connection [desires] to point out that the tolerant attitude shown in the execution of certain United Nations resolutions has been one of the factors contributing to the development of the state of affairs which has resulted in the present situation." The Government of Iraq announced (on July 9) that "it supports the United Nations within the framework of the Charter. At the same time, it insists that the application of the principles of the Charter should embrace the unquestionable rights of the Arabs in Palestine." Yemen just condemned "any attack against any State," and Saudi Arabia requested the Security Council (on July 17) "to take necessary measures to execute their resolutions for prohibiting aggression, whether that be in the case of Korea, or in the case of Palestine, or any other case."

The stress on the Palestine issue made Arab endorsement of United Nations action in Korea somewhat more vague than Israel's reply with all its obvious efforts not to sound clearly hostile to the Soviet Union. Moreover, when it came to answering the question of assistance, Israel, though offering only medical assistance, was the only Middle East country—except for

Turkey, a member of the North Atlantic Treaty Organization (NATO)—that gave a positive answer. (Lebanon alone among Arab countries offered $50,000. The offer was accepted, but the money was never made available.)

On July 4, the Knesset confirmed the Government's decision, which was communicated to the Secretary General of the United Nations. The Minister for Foreign Affairs, explaining the Government's view, declared in the Knesset:

> The principle of nonidentification is Israel's way of serving world peace, of making specific its contribution toward preventing a widening of the breach and perhaps, with restricted means, of helping to narrow and heal the breach. But this principle . . . cannot be perverted into a repudiation of world peace, nor can it serve as a pretext for running away from responsibility toward the United Nations, nor can it be turned into a weapon which, instead of preserving peace, might well affect the security of Israel itself.

There was another paragraph in Sharett's speech, addressed more to Moscow than to the Knesset. It read:

> As a small nation, and more specially as a nation which in the past was itself a victim of aggression, and which is likely any day to be attacked—the singular attitude of Egypt in the Korean question in the Security Council cannot but strengthen these misgivings—Israel cannot under any circumstances willingly reconcile itself to the paralysis of the United Nations and to the surrender of the United Nations' right to intervene for the restoration of international security and the defense of peace, on the sole ground that any nation has chosen to withdraw from its counsels, whatever the reasons for the absence may be, and even though they may stem from a justified grievance.

On July 16, Sharett, answering questions of foreign correspondents, declared that Israel would not feel obliged to enter if "the cold war" erupted into a full-scale conflict. Asked whether Israel would join any extension of the North Atlantic Pact to the Mediterranean if the crisis spread to that area,

Sharett stated categorically that there was no change in Israel's stand against joining any partial combination of powers or any pact against a member of the United Nations. On August 3, after the Soviets decided to return to the Security Council, he wrote explicitly, in a letter to the Secretary General of the United Nations, that "the Government of Israel was gratified to learn that the representative of the U.S.S.R. has seen his way to resume his participation in the work of the Security Council."

All this was to no avail. Israel's stand on Korea transformed the doubts already existing in the minds of the Russians into a certainty that not only could Israel be discounted as a potential ally, but that it could not even be relied upon to remain neutral in a crisis of vital importance for the Soviet Union. The venomous article in *Novoye Vremya* of July 13, stating that Ben Gurion's Government now "went over openly to the side of the American aggressors," did not bode well for Moscow's future attitude to Israel. The fact that, at about the same time (July 18), an anonymous letter, received at the Soviet Legation in Tel Aviv, warned that the Legation would be bombed "if Russia and her satellites do not permit Jews to immigrate to Israel," and that Minister Yershov delivered a protest the same day, made the situation still worse.

In the autumn of 1950, the Israeli delegation voted with the Soviet bloc against the American position on the admission of People's China to the United Nations. It again voted with the Soviets against the United States (which was backed by the Arab States) on the issue of relations with Spain. But even this could not alter the fact that Korea at the time was more important to Moscow than any other item on the United Nations agenda. The prevalent view in Moscow was that the Russian stand and sensitiveness in the Korean conflict was influenced, above all, by the desire to save the unity of the Communist world and prevent a split with Chinese extremists. A different vote on Israel's part would not have changed anything materially because the Soviet bloc remained practically isolated throughout all the votes taken on the Korean issue, but this did not, in the least, seem to weaken Moscow's scorn. Apparently in the hope of smoothing relations, Moshe Sharett contemplated a visit to Moscow, though this was a time when it would hardly have enhanced his or Israel's popularity in Washington, but he was rebuffed by Vyshinsky, who informed him on November 3 that there was no need for such a visit as, after all, they could always meet during the General Assembly session in New York.

Walter Eytan, in his book *The First Ten Years,* summed up the situation in one sentence: "Israel's policy of nonidentification could not survive the crisis of Korea." But was this really the end of "friendly" relations between Israel and the Soviet Union? Was this the fatal turning point in Moscow's attitude to Israel? The record of United Nations discussions between October and December 1950, which concerned Israel directly, bears out this theory only up to a certain point.

On October 5, the Sixth Committee discussed the question of a permanent invitation to the Arab League to attend sessions of the General Assembly. It is true that Israel was alone in voting against extending such an invitation and got no support from the Soviet Union. But the Soviet representative did not lend his support to the Arabs either. He remained silent during the debate and abstained when the vote was taken. Between October 20 and November 17, the Security Council discussed six complaints referring to the operation of the Armistice Agreements between Israel and Jordan and between Israel and Egypt. Again the Soviets did not take the rostrum throughout the debate and abstained from voting. However, on December 14, when the Soviets submitted a draft resolution to the General Assembly calling for the termination of the Conciliation Commission because "it failed to carry out its task of settling disputes between the parties in Palestine," and when their draft was defeated, they suggested an amendment to the Ad Hoc Committee's recommendations, asking for "direct negotiations" instead of "negotiations conducted either with the Conciliation Commission or directly." In his speech on the same day, Tsarapkin criticized the Commission which "has not concerned itself with conciliating the parties . . . [and] has not promoted direct negotiations between the parties, but has concentrated in its own hands the settlement of the whole problem of Palestine and achieved nothing."

Thus it became clear that a new line with regard to Israel had been adopted by Moscow. It was to be a line of passive neutrality. From now on, Israel was not to enjoy active support, but no steps were to be taken openly against it either. In questions that had previously been discussed in the United Nations, however, the Soviet line was, at least for the time being, to stay unchanged even if it were favorable to Israel. The new line— undoubtedly Moscow's reaction to Israel's stand on Korea— was certainly a serious falling away in comparison with the original line. It was a turn of the screw. But it was not yet an open anti-Israeli or pro-Arab policy.

VII

1951
Israel's dilemma over the Middle East Command plan
Russian suspicions
Soviet note of November 21
Israel's reply

The pattern was the same in 1951. In April and May, the Soviet representative again sat silent through four meetings of the Security Council on mutual Syrian and Israeli complaints. When it came to voting, he abstained. Between July and September, during the Suez debate, Tsarapkin did not utter a word. To the great disappointment of the Egyptians, he abstained rather than use his veto to prevent a resolution clearly stating the illegality of Egyptian restrictions on peaceful navigation.

There were other discouraging signs besides the end of active support in the United Nations. On January 15, the Soviet Government, after months of silence—during which period there was no Minister of Israel in Moscow—informed the Government of Israel that it could not agree to the appointment of Zalman Shazar[6] as Head of the Israeli Mission in Moscow. Minister Eliashiv, who was appointed instead, reported repeatedly that his visits to the Soviet Foreign Ministry were monologues. The Soviets listened but seldom answered, and took no action. The Israeli note of January 16, regarding reparations from East Germany—on the same day a note regarding repara-

---

6. Shneur Zalman Shazar has been President of Israel since May 21, 1963.

tions from West Germany was sent to the three Western Powers
—was ignored through the whole year, despite reminders sent
in October and November. At Israel's Independence Day party
in Moscow in May, official Soviet representation was obviously
limited to the minimum. There was not a single member of the
Government, and none of the Soviet public figures who were
invited turned up. There were difficulties in trade relations and
the press continued—to say the least—to be critical and suspi-
cious toward Israel. On April 14, for example, *Izvestia* published a report about a military pact between Israel and Turkey,
and Moshe Sharett subsequently had to ask the Soviet Minister
to deny the report firmly.

Yet, as in the past, there were also encouraging signs. In
conversations, the Russians never admitted any change toward
Israel. In July Gromyko assured Minister Eliashiv that there
was "no reason why relations between the Soviet Union and
Israel should not be normal." True, he did not speak any longer
of friendly, but only of normal, relations. However, in September Vyshinsky, again in a conversation with Eliashiv, certainly
went beyond the official obligation required for normal relations
when he expressed his conviction "that Israel will overcome all
her difficulties." The main source of hope, however, was the
important fact, already mentioned, that the Russians did not use
their veto in the vote on the Suez resolution (September 1).

All the same, another serious crisis of confidence was in the
offing. Shortly after Turkey joined NATO, the three Western
Powers informed the Government of Israel of their decision to
create the Allied Middle East Command, adding that "countries
able and willing to contribute to the defense of the area should
participate." Israel was also informed that in view of "the paramount importance to the Command of bases in Egypt," the
Government of Egypt was invited to participate as a founder-
member, with all the rights of the other founder-members. This
occurred on October 13, 1951. On November 21, Minister
Eliashiv was asked to meet with Gromyko, who handed him a
note denouncing the establishment of the Allied Middle East
Command as an act in preparation of an aggression against the

Soviet Union and threatening world peace, and warning the
Government of Israel that Israel's participation would cause
"serious damage to the existing relations" between the Soviet
Union and Israel, as well as to the interest of keeping peace and
maintaining security in the Middle East. Similar, though not
entirely identical, notes were delivered the same day to the
heads of the Arab missions in Moscow.

Once again Israel found itself caught in a dilemma. There was
no doubt that if Egypt decided to join the Middle East Command as a founder-member, the result would be a significant
strengthening of its military power, which was more likely to be
used against Israel than for the defense of the area. Seen in this
light, a refusal to participate looked suicidal for Israel. Joining,
however, clearly meant inviting an open conflict with the Soviet
Union and the end of any hope for an improvement of relations
with Moscow and the countries of Eastern Europe. Israel's
situation was made even more delicate by a paragraph in the
Western Powers' note of October 13, stating that the Western
Powers were "well aware of the difficulties which will arise over
the association of Israel and the Arab States with one and the
same Command organization." A fortnight later, the Turkish
Minister to Israel, presenting an *aide-mémoire*, made this even
clearer when he explained that his Government regarded the
existence of "tense relations" between Israel and the Arab
States as a "retarding factor" in the realization of the Allied
Middle East Command plan. The Turkish Government, therefore, expected Israel to adopt a "realistic attitude." This meant
that the founding members were obviously more interested in
Arab participation than in Israel's joining at this stage. As Walter Eytan put it, "Israel was left under no illusions. The Middle
East Command would be organized without her, and the Arabs
would be supplied with arms, while she would not." In spite of
this, the Soviet press wrote of Israel's participation as a foregone
conclusion.

The tension did not weaken even when the original plan fell
through because of Egypt's decision not to join the new Command. The three Western Powers—and Turkey—expressed

their regret at Egypt's decision, but made it clear that their plan of organizing the Middle East Command could not be delayed. There were still all the other Arab States which were now being reminded by the Western Powers to "consider seriously what the Middle East Command means in terms of their welfare and security."

The Government of Israel decided to reply to the Soviet note of November 21 by a declaration, the text of which was delivered by the Minister of Israel to Soviet Deputy Foreign Minister Zorin on December 8. The statement explained that Israel, in fact, had never been invited to join the Allied Middle East Command. It was informed about the plan to organize the Command, but was at the same time assured that there was no aggressive intention behind its establishment. The declaration went on to stress that Israel saw the securing of world peace as the most important task facing all nations, and was fully aware that its own existence depended on it. The reports about foreign military bases in Israel were groundless. Rumors to this effect, which had repeatedly appeared in the Soviet press in the course of the last two years, were damaging to the relations between Israel and the Soviet Union. While Israel desired to maintain friendly relations with the Soviet Union, the real danger to its security was posed by the threats coming from the Arab States. As peace is indivisible, it was the duty of all members of the United Nations and, above all, of the Great Powers, to bring an end to this menace to Israel. The Soviet Union was certainly also aware of the basic reason for the establishment of the State of Israel: the return of Jews to their historic homeland and their settlement there. This task, which was compatible with Soviet policy based on the principle of the equality of nations and their right to self-determination, could be realized only in conditions of world peace. Therefore, the Government of Israel used this opportunity also to ask the Government of the Soviet Union to enable Soviet Jews who desired to do so, to immigrate to Israel.

Thus, the Israeli reply was not a direct answer to the Soviet note, and the straight assurance—expected in Moscow—that Israel would not join the Allied Middle East Command was missing. Instead of dissipating Soviet doubts, the declaration probably even helped to reinforce them. Zorin replied only to the part of the Israeli declaration dealing with false press reports. He told Minister Eliashiv that those reports were mostly based on foreign, including Israeli, press sources; that what appeared in the newspapers did not necessarily have to influence relations between the two countries; and that if the press was to be regarded as a policy-making factor, the Soviet Union might possibly have more complaints against Israel than Israel had against the Soviet Union. Eliashiv once more stressed that he had just delivered a declaration by his Government assuring the Government of the Soviet Union that the news reports, whatever their source might be, were not true.

The tension was rather high, but again a year passed without the Soviet Union's taking an openly hostile attitude toward Israel.

VIII

1952–1953
Continued tension over Korea and the Middle East Command plan
The Slánský trial in Prague
The doctors' trial
Sharett's Knesset declaration of February 1953
Moscow's break in diplomatic relations with Israel

Next to the war in Korea, the Middle East Command plan continued to be Moscow's main concern and the principal point of East-West tension in 1952. It reverberated through all Middle East debates in the United Nations.

In January of that year, for example, when the Soviet Union continued its fight against the Conciliation Commission, Tsarapkin declared in the General Assembly (January 26) that the Commission "has in fact been pursuing a policy directly opposed to the interests of the peoples of Palestine" and opposed the Ad Hoc Committee's recommendation for further prolongation of the Commission's life. The recommendation, in the view of the Soviet delegate, purported to maintain a state of affairs which will enable the United States and the United Kingdom to realize their aggressive military objectives in Palestine and in the Near and Middle East.... We should regard the fact that none other than the United States, the United Kingdom, France and Turkey, that is to say the very Powers that are trying to set up the Middle East Command, have submitted the draft resolution for prolonging the life of the so-called United Nations Conciliation Commission for Palestine which, as was established during the discussion in the Ad Hoc Political Committee, has really been acting as a subsidiary organ of the United States State Department.

The theme was taken up again later in the year by Vyshinsky who, in the general debate in the Assembly on October 18 said, among other things:

> The ruling circles in the United States have increased their pressure on the countries in the Near and Middle East to establish a so-called Allied Middle East Command and to induce these countries to join it, and in this way to join the North Atlantic bloc, so that they can use their territories . . . for military bases . . . for the new world war which they are preparing. They allege that such a "Command" must be organized as a means of defense against the Soviet Union, which is said to be threatening the security of the countries of the Near and Middle East. . . . The policy of the Soviet Union toward these countries has been fully in keeping with the basic national interests of the peoples of the Near and Middle East.

Nowhere during all these debates did the Russians make the slightest remark directed against Israel, and that in spite of the fact that Israel found itself that year in a rising number of cases on the opposite side of the aisle. This happened in the voting on methods for maintaining international peace and security (January 12), on South-West Africa (January 19), on Korea (February 5), on the Soviet proposal to invite representatives of People's China and North Korea to take part in the Assembly's discussion (October 21, when the Arab States as well as Israel voted against the motion), on the report of the Director of the United Nations World Relief Agency (UNWRA) (November 6, when the Soviet bloc alone voted against the report), again on Korea (December 3), on the Soviet draft resolution on freedom of information (December 16, with Syria, Iraq and Saudi Arabia voting with the Soviets and Lebanon against, while Egypt abstained), on Morocco (December 19, with the Arab States abstaining), on the Trusteeship Council report (December 21), and the same day on the economic development of under-developed countries (the Arab States, too, voting against the

Soviet Union) and again on Korea (Iraq and Lebanon also voting this time against the Soviets while the other Arab States abstained).

On issues concerning Israel directly, the Russians, in most cases, continued their silence in debates and their abstention from voting. They held aloof from the Ad Hoc Committee discussion of the UNWRA report between October 23 and 30, and took no part throughout twelve meetings of the Ad Hoc Committee on the Conciliation Commission between November 26 and December 11. When the Ad Hoc Committee's draft resolution on the Conciliation Commission came to a vote in the General Assembly on December 18, the Soviet bloc delegations voted together with the Arab States against it, while Israel (together with the United States) voted for it. Yet, in explaining the Soviet vote, Zorin stressed that it was not directed against the contents of the resolution but against the fact that it included paragraphs about the Conciliation Commission, which the Soviet Union did not regard as a body able to promote the settlement of disputes between the States of the Middle East. A few days later, on December 21, when the Assembly, at Israel's request, voted on the Ad Hoc Committee's report regarding the "complaint of violation by Arab States of their obligations under the Charter, United Nations resolutions and specific provisions of the armistice agreements concluded with Israel requiring them to desist from policies and practices of hostility and to seek agreement by negotiations for the establishment of peaceful relations with Israel," the Soviet bloc abstained.

But in spite of the increasing number of cases in which Israel found itself voting against the Soviet Union, there were, in 1952, also cases where, on issues important to the Soviets, Israel voted with them and against the United States. Israel was one of the few States—the others were India, Burma and Sweden—that sided with the Soviet bloc against postponement of the debate on China's admission to the United Nations (October 26) and on apartheid (December 5).

There were other positive signs which seemed to dispel the

prevailing impression of a critical worsening of Israel's relations with Moscow. On February 2, for instance, Abba Eban had a long conversation with Malik, from which he gained the impression, strengthened by Malik's assurances, that the Soviet Union had not in any way changed its attitude to Israel. Soviet support of general Arab movements against the West, in Malik's words, did not "lead to any action at Israel's expense." That was confirmed by the favorable Soviet attitude in the Ad Hoc Committee debate. Malik even spoke contemptuously of the Arab delegations. On October 20, Ben Gurion, in his cable to Stalin congratulating the Soviet Union on the occasion of the 35th anniversary of the Great October Revolution, wrote, among other things:

Dans cette période de développement de notre patrie historique, la part de l'U.R.S.S. dans la défaite de l'ennemi Nazi reste présente à notre mémoire ainsi que la pensée reconnaissante de l'appui de l'U.R.S.S. lors de l'établissement de l'Etat d'Israël. [In this period in the development of our historic fatherland, the role of the U.S.S.R. in the defeat of the Nazi enemy remains alive in our memory as does the appreciative recall of the U.S.S.R.'s support since the establishment of the State of Israel.]

The Russians were apparently pleased and impressed by the message, which was published in the Soviet press almost immediately after the greetings from the Soviet bloc countries. (The year before, Israel's message was printed at the tail end. It is generally believed that such details have a significance in the Soviet Union.) Finally, on November 26, Abba Eban, in a conversation with Gromyko, presented an Israeli compromise plan on Korea. Gromyko's answer was that the plan still contained some American points which were not acceptable to the Soviet Union, but he stressed that he appreciated Israel's efforts.

There were hardly any encouraging manifestations in the day-to-day exchanges between the Israeli Legation in Moscow and the Soviet Foreign Ministry. On February 26, Deputy Foreign Minister Zorin summoned the Israeli chargé d'affaires and handed him a protest against "intolerable sabotage" by Israel in retarding the return of Russian property in Israel to the Soviet authorities. In March, Deputy Foreign Minister Semyen Bazarov invited Minister Eliashiv to convey to him the Soviet Government's reply to the Israeli note on reparations from East Germany. The answer—for which Israel had had to wait fourteen months (since January 16, 1951)—was that the matter could be settled only after the conclusion of a peace treaty with Germany and could be decided by Germany alone. In May, the Legation was informed that the Soviet Academy of Science would be unable to participate in the symposium on "The Conquest of the Desert." On September 16, when Eliashiv handed Deputy Foreign Minister Pushkin a second note on the question of reparations from East Germany, he received an answer on the spot: East Germany was an independent State and the Soviet Government did not see how it could influence Pankow or assist Israel in this matter. The Soviet press, which continued its attacks on Ben Gurion and Sharett and its criticism of Israel's pro-Western leanings, began—while otherwise virtually abstaining from reporting on Middle East debates in the United Nations bodies—to stress the pro-Soviet attitude of Arab countries in the world organization.

All this caused concern. The clouds were visibly gathering. But when the storm came, it broke in unexpected fashion. In November 1952, the world was shocked by the anti-Semite show-trial of Prague. Of the fourteen persons accused in the Slánský trial, eleven were Jews. Of the eleven who were condemned to death and executed, eight were Jews. The trial was not only anti-Jewish, it was also explicitly anti-Israeli. The Soviet press, which so far had tried to avoid direct anti-Semitic outbursts and instead had attacked "Cosmopolitism" and "Zionism," in its reports on the Prague trial became openly anti-Semitic and anti-Israeli. Whatever was said at the trial about the role of Israeli spies and of the Israeli Legation in Czechoslovakia in the alleged "conspiracy" of Slánský and his group was reported and stressed by *Pravda* and *Izvestia* without the slightest reservation. It soon became clear that the Slánský trial was to be just a prelude for the worst tempest of anti-Semitism since Hitler. On December 8, the Soviet press reported the first of a series of trials of "economic criminals." Two of the three men accused and executed in this first trial, which took place in Kiev, were Jews. But the most severe shock was felt on January 13, 1953, when the Soviet press announced the discovery of a conspiracy of doctors, aiming to liquidate Soviet political and military leaders by medical means. The same day, nine leading doctors were arrested. At least seven of them were Jews. Among other things, they were accused of having been in touch with the "Jewish bourgeois-nationalistic organization, Joint" (American Joint Distribution Committee). The press added a charge of contact with the Zionist Organization (World Zionist Organization). The shamelessness of the anti-Semitic attacks reached a nadir unparalleled by anything that had appeared in the Soviet press since 1917. The satirical weekly *Krokodil* became a Russian edition of *Der Stuermer.*

Though Israel was not specifically mentioned in any of the documents connected with the doctors' trial, the Government of Israel could not remain silent. On January 19, Moshe Sharett read a Government declaration in the Knesset which included these words:

In the declaration about the Prague trial, delivered to the Knesset on behalf of the Government on November 24, 1952, it was said:

"In this hour our hearts go to the masses of our brethren who are cut off from the main body of their people, denied any contact with the State of Israel and other sections of Jewry, and are forced to bear their lot in isolation and solitude. Our voice may not reach them, but our hearts are heavy with anxiety for them, their well-being and their future fate.

"This anxiety has proved justified and is now shared by the entire House of Israel throughout the world. . . ."

The report [of accusations against the doctors] shocked world opinion which saw in it, and in the consequences likely to follow from it, a campaign of atrocity, propaganda and terrorization embarked upon by the Soviet authorities against their Jewish nationals.

"This time again, as in the case of the Prague trial, the falseness of the indictments is inherently demonstrated. . . . Under the regime prevailing in the U.S.S.R. and in the States attached to it, the administration of justice is the obedient arm of State power and an instrument of its policy. Just as in all activities of the Government, the investigation of crimes against the regime itself and their exposure in public are done according to plan, with nothing left to chance. It was not accidental that eleven of the fourteen accused and all the witnesses produced in the Prague trial were Jews. The prosecution itself emphasized this point throughout the proceedings, and drew far-reaching conclusions from it. Nor is it accidental that at least seven out of the nine accused physicians in Moscow and their alleged two liaison agents are Jews.

"The denunciation of Zionism and the State of Israel which played so prominent a part in the Prague trial . . . and the slander . . . in Moscow . . . reveal a definite design and clearly show its underlying purpose. . . . The fact that throughout the world outside the Soviet bloc, the Moscow announcement is regarded as a fabrication clearly shows that the whole affair is designed exclusively for internal consumption. Its purpose is . . . to frighten the Jewish community of the Soviet Union and . . . in the States allied to it, and . . . to prepare the population of those countries for possible reprisals against the Jews.

"The State of Israel will not rest silent in the face of an attempt made by any power to defame the name of the Jewish people and of a danger threatening masses of the Jews wherever they may be.

"The Government of Israel has regarded friendship with the

U.S.S.R. as one of the assets of its international position and as a
source of gratification for the whole Jewish people. It views with
deep sorrow and grave anxiety the pernicious anti-Jewish course
officially adopted in the U.S.S.R., which must arouse vehement
indignation and condemnation on the part of the State of Israel and
the Jews throughout the world. . . .

"The Government of Israel will expose in the United Nations and
on every platform the campaign of instigation against the Jewish
people. . . ."

The Government declaration was adopted the same day in
the Knesset by an 89-to-6 vote. Its language was plain. A torrent
of anti-Soviet protests rose all over America and Europe. For
the moment, Moscow seemed taken aback by the strength and
unanimity of the indignation and condemnation expressed by
the entire free world. The Russians found it necessary to defend
themselves against the accusation of anti-Semitism. This, at
least, was the generally accepted explanation of the fact that, on
January 30, Soviet authorities decided to award the coveted
Stalin Prize for the first time to a Jew—Ilya Ehrenburg. Simultaneously, however, the hatred of Israel reached its peak, for
Israel was now regarded as the chief instigator of anti-Soviet
feelings throughout the world. The Soviet press unleashed even
more violent onslaughts against Israel. The article in *Novoye
Vremya* of January 21, in which Ben Gurion and Sharett were
called executors of U.S. State Department orders, Eban and
Shiloah were presented as employees of the British Intelligence
Service, and Eban was accused of acting as an adjutant in British
and American moves to defeat Soviet peace efforts in the
United Nations, will serve as an example of dozens of similar
fabrications that appeared in the press throughout the Soviet
Union at that time.

On February 5, the Government of Czechoslovakia addressed a note to the Government of Israel which, in fact,
extinguished the last hope of finding a way to mend the breach.

The note spoke of "the effrontery and arrogance of the Israeli Zionist agents in Czechoslovakia" and of "the American warmongers and their Israeli stooges," and asserted that "the ruling circles of Israel and the Zionist organisations which they lead and represent, are under the orders of the financially most powerful Zionist groups in the United States and . . . consciously supply a willing instrument for the warmongering policy of American imperialism." The next day the Minister of Israel in Prague, Aryeh Kubowi, was declared *persona non grata.* Two days later, on February 8, Warsaw followed Prague's example. Late in the evening of February 9, a small bomb exploded in the garden of the Soviet Legation in Tel Aviv. Damage was caused to the building and three employees of the Legation were slightly wounded. The President of Israel, the Government and the Knesset straightaway expressed their regret at the incident and condemned it. The Minister of Israel in Moscow tried without success to obtain an appointment with Deputy Foreign Minister Bazarov. Unable to arrange a meeting, he wrote a personal letter voicing his sorrow and dismay. On February 12, he was called to the Ministry of Foreign Affairs and handed a note in which the Government of Israel was informed that, in view of the fact that even the minimal conditions necessary for the activities of a diplomatic mission did not exist in Israel, the Government of the Soviet Union had decided to recall its mission and to break off diplomatic relations with the State of Israel.

In his declaration in the Knesset on February 12, Prime Minister Ben Gurion said: "To our regret, we are unable to see in the note handed to the Minister of Israel in Moscow anything but a further step in the systematic, hostile campaign against the State of Israel, against the Zionist movement and against world Jewry which has been going on in the Soviet press for a long time, and which turned into open, official hostility in the Slánský trial in Prague and in the false accusations published in Moscow on January 13." The same day, Abba Eban, at a meeting of the Israeli delegation to the United Nations, characterized the Soviet decision to break off diplomatic relations with

Israel as "the result of a planned line which has been marked out for a long time." He pointed out that this was not the first time that the Soviet Union had broken off relations with another State when its missions had been attacked. While in the previous cases—Chile, Brazil and Venezuela—the attacks were the real reasons for the break, in the case of Israel the attack was a good excuse for taking a step that the Soviets had obviously decided upon before.

The belief that Moscow would have taken the same drastic action even without the regrettable bomb episode was shared by everyone in Israel.

IX

The severing of diplomatic relations in February 1953 was generally regarded as the point of no return. Moshe Sharett, in interpreting the significance of Moscow's action on March 9, tried to explain it as a logical consequence of the Soviet anti-Zionist line, which had never really changed. The support in 1947 resulted from the hatred of Haman (Britain), not from love of Mordekhai, and it lasted only briefly, because the Soviet Union soon discovered Israel's deeply rooted leanings to Western civilization and Israel's appeal for the Jews of the Soviet Union. The Soviet Union never in truth extended any help to Israel, and the break therefore neither increased nor lessened Israel's dependence on the West. The actual significance of the break lies in the fact that it strengthened the Arabs.

This was Israel's evaluation of the situation created by Moscow's decision, and apparently even the death of Stalin a few days earlier (March 5) was not regarded as a factor that could basically change things. So it came as a surprise when, only two months later, the Soviets put out feelers on the possibility of renewing diplomatic relations with Israel. It is true that shortly after Stalin's death the Kremlin seemed to have called off the anti-Semitic campaign in the Soviet press, but when the first reports on the likelihood of an early resumption of diplomatic relations appeared,[7] they were received with much reserve. Yet they proved correct. In fact, on April 4, less than two months after the break, Mikhail Bodrov, the Soviet Ambassador in Sofia, who had returned to his post from a long home leave in Moscow only ten days after Stalin's death, had approached the Israeli chargé d'affaires at a party at the Hungarian Embassy and asked him about Israeli reaction to the release of the accused Jewish physicians. After this initial contact, further efforts were made through the Polish Ambassador in Sofia, who obviously had been ordered to find out to what extent the Israelis were ready to take the first step. Hints in the same direction were being dropped at the same time by Bulgarian officials and Czechoslovak diplomats in Sofia. Even before the first official meeting between Israel's chargé d'affaires, Gershon Avner, and Soviet Ambassador Bodrov on May 28, it became clear that Moscow had decided to heal the breach, but that the Soviets were looking for a face-saving solution that would give the impression that the initiative came from Israel.

Israel agreed to play the game, and on July 6 Moshe Sharett wrote Molotov a letter whose text had been agreed upon during the talks in Sofia. Sharett pointed out that the Government of Israel had "of late been aware of a noticeable improvement in the atmosphere surrounding international affairs, and of the renewed widespread desire to arrive at peaceful and constructive solutions of major international issues still pending." Referring to the bomb outrage that had given Moscow the basis for the decision to sever relations with Israel, the letter admitted that police investigation had "yielded no tangible results so far" but assured Moscow that the search was being continued "with full vigor." Then came the most important sentence:

7. Among the first was a report by Lajos Lederer in the *Observer*, on April 26, 1953.

Having no hostile feelings towards the Soviet Union but, on the contrary, being anxious to establish and maintain relations of friendship and amity with it, Israel will not be a party to any alliance or pact aiming at aggression against the Soviet Union.

Molotov's reply of July 15 took notice of the apology of the Israeli Government for the bomb outrage and of its declaration that it would be a party to no alliance or pact pursuing aggressive designs against the Soviet Union. Then it continued:

Taking into account these assurances of the Government of Israel, as well as the expression of its anxiety to reestablish relations with the Soviet Union, and following its policy of maintaining normal relations with other countries and of strengthening collaboration between peoples, the Soviet Government, for its own part, also declares its desire to have friendly relations with Israel, and considers it possible to reestablish diplomatic relations with the Government of Israel.

The official announcement of the resumption of diplomatic relations was published in Jerusalem and Moscow on July 20. The London *Times* of July 21 spoke of an enthusiastic reception of the news in Israel.[8] In fact, however, there was more surprise than enthusiasm in Jerusalem, so much so that, even three weeks later, Sharett asked the Research Department of the Foreign Ministry to prepare a study that would try to answer the question of why the Russians were interested in renewing relations with Israel so quickly.

The answer to Sharett's question seems to be fairly clear. No Soviet decision can be evaluated as an isolated step. As with all other Soviet decisions, that to renew diplomatic relations with Israel has to be seen in the context of the overall Soviet policy at the time. It was part of the peace offensive started by Moscow

---

8. The London *Times* report added: "The reestablishment of diplomatic relations with Russia is felt to be of exceptional importance, especially as it also removes the Arab contention—said to have been used cunningly in Washington—that Russia had turned its back on Israel in order to carry favor with the Arab States."

immediately after Stalin's death and was taken simultaneously with the decision to normalize Moscow's relations with Yugoslavia,[9] and with the decision to adopt a policy line which eventually led to the Austrian State Treaty. While both these decisions were fully realized only later, their beginnings can today be traced back to the time when Moscow decided to heal its breach with Israel. It should also be remembered that, in May 1953, Molotov informed the Turkish Government that the Soviet Union was renouncing territorial claims on Turkey, and that in July, Moscow and Athens agreed to exchange ambassadors.

Seen from this perspective, the resumption of diplomatic relations with Israel clearly could not be regarded as anything more than normalization which, though itself a positive step, was not expected to produce any spectacular results. If there was any doubt, it was dispelled by Malenkov's statement of August 8, in which Stalin's successor declared:

> Views expressed by a part of the foreign press, according to which the reestablishing of diplomatic relations with Israel would result in a weakening of the relations between the Soviet Union and the Arab States, are groundless. The activities of the Soviet Government will be directed also in the future to the strengthening of friendly relations with the Arab States. In its efforts to bring about a general relaxation, the Soviet Government agreed to reestablish diplomatic relations with the State of Israel. It took into consideration the Israeli Government's undertaking that "Israel will not be a party to any alliance or pact aiming at aggression against the Soviet Union." We assume that the reestablishment of diplomatic relations will contribute to the cooperation between the two States.

But while there was no room for exaggerated hopes, it was felt that the ground was ready for developing normal relations, and there were even signs that, in the somewhat improved international atmosphere, at least in some fields the relations could bear more fruit than before the breach.

---

9. Moscow's first official approach was made on June 6, 1953.

Minister Eliashiv returned to Moscow on November 29, and his presence was given due publicity in the Soviet press. Soviet Minister Aleksandr Abramov arrived in Israel two days later. The first meetings were somewhat cool on both sides. Molotov, while assuring Eliashiv that he too was pleased that relations were renewed, reminded him that "Israel undertook a certain obligation and the Soviet Government hopes that Israel will keep it." Sharett, on the other hand, used the opportunity of Abramov's question on which was the second language in Israel to explain that "English is the language of the majority of Jews we are in touch with." The speeches delivered during the presentation of credentials in Moscow and Jerusalem, however, gave ground for some hope. A certain significance was attached to the part of Voroshilov's answer to Eliashiv in which he asked him to convey greetings to "the Jewish people of Israel," whereas on the previous occasion Shvernik had spoken of "the peoples of Israel." Especially important was the fact that, in the course of the conversation that followed the official part of the ceremony, Voroshilov spoke with friendship and appreciation of the Jewish people and of the State of Israel and openly derided the Arabs. He declared that Jerusalem was a Jewish city and assured Eliashiv that, with patience, the Jewish people would reach their goal. Abramov, during his speech in Jerusalem, expressed his conviction that the reestablishment of relations would help to develop friendly relations and strengthen peace and international cooperation. President Ben Zwi, in his reply, stressed the support Israel was given by the Soviet Union in 1947 and expressed the hope "that the Soviet Union will show its encouraging understanding also for Israel's efforts to build the country and gather in it the dispersed Jewish people who desire to come and live in it."

This last hope was to be extinguished very quickly. When Eliashiv, in his first meeting with Gromyko (on December 21) after the renewal of relations, once again raised the question of *aliyah* of Russian Jews, the refusal he received was harsher and more resolute than on any previous occasion. Gromyko even expressed his surprise that the question was being raised.

"There is no real basis for discussing it."

However, in all other questions the Russians were showing a more positive attitude. They were ready to talk about expanding trade relations between the two countries and even to back Israel's demand that disputes with the Arab States be settled by direct negotiations. This was, in fact, a continuation of the Soviet line and practice as they were in the period preceding the breach. The Russians would remain neutral or aloof in discussions on problems of the Middle East, but in all questions on which they had taken a position on previous occasions, they would follow the old line.

Consequently, in October, when the Security Council was discussing Qibya,[10] Vyshinsky remained silent throughout, abstained in the vote and did not even explain why, though a special meeting was set aside for that purpose. However, in the discussion on the Syrian complaint against Israel concerning work in the demilitarized zone, he intervened, on December 21, to criticize the Three-Power draft resolution as "calculated . . . merely to evade the really important question of the need for settling the situation that has arisen in the demilitarized zone, by agreement between the parties concerned—Israel and Syria—and by no other means." He even suggested an adjournment of the Security Council "so that Israel and Syria may have a chance to achieve agreement on the present question." (The Soviet press did not, however, even register this intervention.)

Until the end of 1953, the development of relations between Israel and the Soviet Union did not seem to present cause for any serious worry. With the exception of the question of *aliyah*,

---

10. The concentrated military action against the Jordanian village of Qibya, on the night of October 14, 1953, was a retaliatory raid against a marauders' base, from which infiltrators had been penetrating into Israeli territory to perform acts of sabotage and terrorism in Israeli border settlements. Fifty-seven Israelis were killed by these infiltrators in 1953. After Qibya, the number of victims dropped to thirty-four in 1954, and to eleven in 1955. In spite of this proof of effectiveness, the Qibya raid was widely criticized in Israel itself because there were, unfortunately, also women and children among the Jordanian victims. As a result, all later punitive actions have been directed explicitly against military posts and paramilitary personnel only.

which had become tabu, they were following a normal, even a positive, course. In December, a trade agreement was signed according to which the Soviet Union was to buy $3 million worth of Israel's citrus fruit and bananas and to supply 100,000 tons of mazut and 10,000 tons of coal to Israel. The main improvement, however, could be seen in the fact that the Soviet press stopped printing anti-Israeli articles, though its reports about the Middle East often showed a preference for the Arab version.

But the impression of comparative normalcy of relations was short-lived. On January 22, 1954, the Soviet Union for the first time used the veto on a Security Council vote concerning a Middle East issue. The occasion was a Syrian complaint against Israel concerning work on the west bank of the Jordan River in the demilitarized zone, and Vyshinsky explained that the veto was used because, in the opinion of the Soviet Union, the Three-Power draft resolution "fails to eliminate the root cause of misunderstanding. . . . It is impossible without the agreement of both sides to maintain normal conditions in the demilitarized zone. . . . We consider that every step which the Chief of Staff can and should take must be approved by the parties concerned." The use of the veto in a Middle East debate was a dangerous development, but so far—though the only other vote against the draft resolution was that of Lebanon—it could not be labeled as a clearly anti-Israeli move.

That was to come two months later (on March 29), when the Security Council, having discussed (since February 5) an Israeli complaint against Egypt for restricting the passage of ships trading with Israel through the Suez Canal and for interfering with shipping proceeding to the Israeli port of Eilat on the Gulf of Aqaba, came to vote on a New Zealand draft resolution. This resolution condemned Egypt for not fulfilling the Security Council's previous resolution on free passage through the Canal and reaffirmed its obligation of September 1951 to comply with the resolution. Again Vyshinsky used his right of veto. Before the vote, he explained that "when the question . . . was first discussed in 1951, the Soviet Union based its position on the

opinion that the draft resolution submitted to the Security
Council at that time followed a line which would not ensure a
satisfactory settlement of the question." He argued that "the
two years that have elapsed since then have proved the correctness of that statement," and added that "the new draft resolution makes absolutely no change in the attempts—if attempts
they may be called—to help the Arab States and Israel to enter
into conditions of normal coexistence and to establish mutual
peace and friendship." Later, explaining the vote, he repeated
that the 1951 resolution had proved ineffective and that no good
could have come from reiterating it. Even now, he said, the
Security Council was "doing nothing to settle the substance of
a question which needs urgent settlement," and stressed once
more that "the proper method for this is that of direct negotiations between the interested parties. . . . On one side we have
the representative of Israel and on the other the representative
of Egypt. They are sitting opposite one another. Let them sit
down together at one table and try to settle the question which
the Security Council cannot settle now. I am deeply convinced
that they can find a better solution." He further explained that,
in 1951, the Soviet delegation had abstained without making
use of the right of veto "in the hope that it might give some
results, since we did not want to hinder the possibility of achieving positive results." Finally, answering Western criticism of the
Soviet veto, Vyshinsky wound up his speech by asking:

> Do you wish to imply that the Soviet Union by its action is inciting
> Egypt to take some illegal measures? Anyone who says or thinks
> this is taking too much upon himself. We are inciting one particular
> body, and one alone, to take one specific course of action: We are
> inciting the Security Council to deal with the question seriously and
> to find a solution which would lead to the peaceful settlement of this
> problem by means of direct negotiations between Egypt and Israel.

Whatever the degree of sincerity of Vyshinsky's statement, it
remained a fact that in his speech he had called the arguments
brought forward by the Egyptian and Lebanese delegates

"sound enough," that after the vote the Egyptian representative hailed him as "defender of law and justice," and, above all, that this was the first time that the Soviet Union had voted openly against Israel in a matter directly concerning Israel's interest and that it did so clearly knowing that its vote would bring serious harm to Israel.

If, without access to Soviet archives, it is at all possible to put one's finger on the specific date on which the Soviet Union began consistently to follow a line of open hostility to the State of Israel, the date of March 29, 1954, is the most probable demarcation on the calendar of the fatal, final turning point in Soviet-Israeli relations.

X

How Moscow arrived at the point of no return

At this point, to understand the development just described, we must superimpose the sequence of events in the Arab world and anti-Soviet actions of Western Powers in the Middle East upon the chronology of Israeli-Soviet relations. What happened in the Arab world between September 1951 and March 1954 to cause the Soviet delegation, when voting on the same issue, to abstain in the first instance and use the veto in a clearly anti-Israel decision in the second?

The decision of the Soviet Union to put its stakes on the Arabs was not sudden. It was the result of long deliberations, in the course of which, more than once, doubts and hesitations tipped the scales to the other side before the final step was taken. The criterion used to measure the usefulness of either party was the degree of anti-Western orientation and feelings which could be turned to Moscow's profit. In a Russian book on contemporary Egypt (*Sovremennij Egipet*), by Vatolina, we read that already, in 1947, Soviet experts had noted widespread anti-British feelings not only among the "popular masses" but also among the "mercantile bourgeoisie" and even among the big landowners. Just when Israel's relations with London were becoming normal, the anti-British struggle in the Suez Canal

Zone, conducted by Egyptian nationalists, was entering a new phase. In March 1949, the first military revolution took place in Syria, and in 1950, the first signs of a growing pro-Soviet orientation in that country became discernible. The attraction of the Arab countries for Moscow rose considerably in October 1951, when Egypt unilaterally renounced its defense pact with Britain and the agreement on the Sudan condominium. The same month, Egypt refused the Western Powers' offer that it should join the SACME organization (Strategic Allied Command Middle East) as a founding member. News of the Naguib revolution of July 1952 was received in Moscow with a great deal of reserve. But the virtue of the new regime rose in Russian eyes when, a month later, it refused to participate in the second Western plan for a Middle East Command (to be known as the Middle East Defense Organization, or MEDO). Then, in May 1953, John Foster Dulles, U.S. Secretary of State, visited the Middle East. The main subject of his talks was again a collective Middle East security system directed against the Soviet Union. In a speech delivered on June 1, upon his return to Washington, he reported to the American people:

> A Middle East Defense Organization is a future rather than an immediate possibility. Many of the Arab League countries are so engrossed with their quarrels with Israel or with Great Britain or France that they pay little heed to the menace of Soviet communism. However, there is more concern where the Soviet Union is near. In general, the northern tier of nations shows awareness of the danger. There is a vague desire to have a collective security system. But no such system can be imposed from without. It should be designed and grow from within out of a sense of common destiny and common danger.

Three things became clear from Dulles' statement, as it must have been read in Moscow:

1. Arab countries were the real obstacle to the Western plan directed against the Soviet Union. It was therefore important for the Russians to strengthen them.
2. The northern tier countries were, obviously, beginning to give in

to American pressure—the pact between Turkey and Pakistan, signed in April 1954, was certainly already under active consideration, and likewise the pact between Turkey and Iraq, which was to mark the beginning of the Baghdad Pact. This was an additional reason for Moscow to strengthen the countries opposing the plan.

3. Israel's attitude was not even mentioned in Dulles' statement, an omission which could be interpreted by Moscow only in one of two ways: Either Israel was causing no difficulty to the Western plan, or it was regarded by the United States as unimportant. In either event, it was clear that the Soviets should concentrate on securing Arab favor.

This, then, was the basis for the Soviet decision. In October 1953, Moscow sent Daniel Solod as Ambassador to Cairo with the task of preparing the ground for the new Soviet policy in Egypt and in the Middle East. It was a policy of all-out support for the Arab States, especially of Egypt and Syria, in their struggle against the Western Powers. A few days after Solod's arrival in Cairo, Nasser—at that time still Deputy Prime Minister in Naguib's Government—declared that the period when the British were able to treat Egypt's governments "as mere playthings" had definitely passed. "If Britain cannot come to recognize Egypt's full rights, then British reactionary elements should be prepared to face a popular, organized struggle by millions of Egyptians" who would "rally as one man." To Russian ears, this was heavenly music. The Soviets went out of their way to prove that, in pursuing their new pro-Arab line, they would not be deterred even by considerations of the interests of their Egyptian comrades. The Egyptian Communist Party was silently sacrificed. A detailed study of the chronology of events in the Arab world shows, for instance, that the day after more than fifty leaders of the party had been arrested, Moscow did not hesitate to sign an important trade agreement with their jailers.

The evaluation of the reasons and significance of the Soviet veto,.as accepted at the time in Jerusalem, was that it was used:

1. To prove the importance of the Security Council in its present composition and thus to stress the necessity of Peking's admission before the Geneva Conference.
2. To prove that the Soviet Union was a factor in the Middle East and that, without it, it was impossible to solve any regional problem in or outside the United Nations.
3. To strengthen the Soviet interest in keeping unrest and instability in the region, so as to weaken the possibility of establishing anti-Soviet military pacts.

Dag Hammarskjöld believed, at the time, that by using the veto, the Russians:

1. Tried to use opportunities created for them by lack of stability in Egypt and Syria.
2. Wanted to serve notice that they wished to be consulted on all Middle East issues before they were discussed in the Security Council.

Hammarskjöld did not believe that the use of veto was a firm, unalterable Soviet policy, and was optimistic about the possibility of avoiding it in the future, if the initative did not rest solely with the Western Powers. It seems, however, that Minister Eliashiv was nearer to the truth, when (on March 31, 1954) he summed up his evaluation in one sentence: "The elimination of British influence in the area is the principal goal, and to reach this aim, the Soviet Union will support Egypt in everything, just as it supported us, for the same reason, in 1947."

XI

From then on, relations with Israel became for Moscow just a useful lever and regulating device for its relations with the Arab States, and particularly with Egypt. When the Egyptians agreed to resume the talks with Britain about the Suez Canal Zone, which had been broken off in May 1953, the Soviets informed Israel—first unofficially on April 27, 1954, then officially in a note handed to Moshe Sharett by Ambassador Abramov on May 13, 1954—of their willingness to raise the status of the diplomatic missions to that of embassies.[11] When the British-Egyptian agreement was signed in October of that year, the Polish Government informed Israel that it intended to open a legation, headed by a minister, in Tel Aviv.

This also explains why, in spite of all these improvements, the relations between the Soviet Union and Israel—with the exception of trade, which showed a certain rise after the resumption of diplomatic ties—were still lacking in substance. Abramov, while presenting his credentials after the resumption of diplomatic relations, stressed the intention of developing cultural relations between the two countries. The Israeli Legation—and

---

11. The official announcement was published simultaneously in Moscow and Jerusalem on May 17, 1954.

later the Embassy—spent an entire year negotiating with the responsible Soviet authorities without the slightest results. There were practically no exchange visits. In July 1954, the Soviet Minister of Agriculture invited an Israeli delegation to the Agricultural Exhibition in Moscow, but when the Government of Israel decided to reciprocate and invited three agricultural experts to visit Israel, the invitation was declined. Ambassador Abramov made it clear, in a talk with Moshe Sharett, that it was unlikely that such invitations could be accepted "in the near future." The only delegations the Russians were ready and interested to send to Israel were those invited by the Communist Party or its affiliated organizations. Israel's refusal to grant visas to some of those invited led to sharp criticism from Moscow. Talks held with the Russians in Jerusalem, Moscow and New York became monologues even more often than they had been in the past. The Soviet interlocutors listened to what the Israelis had to say but hardly ever reacted. They would report to their superiors, who would make the decisions. When presenting his credentials as Ambassador, Eliashiv said that the raising of the status of representation should be regarded as an expression of "mutual will to strengthen the friendship" between the two countries, and Vice President Sharif Rashidov, in his reply, agreed that it would "help develop mutual friendship." It remained wishful thinking on the part of Israel. On the Soviet side, it proved an empty phrase.

Between April 1954 and December 1955, questions connected with the Israeli-Arab conflict were brought before the Security Council on six different occasions. Whenever the complaining party was Israel, the Soviet delegation ignored Israel's claims; when, on the other hand, the Arab States complained, the Soviet delegates would, unfailingly, lead the attack against Israel. Thus, after the *Bat Galim* incident,[12] when Israel, on

---

12. *Bat Galim*, a small Israeli merchant ship, was sent, in November 1954, through the Suez Canal. The action was in defiance of the Egyptian blockade which had continued, contrary to the decision of the Security Council of September 1, 1951, calling upon Egypt to terminate restrictions on the passage of all international shipping and goods wherever bound. The ship was

October 14, 1954, lodged a complaint against Egyptian restrictions on the passage of ships trading with Israel through the Suez Canal, the Russians remained silent throughout the debate. When, in March 1955, Israel and Egypt complained of reciprocal violations of the Armistice Agreement, the Soviet delegate, Arkadi Sobolev, disregarded the Israeli complaint entirely but expressed "sympathy to the Government and people of Egypt in connection with the Gaza incident and the resulting loss of life" (March 4) and asked the Council to censure the Israeli action. When, on April 6, 1955, the Council discussed Israel's complaint against Egypt "concerning repeated attacks by Egyptian regular and irregular armed forces and by marauders from Egyptian-controlled territory against Israeli armed forces and civilian lives and property in Israel," Sobolev dismissed the issue by stating that previous resolutions constituted "a sound basis for the settlement of disputes arising near the demarcation line between Egypt and Israel," and that therefore no action by the Security Council was necessary. However, when Syria complained (December 16, 1955) against an Israeli retaliatory action, Sobolev rendered his delegation's condolences to the Government and people of Syria, and paid "tribute to the restraint shown by the Government of Syria" (January 12, 1956); he defined the Israeli action as a "gross violation of the United Nations Charter" and as "a completely unprovoked and deliberate attack," asking the Council not only to condemn Israel but also to warn it solemnly "of the dangerous consequences of such attacks" and to request it to pay compensation to Syria. When, on that occasion, Shukairy[13] submitted one of

---

detained, her cargo confiscated and her crew arrested on a trumped-up charge of having fired on an Egyptian fishing boat and killed some fishermen. The charge was dropped three months later, and members of the *Bat Galim* crew were repatriated. Walter Eytan summed up the world reaction to the incident thus: "The Great Powers appeared to be less vexed with Egypt for this violation of Israel's rights than with Israel for provoking it." (W. Eytan: *The First Ten Years*, p. 101.)

13. Ahmed Shukairy, perhaps the most vociferous, demagogic, violently anti-Israeli Arab politician, acted first as Saudi Arabia's, later as Syria's, Permanent Representative to the United Nations. At the Arab League Conference in

the most vituperative draft resolutions ever tabled in any United Nations body, Sobolev found that it "warrants the most careful consideration" (December 22, 1955) and submitted the same draft in a somewhat mutilated form (January 9, 1956) as a Soviet proposal. He did not mention Israel's arguments at all and explained, on January 12, that in the opinion of the Soviet delegation, "the Security Council would not be justified in, and cannot agree to, shifting some of the blame to Syria, even in a disguised form."

Abba Eban, speaking of the Soviet draft resolution on January 17, said:

This draft resolution does not make any claim to objectivity. The Soviet representative has simply copied down certain extreme and partisan views of the Syrian Government, and has put the name of his delegation to Syrian views. . . . The Soviet draft resolution completely ignores the important passages of the Chief of Staff's report which refer to contraventions of the Armistice Agreement by Syria. . . . Similarly, the Soviet draft resolution refuses to say anything requiring Syria to respect the Armistice Demarcation Line and to avoid firing across it. . . . Ignoring the equality of rights of Israel and Syria under the Armistice Agreement, and thereby discriminating against hundreds of Israelis who have lost their lives at Arab hands, the Soviet draft resolution precludes an injunction . . . on how the indemnification problem [may] be solved without agreement between sovereign states. . . . Israel deeply regrets this unbalanced approach. We see here the unfortunate extension of an attitude previously expressed in the vetoing of two important draft resolutions before the Security Council, for no other reason than that they emphasized an Arab duty to observe Charter obligations and treaty obligations towards Israel. . . . Ever since the veto frustrated two basic Security Council decisions in 1954, we have been gravely aware of the effects of this imbalance. Israel here comes

---

Alexandria in September 1964, at his suggestion, it was agreed to form a "Palestine Entity" with its own "Palestine Liberation Army" politically directed by a "Palestine Liberation Organization" (PLO). He was appointed head of that organization. On December 24, 1967, he was dismissed from the leadership of the PLO.

before a tribunal where the only alternative, whatever the merits of the case, is a verdict for the Arabs or no verdict at all.

This brought an answer from the Soviet delegate the next day, which only furnished additional proof of Eban's remarks. The gist of Sobolev's reply was: "In view of the fact that the State of Israel, since the very first days of its existence, has pursued a threatening policy toward its neighbors, the Security Council cannot confine itself to merely noting the facts. It must issue a very serious warning. . . . The inclusion in the draft resolution of the Western Powers of a paragraph dealing with the responsibility of Syria is completely incomprehensible."

All this was merely an expression of the line adopted, for reasons already explained, sometime at the beginning of 1954. The events of 1955, seen through Russian eyes, seemed to supply further justification for Moscow's apprehensions and decisions. On the one hand, the West went on with its policy of forging a chain of anti-Soviet military pacts in the Middle East. (On February 24, the Turkish-Iraqi pact was signed. On April 5, Great Britain added its signature to it. On the same day, the Pakistani Foreign Minister announced that his country was invited to join. Pakistan actually joined the Baghdad Pact on September 23, and was followed by Iran on October 11.) On the other hand, the front of the so-called nonaligned countries was being formed, most of them only recently liberated from subjugation to colonial powers and others still fighting for their independence. The post-Stalin, nondogmatic rulers of the Soviet Union were quick to recognize their chance of using the nationalist sentiments of the "liberation movements" in these young nations for their own purposes. When the Bandung Conference opened on April 18, 1955, it had Moscow's blessings and the Russians made sure to have a finger in the pie.

In both these developments, Egypt played a role which further increased Nasser's importance in Moscow's eyes. On January 22, 1955, the Egyptian Foreign Minister announced that Egypt refused to join the Turkish-Iraqi Pact or sign any similar pact, claiming that the pact between Arab countries gave sufficient security to the area. At Bandung, Nasser emerged as one of the leading figures of the nonaligned camp. Even before Bandung, it became clear that the Arabs, and above all Nasser, would be playing an important part in this new grouping, thereby strengthening those among the Kremlin leaders who, a year before, had advised betting on the Arab horse. In Molotov's foreign policy declaration of February 10, 1955, the Arabs were mentioned twice. In one place, he said:

> The relations between the Soviet Union and the Arab States—with the exception of Iraq—have lately been marked by some positive facts. The breaking of diplomatic relations with Iraq resulted from the Iraqi Government's readiness to dance to the tune of Western imperialists. The rest of the Arab countries are aware of the friendly feelings of the peoples of the Soviet Union, and they know that the Soviet Union is supporting and will continue to give them safe support in defending their national independence.

At another point, he declared:

> The national liberation movements in Arab countries have not yet reached the same impetus as in many Asian countries. There are still Arab States, owning rich oil resources, which are heavily dependent on the West.

It was a clear warning that those of the Arab States whose relations with Moscow were "marked by the positive facts" were to be fully supported, while pressure was to be exercised on those "still heavily dependent on the West." On March 27, Molotov summoned the Syrian Minister in Moscow and handed him a statement declaring that the Soviet Union fully supported Syria in its struggle against Turkish threats and in its opposition to military pacts outside the framework of the Arab League. On April 16, the Soviet Foreign Ministry published a statement branding Western-sponsored military alliances in the Middle East as a threat to Soviet security. The statement did not mention Israel, but warned those of the Arab States that might still be deliberating whether to join these pacts. In June, the Soviets invited a Syrian parliamentary delegation to visit

Moscow in July. On its departure, the delegation, in a press conference on August 1, 1955, expressed satisfaction over the understanding it had found in conversations with Bulganin and Molotov. The press conference was at the same time exploited, without Soviet objection, for attacks against Israel, which it called "a danger to peace and a servant of imperialists."

The reverse side of closer Russian ties with the "progressive" Arab countries was, of course, a further worsening of relations with Israel. It took many forms. The Soviet press accused Israel of negotiating a military pact with Turkey (March 7, 1955), and when the Israeli Embassy denied the rumor and asked the Soviet Foreign Ministry to publish a démenti, the request remained unanswered. The same happened when the press published a report from Beirut (April 28, 1955) about the amnesty granted to a group of Israeli terrorists who were allegedly responsible for the attack on the Soviet Embassy in April 1953 (which had led to the rupture of diplomatic relations) and described the release as an unfriendly act. Ambassador Yosef Avidar, only a fortnight after he had presented his credentials, stressed in vain that those released had been arrested for other crimes. Deputy Foreign Minister Vladimir Semyonov turned a deaf ear to his assurances and reminded him of the promise given by the Government of Israel at the time of the resumption of diplomatic relations. Far from retracting its charge, the press renewed it a few days later (May 25) in an even stronger form. At the same time, it started elaborating the thesis that there was a direct connection between American pressure on Arab countries to join anti-Soviet military pacts and Israeli attacks on Egypt—an argument later used by the Soviet delegate in the Security Council debates. On June 16, the press published a TASS report from Cairo that the United States had offered a military pact to Israel. Even before then, on June 11, *Izvestia*, in a leading article, spoke of American efforts to bring Israel into the chain of anti-Soviet military pacts. The article reminded Israel that such a step would be incompatible with its undertaking, at the time, of the resumption of diplomatic relations. On July 7, *Novoye Vremya* already spoke of a U.S.-Israeli pact as an accomplished fact and accused

Israel's leaders of having lost all sense of national independence.

There were other events giving expression to the deterioration of relations. The Independence Day reception at the Israeli Embassy in Moscow that year was not attended by a single member of the Soviet Government, and the Foreign Ministry was represented by a lower-grade official of the Protocol Department. On the other hand, Kaganovich and Mikoyan attended the Egyptian national celebrations. On August 18, Deputy Foreign Minister Zorin called in Ambassador Avidar to inform him that three members of the Israeli Embassy had been declared *personae non gratae.* And so on, and so on.

All this, however, was just the prelude to far more serious steps. On August 27, the French economic paper *Les Echos* published a leading article claiming that the Soviet Ambassador to Cairo, Solod, had made the Government of Egypt an offer to arm Egyptian forces with modern weapons and to build a steel plant and several armament factories for Egypt. (The paper further reported that the Egyptians, while starting to negotiate with the Russians, at the same time informed the United States that they would not accept the Russian offer if they could get the same from America. According to the report, the American Ambassador asked for detailed lists of Egyptian requirements.) Ambassador Avidar was instructed to ask for an explanation. All he was told (September 12, 1955) by the Director of the Middle East Department of the Foreign Ministry, Zaitsev, was that there was no ground for reports about sales of weapons by the Soviet Union. Purchases of defensive weapons on a commercial basis were, of course, regarded as legitimate; but no such deals were being transacted by the Soviet Union, and he, Zaitsev, did not know of any such deal between Arab countries and any of the People's Democracies.

A fortnight later, on September 27, Nasser officially announced the Czech arms deal. There was an outcry in the West, to which Moscow responded in a TASS statement on October 2:

The Soviet Union holds that every State is entitled to see to its
security and purchase arms for its defense from other countries on
normal commercial conditions, and no State has the right to interfere and to raise one-sided claims which are bound to undermine the
rights and interests of other States.

On October 4, the Soviet press published the full text of
Nasser's speech on the arms deal, together with the declaration
by the Government of Czechoslovakia refusing to yield to
Western interference and to the request that the deal be can-
celed.

The Government of Israel reacted in a note handed to
Deputy Foreign Minister Semyonov by Ambassador Avidar on
October 24. The note, addressed to Molotov, drew the Soviet
Government's attention to "the grave threat to the security of
Israel" arising from the conclusion of the agreement for the sale
of Czechoslovak arms to Egypt. Recalling Avidar's meeting
with Zaitsev on September 12, the note referred to the "numerous declarations made by members of Arab Governments, including that of Egypt, to the effect that the annihilation of Israel
was a major objective of their foreign policy and that it was their
resolve to launch a new war against Israel as soon as they were
ready for it." The note recalled the Arab boycott, the armed
raids into Israeli territory and Arab propaganda incitements
against Israel, and went on to point out:

These activities clearly revealed the aggressive policy pursued by
Egypt against Israel. In these circumstances the sale of arms to
Egypt was bound to further these hostile designs and to enable the
Egyptian Government to launch a new war against Israel. . . .

The Government of Israel does not dispute that, in principle, every
State has a right to enter into commercial transactions, including
arms sales, with other States. It does not consider, however, that a
State doing so will escape responsibility for the consequences, when
the recipient State has made no secret of its aggressive intentions
against another State, and it is to be anticipated that the arms sold

will be used to further aggressive intentions. The Government of Egypt has made no secret of its aggressive designs against Israel.

Giving a number of quotations from Nasser's speeches on the necessity to liquidate Israel, the note continued:

These and similar statements made by the Prime Minister of Egypt leave no doubt as to his warlike intentions. In addition, representatives of Egypt have made a point of stating at meetings of the Security Council and elsewhere that Egypt regards itself to be in a state of war with Israel. The Soviet Government has on many occasions expressed itself emphatically in favor of the promotion of international peace and disarmament and against the conclusion of treaties involving aggressive designs against other States. Your Excellency, in an address to the current U.N. General Assembly, stressed that "under present conditions the termination of the armament race must be regarded as the primary objective." My Government viewed these expressions of policy with much satisfaction, both on account of world peace and of its own experience of the dangers threatening the internal peace of the Middle East.

Israel was the victim of Arab aggression in 1948 and has been the target ever since of persistent Arab enmity. Every effort which Israel has made to compose the problems outstanding between it and the Arab States by methods of peaceful negotiations has been rejected and encountered by a new outburst, in ever more serious forms, of organized Arab hostility. In these circumstances, Israel has perforce been particularly alert to the perils with which the supply of arms to the Arab States from any quarter is fraught, and it has at all times been firm in its opposition to the supply of arms to any Arab Country by any country within any framework, as long as the Arab States refuse to make peace with their neighbor.

It will therefore be understood why Israel has viewed with gravest anxiety the announcement of an agreement between Egypt and Czechoslovakia, which under the Warsaw Pact is a close military ally of the Soviet Union, for the supply of modern weapons to

Egypt. Nor can the Government of Israel fail to be concerned by
the reports which have recently appeared in the Arab press to the
effect that the Soviet Union and countries allied with it contemplate
the supply of arms also to other Arab States, whose implacable
hostility toward Israel is no less manifest than that of Egypt.

The supply of arms to Egypt, whatever its declared justification, can
only have the effect of encouraging the aggressive designs of Egypt
and other Arab States against Israel, plunging the Middle East into
a competitive arms race, diverting valuable resources from constructive purposes to the preparation of war, menacing the security
and very existence of Israel, undermining the foundations on which
the hope for peace in the Middle East could be based, and gravely
prejudicing the efforts now in progress for the relaxation of world
tension and the promotion of international peace and stability. No
greater misfortune could, indeed, befall the peoples of the Middle
East, who are striving hard to improve their lot, than that their scant
financial resources should be dissipated on a ruinous arms race, and
that its progress should result in a renewed conflagration. It would
be the very denial of the spirit of international cooperation and
goodwill which inspired the recent Geneva Conference, and on
which all peoples of the world have placed their hopes for peace and
security.

In the light of this grave turn in the fortunes of Israel and the Middle
East, the Government of Israel addresses a most urgent appeal to
the Government of the Soviet Union to use its influence to prevent
the supply of arms by its allies to Egypt or to any other Arab State
which, by its relentless hostility and aggressive policy, threatens the
security of Israel.

The answer given by Semyonov to Avidar there and then was
that the Soviet Union had no agreements about arms supply to
Middle East countries, that in the opinion of the Soviet Union
Israel had no reason to be worried, and that, as a matter of fact,
the United States and Britain were also ready to sell arms to
Egypt, only they asked the price of joining Western military
pacts, and it was therefore understandable that the Egyptians

gave preference to the Czechoslovak offer, free of any ties.

A few days earlier (on October 21), Gideon Rafael, a member of the Israeli delegation to the United Nations, asked Sobolev in New York how the supply of arms to Arab States was compatible with declared Soviet policy in the disarmament talks. Sobolev answered that, for the time being, only the reduction in armament of the Big Powers was being discussed, and claimed that the Soviet bloc arms suppliers had the same rights as American and British arms dealers. He added an assurance that the Czech deal was not directed against Israel and that every State that wished to buy arms from the Soviet bloc could do so. To the question of whether this also applied to Israel, Sobolev replied, "Why not? But you never asked."

On November 2, 1955, Moshe Sharett met Molotov in Geneva, and the next day he received a letter in which the Soviet Foreign Minister summed up Moscow's position as follows:

> The Soviet Union, as a peace-loving country and, as a result of that, a country defending the interests of freedom and independence of nations, understands the efforts to assure security. . . . As for bad relations between Israel and Egypt, it has to be said that the solution depends on both sides, and that the possibilities existing for reaching it must be utilized without threats and suspicions. All peace-loving States will assist such an agreement.

The words of Sobolev and Molotov attempted to play down the significance of the Czech arms deal and of the worsening relations with Israel, but the intended soothing effect was wiped out by a new crescendo in the anti-Israeli tone of Khrushchev's speech before the Supreme Soviet on December 29. Speaking of the Baghdad Pact, Khrushchev attacked Turkey, Iran and Pakistan—without mentioning Iraq—and lauded the refusal of the Arab States to join it. Then he launched an attack on Israel:

> Deserving condemnation are the activities of the State of Israel, which from its very first days began to threaten its Arab neighbors and to behave in an unfriendly way toward them. It is clear that such a policy does not serve the national interests of Israel and that,

behind those who are pursuing such a policy, there are imperialist States known to everybody. They are trying to use Israel as their own weapon against Arab nations, bearing in mind nothing but their own use of the oil riches in the area.

The next day, Sharett summoned Ambassador Abramov, asked for the official text of the speech and added that, if the version distributed by Reuter's proved correct, the Government of Israel would demand an explanation of the falsification of truth in connection with Israel's alleged hostility toward the Arab States, and the role it played in abetting Western pressure on Arab countries.

The situation created by Moscow's opposition to Western pacts in the Middle East on the one hand, and by the Western and Israeli criticism of the Czech arms deal on the other, was the main theme of the Middle East discussions in 1956 as well as up to the time of the Suez crisis.

On February 1, 1956, Ambassador Avidar, who had been present at Sharett's Geneva talk with Molotov, went to see the Soviet Foreign Minister once more, to try—before departing from Moscow on home leave—to obtain a clearer reply on what steps Israel could take to improve its relations with Moscow. Molotov's long answer helped little to clarify things. He surveyed Israeli-Soviet relations from the beginning but evaded concrete issues. The Soviet Union was ready to maintain close and friendly relations with Israel. Even with Finland, a country they had had to fight three times, the Soviets now had excellent relations. Israel had no reason to doubt that Moscow wanted good relations both with it and with the Arab States. The Czech arms deal and Khrushchev's statement? Israel was inflating the importance of these issues out of all proportion and, by doing so, was moving closer and closer toward the West.

On February 14, 1956, the Soviet Foreign Ministry issued a policy statement on the Middle East. After a survey of the history of Western interference in the affairs of the region— from the 1950 Tripartite Declaration to the Baghdad Pact—and after charging that the Western Powers, while pretending to be trying to help solve the Arab-Israeli dispute, were, in fact, pursuing their own strategic and oil interests, the statement said that the Soviet Union was justifiably concerned about this development. It declared that the Soviet Union would continue to support and defend the freedom and independence of the peoples of the area, and would oppose foreign interference in the internal affairs of Middle Eastern States. On February 16, *Pravda* devoted much space to the positive Arab reaction to the statement. On February 23, *Literaturnaya Gazeta,* under the heading "The Soviet Union—Friend of Arab Peoples," wrote:

> Not a long time ago, the Arab States were asking Western Powers for their approval of any step they intended to take. Arab States were getting blow after blow from Israeli aggressors and were addressing their complaints to the Western Powers, asking them to condemn Israel. Now we know that behind every Israeli aggressive act against Arab countries, there were guarantees of the imperialists. In spite of all complaints and requests by Arab States, addressed to the Western Powers to bring about compliance with U.N. resolutions on Palestine, no steps were taken. The West continued to interfere, using to that end the Three-Power Declaration of 1950. . . . But now Egypt has signed a commercial agreement about an arms supply from Czechoslovakia, and the West is becoming wild with fear that the Arab world is getting out of its hands.

Other Soviet papers went even further in their hostility to Israel. On March 19, *Izvestia* spoke of Israel as having become a victim of war hysteria.

This was also Molotov's theme in his conversation with Avidar on April 3. In Moscow's opinion, the Arab States were not preparing an attack against Israel; on the contrary, Israel, which was stronger than the Arab States, was preparing for war and this would not bring it any good. The Soviet Union was interested that the parties in the area should solve their problems among themselves, but the war preparations on the part of Israel were worrying its neighbors and increasing their suspicions of Israel's intentions. If Israel wanted peace, it was not enough to make declarations about its readiness to negotiate. It would have to abstain from taking unilateral actions like, for example, preparatory work to divert the Jordan waters without the Syrians' approval, which might lead to war.

The conversation confirmed that the Soviet Union could be expected to continue to give full support to the Arab States, without taking Israel's interests into consideration at all.

However, on April 17 the Soviet Foreign Ministry published another policy statement on the Middle East, which raised some hopes. The statement read, in part:

> The establishment of military pacts in the Middle East caused an increase of tension in the area, and is a factor in sharpening the conflict between the Arab countries and Israel and Turkey, between Pakistan and Afghanistan, between Pakistan and India. Certain circles in countries that are not interested in strengthening international peace are trying to use the Arab-Israeli conflict for their aggressive aims, even up to sending foreign armies to territories of States in the area and to creating military complications.

The statement then enumerated States in the area, mentioning also Israel, whose independence the Soviet Union had supported, but continued:

> As a consistent supporter of these principles (independence, freedom, integrity, noninterference), the Soviet Union always supported and now supports the efforts of Arab States further to strengthen their recently gained independence and their economic advancement. . . .

> The Soviet Union believes that an armed conflict in the Middle East can be avoided and that it is in the interest of all States in the Middle East not to let themselves be provoked into involvements in military actions. At the same time, the Soviet Union regards as illegal, and prohibited from the point of view of support of general peace, the attempts to use the Arab-Israeli conflict as an excuse for foreign interference with internal affairs of independent Arab States, or for the entry of foreign troops into the Middle East.

The statement also declared:

> The Soviet Union will support steps by the United Nations directed to the strengthening of peace in the Palestine area and decisions of the United Nations appropriate for that end . . .

> The Soviet Union holds the opinion that, in the nearest future, steps should be taken to alleviate the tension existing in the Palestine area, without outside intervention executed against the will of Middle Eastern States and against United Nations principles.

> The Soviet Union calls on the interested parties to abstain, in accordance with the lines included in the Armistice Agreements between the Arab countries and Israel, from all actions liable to lead to an increase of the seriousness of the situation, and also to make all necessary efforts to improve the difficult lot of hundreds of thousands of Arab refugees deprived of homes and means of existence.

> The Soviet Union is of the opinion that in the interest of the strengthening of international peace and security, it is necessary to work for an effective peace agreement on a mutually acceptable basis, taking into account the just national concerns of the interested parties. The Soviet Union on its part expresses its readiness to assist, together with other States, in efforts to reach a peaceful solution of the outstanding problems.

The statement was regarded as containing a number of positive points. Foreign diplomats in Moscow even saw it as an achievement for Israel. It did not speak of Israel as an aggressor, as Khrushchev had done less than four months earlier and as the Soviet press had continued to do even a few days previously. It said that not only Israel, but also the Arab States had to avoid actions bound to increase tension in the area and it spoke of the need to improve the lot of the refugees, but not of their return.

Finally it stressed that the peace agreement must be acceptable to all interested parties.

Various explanations were offered. Some saw in the statement the result of Soviet embarrassment in the face of Western and Israeli criticism of the Czech arms deal; others, the result of tactical discussions in the Kremlin before the visit of Bulganin and Khrushchev to London. Certain interpreters considered Moscow's fear that an open Arab-Israeli conflict could give the West a pretext for sending troops to the Middle East to be the motivating factor, while contrary ideas that it was a Russian attempt to enter the area under the pretext of trying to find a solution for the existing tension were also expressed. It may be interesting to mention here Dag Hammarskjöld's evaluation at the time. In his opinion, the Russians were not interested in a war in the Middle East, but tension was good for them since it made it easier for them to prevent Western Powers from gaining ground in the area.

Hopes were fighting skepticism in most interpretations. The Israeli Embassy in Moscow had some additional reasons for optimism. It happened that the date the statement was published coincided with Israel's Independence Day. To the great surprise of the Israelis, the reception at the Embassy this time was attended by Molotov and Mikoyan. On April 19, the Soviet press quoted Israel's positive reaction to the Soviet statement. On the same day, the slogans for First of May celebrations were published. They did not mention the Arab States but, instead, included greetings to Middle Eastern countries in general. Deputy Foreign Minister Semyonov made a point of thanking Avidar for the positive reception the statement was given in Israel. It is easily understandable that Avidar felt that "possibly some change has occurred" in the Soviet attitude toward Israel.

On April 22, Abba Eban met Sobolev in New York. He expressed Israel's appreciation of the positive points in the Soviet statement, but asked what concrete steps would be taken to restore the equilibrium distorted by the Czech arms deal, and if the Soviet Union would adopt a more balanced position or would leave the Arabs convinced that they could always count on a Soviet veto. Sobolev answered he was sure that Israel would be able to procure arms. To the second part of the question, he replied it was wrong to believe that the Soviet Union would support the Arabs if they were the aggressors. The Soviet Union would always support the side attacked and there was, therefore, no need for seeking defense arrangements outside the United Nations. When Eban mentioned that Israel found it very distressing that, during the Suez debate in the Security Council, the Soviet Union did not oppose Egypt's contention that it was in a state of war with Israel, Sobolev answered that the meaning of the statement was to stress Israel's right to exist as a sovereign state that must not be attacked by force. He added that the aim of the Czech arms deal was not to change the equilibrium or to increase the danger of an attack on Israel. In response, Eban pointed out that not the intentions but the results were important. While in the past, despite all frontier incidents, nobody thought that there was a real danger of a full-scale war, such a danger existed now after the Czech arms deal, which was certainly not "a measure directed at relaxation of international tension." To the question of whether the Soviet Union still supported direct negotiations, Sobolev answered with an emphatic *yes*. Finally he added that in the opinion of the Soviet Union, the Arabs were beginning to understand that they had no choice but to seek an arrangement, and the Soviet Union believed—and had said so in the statement—that the arrangement had to be agreed upon and not dictated.

Two days later, Sharett called in Ambassador Abramov to ask him a few more questions with regard to the statement. The talk did not go as well as had Eban's with Sobolev. Sharett's questions were very explicit. Had Israel to expect the continuation of a one-sided arms supply to Arab countries? Why did the statement speak only of Soviet support of the efforts of Arab States to strengthen their independence, and not of Middle Eastern States in general? Why were direct negotiations not specified as the right way of reaching peace? Did or did not the Soviet Union include the Security Council decision on freedom of navigation among those that had to be complied with?

Abramov answered stiffly that all Sharett's questions were controversial and defined them as proving that Israel did not want to understand the real meaning of the Soviet statement. Sharett took objection to the "inadmissible tone" of Abramov's answer, and the conversation ended in a bad atmosphere.

Others were asking questions, too. During the visit of Khrushchev and Bulganin to London at the end of April, the British asked the Russians to stop their one-sided arms supply to Arab countries, and to try to bring the Middle Eastern States to a peace settlement. In May, when asked about the meaning of the Czech arms deal, Khrushchev bluntly told a delegation of French Socialists headed by Guy Mollet: "I could avoid the answer by saying that we were not the suppliers, but I shall not do so. It so happens that some Arab States have identical interests with the Soviet Union, and it is, therefore, only natural that we should supply them with arms." On the same day (May 23), however, Molotov, talking to Ambassador Avidar, expressed his belief that Hammarskjöld's visit to the Middle East had had a calming effect and would make it possible to continue efforts to attain a decrease of tension.

Khrushchev's "identical interests" proved to be stronger than Molotov's "efforts to attain a decrease of tension." In June, the new Foreign Minister Shepilov visited Cairo. As soon as the plan of his trip became known, the Government of Israel informed Moscow that he would be a welcome guest, if he should find it possible to include a visit to Israel. The answer was negative. On the day when the reply was conveyed to the Ambassador of Israel, *Izvestia*, in a report on Sharett's resignation,[14] said it could now be expected that "Ben Gurion's Government will follow a harder line toward the Arabs." On June 20, all Soviet papers published Shepilov's speech in Cairo, stressing Soviet friendship with the Arab States. In the following days, anyone reading the Soviet press must have received the impression that Arab friendship was the point of supreme

---

14. Moshe Sharett resigned in June 1956 and was replaced as Foreign Minister by Mrs. Golda Meir.

importance in the whole structure of Soviet foreign policy.

For some time, the friendship with the Arab States was not openly connected with hostility to Israel. In June, Walter Eytan, then Director General of the Israeli Foreign Ministry, visited Moscow and was received by Semyonov. As late as July 6, Avidar heard from Dag Hammarskjöld, at a Kremlin reception in the Secretary General's honor, that he was satisfied with the talks he had had with the Soviet leaders and that "the Government of Israel will also be satisfied." He added that the Russians had confirmed to him that they were still holding to the policy of the statement of April 17.

Hammarskjöld—and he was not alone—apparently underestimated the degree of Soviet susceptibility to Arab opposition. Once they had decided that Arab friendship was what they needed, the Soviet rulers became extremely sensitive to the slightest sign of possible danger to that friendship. Immediately after the publication of the Soviet statement, at the first negative reaction from certain Arab quarters, the Russians hastened to assure the Arabs of their unchanged attitude toward Israel. On April 21, *Izvestia* published a long article stressing that the Western Powers, "in agreement with certain circles in Israel which are in a war mood," were trying to use the Arab-Israeli conflict for the purpose of their anti-Arab policy. The article reminded the Arab States that the Soviet delegation at the Security Council had defined Israeli actions as "violating the Charter and leading to a worsening of the situation on the borders," and concluded by stating that the Soviet Union continued to see in Israel an instrument which the imperialists were trying to use against Arab peoples.

In the generally optimistic evaluation of the significance of the Soviet statement, the *Izvestia* article was a solitary cloud and passed almost unnoticed. Soon, however, there were more disturbing signs. On May 20 at a Kremlin reception Khrushchev went out of his way to assure Arab ambassadors, in front of a group of journalists, that the Soviet Union was supporting the Arab States. In July, when the Arab opposition to some parts of the statement became more vocal, the Russians decided that they had to make their position even clearer. On July 26, *Izvestia* wrote that the West was trying to present the statement as a change of Soviet policy toward the Arab States, but "lies have short legs." On July 29, the same paper published an attack on Israel, singling out Ben Gurion, Abba Eban and Yigal Alon as warmongers threatening the Arab States. The article warned Israel against any unwise step "as a result of which Israel would suffer most." Finally, on July 31, all Soviet papers came out in full support of the nationalization of the Suez Canal, glorifying the Egyptian act as a great victory of the Arab fight for independence, in which the Soviet Union had always stood on the side of those who were struggling to throw off the fetters of imperialist domination.

On the same day, Khrushchev made a declaration regarding the Suez Canal, in which—while not explicitly mentioning Israel—he said that "the Soviet Union stands for the freedom of navigation for all." However, a Soviet note defending the Egyptian position and explaining the Soviet Union's support of it, which was sent to the Embassy of Israel on August 8, claimed that "the principle of freedom of navigation through the Suez Canal, as adopted in the Convention of 1888, was intact and was being fully complied with." On August 21, the Government of Israel expressed its surprise at this claim and its disappointment that the Soviet Union was ignoring Israel as a factor in settling the Suez Canal problem, though Israel was nearer to, and more interested in, Suez than any other country. On September 16, the Soviets issued another note about the Suez Canal, again completely ignoring Israel's existence and interest in the question. On September 21, Israel once more expressed its surprise and disappointment.

It was futile to expect any positive reply from the Russians. Khrushchev was more than outspoken when, formulating the Kremlin's evaluation of Israel in a talk with a French delegation visiting Moscow, he said, "Let's be frank. Israel is a State which could not exist economically without American aid, and it is, therefore, clearly a stronghold of imperialism." On September 22, Ambassador Avidar was invited to meet with Deputy Foreign Minister Zorin, who handed him a statement enumerating Israel's attacks against Egyptian and Jordanian territory, quoting an alleged remark by the French Ambassador in Israel to the effect that Israel would fight together with the Western Powers against Egypt, and warning Israel of the serious consequences if such a policy were continued.

Foreign Minister Golda Meir met with Ambassador Abramov (September 26) and expressed Israel's dismay at Zorin's statement. How was it possible to speak about Israel's actions without even mentioning Arab attacks which had provoked them? How was it possible not to mention Israel's losses? She handed the Ambassador a long list of frontier incidents in which Arab States had been condemned by the Mixed Armistice Commissions and added that, as the Soviet Union's friendship to the Arab States was a well-known fact, it gave Moscow the possibility of influencing the Arabs in the right direction. This was repeated in a note handed to the Foreign Ministry in Moscow (September 28), which added that the remark by the French Ambassador, quoted in Zorin's statement, if indeed it had been made, was the sole responsibility of the Ambassador, and it was not for the Government of Israel to deny it. The note stressed that the responsibility for the unrest in the frontier areas lay with the Arabs and expressed the hope that the Soviet Union would try to use its influence with the aggressive Arab governments.

On October 2, Avidar saw Zorin again in a frustrating last attempt to change the Soviet attitude on the Suez Canal issue. Zorin showed complete lack of understanding for Israel's views on freedom of navigation and for its request to be permitted to participate in the Security Council debate on a subject of paramount importance to it. Instead of reacting to Israel's request, Zorin plunged into an attack on the Government of Israel which, in the opinion of the Soviet Union, was "showing no will to peace, which is not good for Israel."

Far from using their influence to keep the Arab States off the warpath, the Russians were, in fact, giving them at least indirect encouragement by their unlimited support in the United Nations. In the Security Council Suez debate, which started on October 5, Shepilov became the main advocate of Egypt. He declared, for instance, that "in practice Egypt was actually guaranteeing freedom of navigation through the Suez Canal in accordance with the 1888 Convention," defended Egypt against the proposals of the Menzies mission's proposals,[15] objected to their being imposed on Egypt by the Security Council, and finally, on October 13, used the veto. A week later (October 19), when the Security Council was discussing reciprocal Israeli and Jordanian complaints, Sobolev, ignoring completely the complaints proffered by Israel, asked for "energetic intervention by the Security Council ... with a view to adopting effective measures to put an end to Israel's systematic violation of the Armistice Agreement and the Security Council resolutions."

It is even doubtful whether Soviet encouragement of the Arab States at that time can be described as only indirect. It is hard to believe that the October 24 decision to establish a unified military command of Egypt, Jordan and Syria—the ultimate factor in Israel's decision to mobilize—could ever have been taken without Moscow's full knowledge and condonation.

---

15. The Right Honorable Robert Menzies, Prime Minister of Australia, was charged with heading the delegation representing eighteen countries which participated in the London Conference of Canal-User Nations in August 1956. He subscribed to a declaration proposing the negotiation of a new Suez Canal convention. Under the new convention, the running of the Canal was to be entrusted to a board on which, in addition to Egypt, there "would be other States chosen in a manner to be agreed upon among the States parties to the Convention ... the composition of the Board to be such as to assure that its responsibilities would be discharged solely with a view to achieving the best possible operating results without political motivation in favour of, or in prejudice against, any user of the Canal." The Committee negotiated with Nasser between September 3 and September 7 without any positive results. The failure of the mission led directly to the Suez campaign.

XII

1956–1957
The Sinai Campaign
Bulganin-Ben Gurion correspondence
Russia's leadership in attack on Egypt's behalf
Khrushchev's speech in November 1956
Izvestia: "The Way to Suicide"
Moscow's embrace of Arab thesis regarding Israel

Operation Kadesh (Israel's code name for its Suez campaign) was launched on October 29, 1956. By that time, the Russians already had their hands full with the Hungarian uprising. Therefore, the almost hysterical campaign which at once started in the entire Soviet press, and the round-the-clock attacks on Israel, Britain and France that were broadcast in all languages from Moscow, served the purpose not only of lending support to Egypt but also, and perhaps even more important, of creating a smoke screen for the humiliating developments in Budapest. Israeli operations in Sinai ended on November 4, the very day when the Soviet troops began their bloodiest counterattack against the Hungarian revolutionaries. To save Soviet prestige at all costs, the smoke screen had to be continually thickened.

On November 5, large-scale demonstrations took place in front of the Israeli Embassy in Moscow. On a bitterly cold and snowy day, factory and office workers were ordered to the streets for hours on end to shout slogans against "Israeli Fascists." After midnight, the Israeli chargé d'affaires, Aviezer Chelouche, was called to see Gromyko, who handed him a note from Marshal Bulganin, Chairman of the U.S.S.R. Council of

Ministers, to Prime Minister Ben Gurion. Referring to the declared Soviet attitude toward the attack on Egypt and its condemnation in the General Assembly, Bulganin's note chastised the Government of Israel, which

> without heeding the warning, continues to act as an instrument in the hands of extremist imperialist Powers [and] continues the illogical adventure of challenging all Middle Eastern countries which are fighting against colonialism for their freedom and independence, challenging indeed all peace-loving peoples of the world. These Israeli actions show clearly what is the value of all those past declarations about Israel's being a peace-loving country and about its desire to co-exist peacefully with Arab countries.

The note spoke of "treacherous attacks" on Israel's neighbors and culminated in a solemn warning:

> The Government of Israel is playing with the fate of the whole world, with the fate of its own people. It is sowing hatred of the State of Israel among the peoples of the East. Its actions are putting a question mark on the very existence of Israel as a State. . . . We suggest that the Government of Israel should weigh its action as long as there is still time, and stop all military movements against Egypt.

The note ended by informing the Government of Israel that, "in view of the situation that was created, the Soviet Government decided to instruct its Ambassador in Tel Aviv to leave Israel and return at once. "We hope that the Government of Israel will understand and properly evaluate the significance of this step." (Copies of the note were distributed to journalists even before it was handed to the Israeli chargé d'affaires. However, at a press conference on November 6, when asked if the recall of the Ambassador was to be interpreted as a preliminary step to the breaking off of diplomatic relations with Israel, the spokesman of the Soviet Foreign Ministry answered, "Certainly not. Those are two different things and there are no connections between them.")

Ben Gurion answered Bulganin's note on November 8. He expressed his regret at the fact that, on certain points, it was obviously based on wrong or incomplete information. He reminded Bulganin that for more than two years Nasser had been organizing a special army of *fedayeen*, [16] and that in the last few months these murder gangs, operating from Jordan, Lebanon and Syria, had been daily harrassing Israelis living in the frontier areas. He quoted passages from Egyptian army orders on the necessity for preparedness to liquidate Israel. He further recalled that, in spite of Security Council resolutions on freedom of navigation through the Suez Canal, Nasser had declared he would continue discriminating against Israel.

Therefore, the action we decided to take at the end of October was in self-defense and not an act performed according to foreign will, as it was presented to you. At the request of the General Assembly, we have agreed to cease fire, and for some days now there have been no armed hostilities between Israel and Egypt. Yesterday I informed the Knesset that we are ready to enter immediately into direct negotiations for a stable peace and cooperation, without any prior conditions. We hope that all peace-loving States, and especially those with friendly relations with Egypt, will use their influence to bring about direct peace talks.

And Ben Gurion concluded:

In the end, I cannot but express my surprise and regret at the threat to the integrity and very existence of Israel contained in your note. Our foreign policy is dictated by our vital interests and by our desire to live in peace, and no foreign factor determines it or will determine it in the future. In a sovereign State we decide our ways

---

16. The Arabic word *fedayeen* has no exact analogy in English. It means a group of persons ready to sacrifice their lives for those close to them. Arabs themselves, in their English-language broadcasts, translate the word as "commandos." Sent to Israel with the task of performing acts of terror and sabotage, they started operating under this name in August 1955. There is plenty of evidence that they formed, in fact, units of the Egyptian Army. Egyptian propaganda widely glorified their exploits. Their activities were stopped after the Suez campaign of 1956.

ourselves, as partners of all peace-loving peoples in the world, fur-
thering relations of peace and justice in our region and in the world.

This was not the end of the correspondence. On November
15, Gromyko handed the Israeli chargé d'affaires another note
from Bulganin to Ben Gurion, which (in a Soviet translation of
the Russian original) read as follows:

The Soviet Government's position on the situation in the area was
set forth in my letter to you of November 5. Since in your letter of
reply you try to defend the actions taken by Israel against Egypt,
I have to reply in brief to your arguments. You allege in your letter
that the invasion of Egyptian territory by armed forces was due to
self-defense, mentioning in this connection the existence on Egyptian territory of some danger to Israel. In fact, as a number of
Security Council decisions say, it was precisely Israel and not the
Arab States that launched many armed attacks upon the neighboring Arab countries. The Security Council expressed serious anxiety
over the nonfulfillment by the Israeli Government of its obligations
under the Armistice Agreements, urged the Israeli Government to
fulfill these obligations, in the future threatening Israel to apply
appropriate sanctions under the United Nations Charter. Even your
allegations that Israel launched an armed attack on Egypt because
it was allegedly threatened by Egypt mean that the Israeli Government does not want to take into consideration the demands of the
United Nations Charter, prohibiting United Nations member-States
from using force and demanding settlement of their disputes solely
by peaceful means.

The Soviet Government cannot disregard the fact that the Israeli
Government, far from complying with the call of the U.N. General
Assembly for an immediate cease-fire and withdrawal of the forces
that have invaded Egypt, even openly announced its annexationist
intentions with regard to Egypt, the preparatory plans of joining to
Israel the Gaza area, the Sinai peninsula, the Tiran and Sanâfir
islands in the Gulf of Aqaba. In your speech in the Israeli Parliament, you referred to the "invalidity" of the Armistice Agreements
concluded between Israel and the Arab States. It is worth noting

that the Israeli Government, even after being compelled to take a decision on the withdrawal of its forces from Egyptian territory, still tries to make the fulfillment of this demand conditional upon the conclusion of "satisfactory agreements with the United Nations" with regard to the entry of international forces "in the Suez Canal Zone," which is known to be an integral part of the sovereign State of Egypt. All this, obviously, contradicts the assertions in your letter that the Israeli Government policy is allegedly prompted by the "desire for peace" and "the vital needs" of Israel.

The Soviet Government is convinced that Israel's present policy, resting on the fanning of hostility against the Arabs and their oppression, is in fact dangerous to universal peace and fatal to Israel. Such a policy, as recent events have confirmed, indeed accords only with the interests of outside forces that seek to reestablish colonial order in that area, but it is our profound conviction that it is alien to the interests of all the Near and Middle East peoples without any exception.

The Soviet Government warned the Israeli Government of the consequences dangerous to Israel, in case of the opening of aggressive armed actions against the Arab States. We regret that you did not pay attention to this. As a result of the aggression against Egypt unleashed by Israel, Egyptian towns and populated locations were ruined, thousands of innocent people were killed or mutilated, damage was inflicted on the communications, trade and economy of Egypt. But what did Israel achieve? One has to be blind not to see that aggression has brought nothing good to Israel. Aggression against Egypt has undoubtedly undermined the international position of Israel, aroused profound hatred of the Arabs and other peoples of the East toward Israel, worsened her relations with many States and entailed more economic and other difficulties in the country.

The Soviet Government takes into consideration that the Government of Israel ceased fire and then announced the forthcoming withdrawal of the Israeli forces from Egyptian territory. It goes without saying that the armed forces of Israel must be withdrawn from the territory of Egypt without delay. At the same time, to stabilize the situation in the Near East area and to eliminate the consequences of the aggression against Egypt, the Soviet Government deems it necessary to take such measures as would preclude the possibility of fresh provocations by Israel against neighboring States and would ensure durable peace and tranquillity in the Near East. Justice also demands that Israel, as well as Britain and France, should compensate Egypt, as the victim of unprovoked aggression, for damage resulting from destruction of Egyptian cities and populated localities, from discontinuation of the functioning of the Suez Canal and from demolition of its structures. Moreover, Israel must return to Egypt all property taken from Egyptian territory by Israeli armed forces which invaded the country. The international U.N. Forces, to the formation of which the Egyptian Government has consented, as follows from the U.N. decision, must be located on both sides of the Demarcation Line between Israel and Egypt, established by the Armistice Agreement. I should like, Mr. Prime Minister, to express the hope that the Government of Israel would draw appropriate conclusions from the lessons of recent events in connection with its participation in the aggression against Egypt.

There was no further reply from Ben Gurion. The complete disregard of Israel's interests and arguments in Bulganin's second communication made it only too obvious that any renewed attempt to change Moscow's mind would be futile.

The Russians continued to speak on behalf of the Arabs in the United Nations. A few quotations from their speeches in the Emergency Session of the General Assembly in November 1956, and in the regular session between November 1956 and March 1957, will suffice to show the completely biased attitude of the Soviet Union:

Shepilov (November 11, 1956):

The Soviet delegation considers it imperative that measures be taken to prevent Israel from further provoking its neighbors and to ensure peace and tranquillity in the Middle East.

Shepilov (November 23, 1956):

Israel has played a particularly unedifying, and I might even say provocative, role in the sinister political game of the imperialist forces.

Byelorussian delegate Kiselev (November 27, 1956):

As regards Israel, the policy of its extremist groups intent on fanning hostility towards the Arabs and crushing them in reality endangers the cause of peace and is fatal to Israel itself. It is a policy which is solely in the interest of reactionary groups in the United Kingdom and France, anxious to restore colonialism, and contrary to those of all peoples of the Middle East, including the people of Israel.

Ukrainian delegate Palamarchuk (December 5, 1956):

Israel was cast in the role of the initial aggressor by the United Kingdom and France, on the ground that it was entitled to start a preventive war.

Kuznetsov (January 17, 1957):

The invading forces of Israel are still on Egyptian territory.... The ruling circles of Israel are planning the annexation of territory belonging to neighboring Arab States. That policy is a challenge to the peoples of the East.... the continuation of such a policy can only worsen the position of the State of Israel.

Kiselev (February 18, 1957):

Mr. Fawzi [a member of the Israeli delegation to the United Nations] rightly considers that Israel should not be allowed to reap any fruits or gain any advantage from its aggression against Egypt, or to continue committing atrocities and acts of destruction . . . in the territory it has occupied. . . . The ruling circles in Israel are more willing to unleash a new war against Egypt than to withdraw their forces from Egyptian territory.

So much for Soviet labors on behalf of the Arabs in the United Nations. The Russians did not, however, neglect any other opportunity to express their full support of the Arab fight against Israel. On November 11, 1956, Syria opened negotiations for additional arms supplies (the Syrian President had visited Moscow on October 31 during the Sinai campaign), and the deal, on this occasion made publicly and directly with the Soviet Union, was concluded on December 2. At the same time, the Russians stopped all trade with Israel, which included the cancelation of the agreement for the supply of crude oil that was scheduled to continue till 1958. On November 17, Khrushchev, at a reception in honor of Gomulka, spoke of the acts of "Israeli, British and French robbers" against Egypt. Soviet workers "donated" $15 million to Egypt. Komsomol, the Soviet youth organization, started registering volunteers to fight with Egypt against Israel. On November 18, Khrushchev, at a reception at the Polish Embassy, said:

> What is Israel? A country without any great importance in the world, whose only task is to play the role of provocateur before an aggression. If the Israelis did not feel that they had the support of the Great Powers, they would be sitting quietly like little boys.[17]

The nadir—below which Soviet behavior was not to fall until ten years later, during and immediately after the Six-Day War —was probably reached in the leading article of *Izvestia* on November 29, 1956. Under the heading "The Way to Suicide," it said:

> By challenging Arab peoples and all peoples struggling against colonialism, Israel is digging its own grave. When in 1947 the

---

17. *Pravda*, the only Soviet paper published on Sundays, appeared very late the next day, because it was believed necessary to make a number of changes in the published version of Khrushchev's speech. The cited passage was omitted. So was another, in which Khrushchev said: "Politically and ideologically, Nasser is nearer to those who fought against him than he is to us. In Egypt, Communists are in jail. Why do we support him? Because he is a national hero, because he was the leader of the Egyptian people in their struggle against the British, French and Israeli armies."

United Nations General Assembly decided to establish the State of Israel, the world expected and hoped that Israel would develop on the principles of democracy and peace and would work for peaceful coexistence with its neighbors. These hopes and expectations were not fulfilled. From the very first days of its appearance on the international stage, the State of Israel began threatening its neighbors, following an unfriendly policy toward them, and "Socialists" of the type of Ben Gurion put into motion slogans of extremist and aggressive Zionism, placing themselves fully at the disposal of imperialist forces and serving them in all possible ways. The rulers of Israel became the gendarmes of the colonial powers in the Arab East.... With the appearance of the State of Israel, where the power fell into the hands of a group of irresponsible adventurers, the East turned, in fact, into a powder keg.

After more attacks on Ben Gurion, whose policy, according to the newspaper, led to mounting hatred of Israel among the Arabs, the article concluded with a warning, already familiar from Bulganin's letters and Shepilov's speeches in the General Assembly: "The ruling circles of Israel must stop playing with fire, as long as there is time. . . . The very existence of Israel as a State is at stake."

The warning was less important and less horrifying than the fact that the Russians finally embraced the Arab thesis that the existence of the State of Israel, which they had helped to establish only nine years earlier, was the root of all evil in the Middle East.

PART
II

1957-1967

XIII

The second decade, a continuation of the line adopted in 1954
Gromyko: Israel hacking at the branch on which it is sitting
Moscow spreading false accusations against Israel

The second decade of Soviet-Israeli relations, the years between 1957 and 1967, was merely a continuation of the line
adopted by Moscow early in 1954. There was no basic policy
change on the Russian side during this period. All actions of the
Arab States, especially of Egypt and Syria, were in Moscow's
eyes worthy and deserving of support, or at least of defense.
Everything done by Israel was to be condemned. Cooperation
and mutual understanding in the relations between Moscow
and Jerusalem were practically nonexistent. Since 1956 there
had been no trade, cultural ties had been limited to the minimum, and political connections could best be described as existing not per se, but as a function of Moscow's increasingly active
relationship with the Arab States. However, precisely because
Soviet policy was used as a regulating device, it may be a subject
deserving study not only because the Soviet attitude toward
Israel was an exact negative of the picture of its relations with
Arab countries, but also because it indirectly indicates Russia's
strengths and weaknesses in the Middle East and gives some
insight into Soviet intentions there.

The evaluation of the situation by Israel's Ministry for For-

eign Affairs at the beginning of the period may be summed up
as follows:

1. The Soviet Union adopted an anti-Israeli line as a matter of
   long-term policy.
2. This policy was an integral part of the Soviet effort to prevent the
   United States from becoming the heir of Britain and France in
   the Middle East.
3. In the competition to fill the vacuum created by the decline, if
   not the end, of British and French influence in the area, the
   Soviet Union saw itself handicapped by the enormous economic
   potential of the United States. Therefore, while also giving the
   Arab States some economic assistance, it concentrated mainly
   on extending political and military aid. This was a sphere in
   which Washington was unable to outdo Moscow, because
   American public opinion would not permit the Government to
   take openly anti-Israeli steps.

Ample proof soon showed the accuracy of this estimate. The
Soviets were now ready to extend unlimited and unrestrained
political help to the Arab States.

Though in 1957 the Security Council was occupied mainly
with the problem of India and Pakistan, it had to deal with the
Middle East on three different occasions. In April, when France
and Australia opposed the Egyptian claim that the Convention
of 1888 entitled Egypt to prohibit Israeli vessels from passing
through the Suez Canal, the Soviet delegate Sobolev (April 26),
without entering into discussion of the aspects of international
law governing the matter, simply declared:

The failure of the armed attack on Egypt by the United Kingdom,
France and Israel proved, as nothing else could have done, the utter
futility of the imperialist powers' efforts to impose upon the Egyptian Government by force disadvantageous conditions with respect
to the operation of the Suez Canal.

A few weeks later in the continuation of discussion on the same issue, Sobolev, on May 20, went a step further:

I am compelled to draw attention to another purpose sought by raising the question in the Security Council and one which is, in our view, fraught with serious dangers, namely, the fact that aggressive circles are inciting Israel to commit new, provocative acts against Egypt, such as the widely discussed attempt by an Israeli vessel to force its way through the Canal as a test of the firmness of Egypt's position. . . . There can be little doubt that such a policy is aimed not at creating conditions for the restoration of peace in the Near and Middle East, but at maintaining a center of unrest in that area and creating the necessary conditions for intervention in the internal affairs of the Arab States. The Soviet delegation considers that the Security Council should not tolerate the intervention of any country in the domestic affairs of the sovereign Arab States on any pretext whatsoever. By taking such a stand the Security Council would make a significant contribution to the cause of peace and would forestall the provocative actions that are being prepared on the Arab-Israeli frontiers or even in the territorial waters of Arab States.

The same month the Security Council discussed the Syrian complaint "concerning the construction of a bridge in the demilitarized zone," and again Sobolev's help went wholly to the Arabs. He declared on May 28:

The Israeli authorities, in defiance of the clear and specific provisions of the [Armistice] Agreement have in various ways acted unilaterally in the demilitarized zone, in particular by building a bridge at the southern end of Lake Rula, which is essentially strategic and gives Israel a military advantage. . . . The unilateral actions of the Israeli authorities . . . constitute a serious violation of the Armistice Agreement and are, in fact, a military threat to Israel's neighbor, Syria . . . Syria has every justification for showing alarm at Israel's new violations of the provisions of the Armistice Agreement since it has in the past, on more than one occasion, been the victim of aggressive activities on the part of Israel. . . . The events of the past months, and in particular the unprovoked aggression against Egypt, show that Israel's leaders will go to any length in their endeavors to carry out their extremist plans directed against their Arab neighbors. . . . The Council ought, in our view, to put a stop to Israel's attempt to sabotage the present armistice and to provoke fresh conflict and friction with neighboring States. . . . In the Soviet delegation's view, it is impossible not to support the Syrian representative's appeal to the Council to condemn Israel's violation of the provisions of the Armistice Agreement and of the Security Council's resolution.

On the third occasion that year, the Security Council was debating (September 6) reciprocal complaints of Jordan and Israel. Even Hussein's kingdom, which only a few years prior was to Moscow a "British puppet," had by now graduated to the rank of an Arab State deserving Soviet support against Israel. Overlooking Israel's complaint entirely, Sobolev said:

The Soviet delegation understands Jordan's concern in connection with this as yet bloodless but serious violation of the Armistice Agreement, because it occurred after repeated warnings to Israel from the Security Council and when all peace-loving States are endeavoring to reduce tension in this area of the world. . . . What is the purpose of these incessant provocations by Israel on its neighbors' frontiers, accompanied by a campaign of threats and saber-rattling directed at the Arab countries? There can only be one answer: The continuation of strained relations between Israel and the Arab countries and the incessant frontier incidents are of advantage only to the aggressive circles in certain States, that use Israel as a tool in their far-reaching plans which are not concerned either with the interests of the peoples of Arab countries or with the maintenance of peace. It is not by chance that the present increase in tension between Israel and the Arab countries coincides with the pressure that is being exerted by the United States on certain Arab countries.

The anti-Israeli Soviet pronouncements that year were, however, climaxed not in the Security Council but in the General Assembly. There Gromyko spoke twice about "the situation in the Middle East, where almost before one military conflict has been settled a new crisis fraught with the danger of fresh hostilities is already gathering to a head." In his first speech (on September 20), Gromyko did not mention Israel by name. The attack was concentrated on the United States and only implied that Israel was being used as a tool.

> The Egyptian gamble failed because the forces of peace proved stronger than the forces of war. . . . Today . . . it is Syria which has been selected as the victim of imperialist intrigues. . . . The Soviet Union cannot remain indifferent and observe from afar the attempts that are being made to turn the Near and Middle East, an area adjacent to its own territory, into a permanent hotbed of armed conflict.

In his second speech, Gromyko, on October 22, began with an attack against the United States and Turkey, which "was chosen because there were no volunteers for the thankless task of executing the design of foreign imperialist circles in regard to the Arab States, among the other States of the Near and Middle East." But then he continued:

> Israel has discredited itself too deeply as a result of last year's adventure against Egypt. Nevertheless, a definite role has also been assigned to Israel in the plans against Syria and the other Arab States. It was anticipated, when the U.S.-Turkish plan of attack upon Syria was discussed, that Israel, too, would participate in certain stages of these operations. Experience has shown that Israel, in pursuing its present policy, gives little heed to the course of its future development or to its very existence as a State. Israel appears to be hacking away at the branch on which it is sitting.

Gromyko's questioning of the very existence of Israel was not the only threat Israel was to hear from Soviet sources during that year. It was the year of the Eisenhower Doctrine, which may been responsible for stepping up Moscow's sensitivity in matters concerning the Middle East. "Israeli activities during the Jordan crisis," wrote *Pravda* on May 24, "the provocations against Egypt and the acceptance of the Eisenhower Doctrine prove that Israeli ruling circles guide their country on a dangerous path that does not promise any good to Israel. All the responsibility for the results of this shortsightedness will fall on these ruling circles." *Pravda* went so far as to claim that Israel's adherence to the Eisenhower Doctrine was "in direct contradiction to Israel's obligations to the Soviet Union." Even earlier, on April 19, TASS claimed that "it is known that open and demonstrative war preparations are taking place on the border of Jordan, and that this time Israel plays a specially shameful part."

The spreading of false rumors with a clear intention to incite the Arab States and thus increase their dependence on the Soviet Union was not invented by Moscow in May and June, 1967. Ten years earlier, on July 7, 1957, for instance, the entire Soviet press and radio publicized the news that Israeli authorities evacuated Eilat to turn the region into an American military base.[18] Throughout July, the Soviet press continued to accuse Israel of "preparing an aggression against Syria with the help of the United States" and to urge the Syrian people to "defend their independence well, in spite of all the intrigues of the American imperialists and their puppet, Israel." On July 21, the Moscow radio added: "Israeli ruling circles should not forget that there are powers that are capable of making them abandon the policy of intimidation which threatens peace and security in the Middle East."

After Gromyko's second speech in the General Assembly, Golda Meir talked with him in New York. The meeting was not even mentioned in the Soviet press, while Gromyko's conversations with Arab statesmen were given wide publicity. Attacks on Israel continued with ever greater intensity. *Komsomolskaya Pravda* (October 15) wrote: "In submitting to the will of

---

18. The behavior of Soviet Ambassador Abramov, when the then Director General of the Foreign Ministry, Walter Eytan, suggested to him, on this and other occasions, that he could easily find out for himself that the rumors spread by the Soviet press were completely unfounded, was identical to that of Ambassador Chuvakhin ten years later. See page 194.

their foreign masters, the Israelis purposely create the tension which reigns in the Middle East and insults the peace policy of the Soviet Union." *Literaturnaya Gazeta* (October 29) wrote:

> American imperialism increased its activities in Israel and changed it, in fact, into one of its colonies and a strategic military base in the Middle East, the jumping board for its offensive wars. The leaders of the country smashed the progressive and democratic forces and stirred up national troubles, oppressing the Jewish workers and suppressing all rights of the Arab population.

And the Red Army paper *Krasnaya Zvezda* (November 22) summed it up as follows:

> Israel is backed by the Western Powers which consider Israel as an instrument for their colonialist policy, for their pressure on the Arab countries. They encourage their lackey's aggressive ambitions and support and arm Israel. . . . Israel's present policy is foolish and adventurous. The continuation of this policy constitutes a threat to the very existence of Israel as a State. It looks as though it cuts the branch on which it sits.

In answer to all previous and later protests against the Soviet press, the Israeli Embassy was invariably told by the Soviet Foreign Ministry that the press in the Soviet Union was independent from government authorities. This time the official organ of the Red Army branded its own Government's lie by using the very words that Gromyko had spoken.

On October 30, the Israeli delegation to the United Nations issued a statement in answer to Gromyko's speech. It read as follows:

> The Israeli delegation took no part in the discussion or voting on the Syrian charges against Turkey and the United States, to which full response was made by the Governments concerned. The only reference to Israel requiring public comment is the brief allusion to Israel by Mr. Gromyko in his speech on Ocober 22, which was echoed by some others. In connection with that statement, the Israeli delegation wishes to state:

1. It is untrue to assert (as Mr. Gromyko did without a shred of evidence) that Israel has ever been involved in the Syrian crisis or in some alleged plan of aggression conceived by the United States and Turkey. This assertion does not deserve to be taken seriously and is not taken seriously anywhere. But it is regrettable that the United Nations should be used at all for such a baseless statement.
2. Israel's policy is one of peace in the Middle East based on mutual recognition and respect for the independence and integrity of each of its States.

Even when not addressing the gallery, Soviet diplomats did not change substantially the tenor of their utterances. Here and there, one might detect a trace of apology, but the final summing up was always the same: Israel was responsible for the tension in the Middle East and for the worsening of its relations with the Soviet Union. Ambassador Abramov returned to Israel in April; on June 28 he was called in by Golda Meir. She told him that she had hoped his return would mean the beginning of a new chapter in Israeli-Soviet relations, but actual happenings did not reveal any signs of improvement. She said she would like to know the sources and reasons for the increasingly hostile Soviet attitude to Israel, and to have the Ambassador's opinion as to what could be done to arrive at normal, if not friendly, relations. Abramov did not answer the questions. He simply replied that he too had returned with great optimism which, however, had evaporated very quickly after the anti-Soviet attacks by the Israeli press. He had nothing to say about the attitude of the Soviet press to Israel. When Mrs. Meir mentioned the sending of submarines to Egypt, Abramov parried by saying that they had been supplied only after large shipments of arms had been sent by the Western Powers to Turkey, Iraq, Saudi Arabia and Israel. Gromyko was more outspoken. When Ambassador Avidar asked him, on March 16, about the chances of improving relations between Moscow and Jerusalem, he admitted that there had been a deterioration but added bluntly that the reason for it was solely Israel's behavior in opposing peace with its neighbors; it should be clear that Israel's present policy was against its own interests.

The futility of Israel's attempts to come to a dialogue with Moscow was expressed even more clearly in Gromyko's conversation with the ambassador of a country friendly to Israel. When asked if he did not see a possibility for a constructive reassessment of the Middle East situation and especially of the Soviet attitude to Israel which might lead to a lessening of tension in the area, Gromyko answered, "What hopes are you putting on Israel? Israel is just an agent of American imperialism."

From certain conversations the impression could still be gained that Moscow's position was not altogether petrified. Thus, for instance, the following interesting dialogue took place between Gideon Rafael and the Soviet delegate to the United Nations, Sobolev, on February 5:

Sobolev: Our friendship with Israel continued, in fact, up to your attack on Egypt [in 1956].

Rafael: Perhaps it had already ceased when the Czechs supplied arms to Egypt?

Sobolev: What was all the excitement about? The events have shown you clearly that you had nothing to fear from these arms, which are now in your hands.

Rafael: And what have you gained? The United States, which, till then, did not want to take upon itself the responsibility for security in the Middle East, has now strengthened the Baghdad Pact, to which Israel objects.

Sobolev: We have no special interests in the Middle East. We only react to the policy of imperialists in the region.

But the conversation ended by Sobolev's asserting that there was "no hope for peace as long as Israel follows its militant policy." In September of that year, Ambassador Abramov called in Dr. Nahum Goldmann, President of the World Jewish Congress, and bitterly complained that he was trying to work for an improvement of relations between the Soviet Union and Israel, but found no understanding in Jerusalem. The Soviet

Union was against an arms race in the area, but it had to follow the United States. Should Washington stop supplying arms to the Middle East, Moscow would stop too. Anyway, arms supplied to Arab countries were not directed against Israel. When arms were supplied to Cairo, Egypt was warned that the Soviet Union would go to Israel's aid should Egypt attack Israel. As the attack came from Israel, the Soviet Union helped Egypt. Abramov's argument was misdirected for Dr. Goldman was known at the time to be advocating a change in Israel's foreign policy toward greater neutrality, a line attractive to the Russians, who therefore had good reason to use a different language with him from that used with official representatives of the State of Israel. The voice of Gromyko was not only more authoritative; it was also closer to expressing the true thoughts and feelings behind Soviet policy toward Israel.

Israel's first Envoy to the Soviet Union,
Mrs. Golda Meir, presenting her Letters of
Credence to Deputy Chairman of the
Supreme Soviet Vlasov. Deputy Foreign
Minister Zorin (*left*) attended the ceremony.
(September 10, 1948.)

President Ben Zvi in conversation with
Minister Yershov during the first reception
for the Diplomatic Corps given after the
President's election. Director General of the
Foreign Ministry Levavi in center
(January 8, 1953).

On the second anniversary of Israel's
independence, President Weizmann enjoys a
joke with the Soviet Envoy Yershov and the
American Ambassador Macdonald.

Ambassador Abramov with President
Ben Zvi and Foreign Minister Sharett. (*right*)
after the accreditation ceremony in
Jerusalem (February 4, 1953).

Foreign Minister Golda Meir and
Ambassador Bodrov raising their glasses
after signing the agreement on the sale of
Russian property in Jerusalem to the
government of Israel (October 7, 1964).

Ambassador Bodrov greeted by
Prime Minister Ben Gurion at their first
meeting in Jerusalem. (July 17, 1958.)

President Shazar and Foreign Minister
Abba Eban raising their glasses to
Ambassador Tchouvakhin (*left*) after he
had presented his credentials in Jerusalem
(November 26, 1964).

Israel's Permanent Representative to the United Nations Gideon Rafael (*left*) in conversation with the Soviet representative Ambassador Fedorenko before the Security Council met to discuss "the extremely grave situation in the Middle East" (May 24, 1967). Ten days later, the Six Day War broke out.

Chairman of the Supreme Soviet Anastaz Mikoyan receiving in the Kremlin Israel's last Ambassador to the Soviet Union Katriel Katz (*left*) (July, 1965).

On June 7, 1967, the Security Council
adopted a Soviet draft resolution on a
cease-fire. Israel's Permanent Representative
Gideon Rafael (*right*) is seen here conversing
with the President of the Council on that
occasion, the Danish representative
Hans Tabor.

Foreign Minister Abba Eban addressing the
Security Council on November 13, 1967.
(In the foreground, back to camera, the
Egyptian Foreign Minister Riad (*left*) and
the Jordanian Foreign Minister Rifai.)

XIV

1958–1960
Israeli note of January 1958
Ben Gurion
Bodrov meeting of July 17, 1958
Abba Eban's and Golda Meir's answers to Gromyko
Lost hopes

In December 1957, the Soviet Government sent a note to the Governments of other United Nations member-States which, while painting a one-sided picture of the causes of world tension, nevertheless encouraged some hope by its enumeration of general principles to be maintained for the relaxation of the tension. The Government of Israel replied to the Soviet note on January 21, 1958. The text of the reply handed to Ambassador Abramov by Foreign Minister Golda Meir on that day was as follows:

The Government of Israel has given serious consideration to the note of the Government of the Soviet Union of December 10, 1957. The Government of Israel is pleased to record its full agreement with the Government of the Soviet Union regarding most of the constructive principles contained in its note which are designed to strengthen peace in the world and in the Middle East in particular.

Israel, being a small country that is not connected by any political pact with any Power or group of Powers in the world, abstains from expressing opinions regarding the causes and factors of interna-

129

tional tension, though not necessarily because it agrees with all the points in the Soviet Government's note regarding this issue. At the same time the Government of Israel wholeheartedly endorses the assumption of the Soviet Union that the Government of Israel, cognizant of Israel's responsibility as a member of the United Nations, will on its part do all in its power to assist in the prevention of a new war and in the strengthening of peace and friendly cooperation among the nations.

The Government of Israel views with anxiety the sharpening of international tension as well as the danger of the outbreak of a war liable to bring unparalleled disaster to the whole of humanity. Israel believes that peace is indivisible and that, therefore, peace must be maintained everywhere, for any "small" or "local" war is likely to spread into a worldwide conflagration.

The Government of Israel wholeheartedly welcomes the opinion of the Government of the Soviet Union that "relations among nations must be based on the mutual maintenance of sovereignty and territorial integrity, on the principles of nonaggression and noninterference in each other's internal affairs, on equality and mutual benefit—in sum, they must be based on the principles of coexistence in peace and cooperation."

When President Eisenhower's representative, James P. Richards,[19] visited Israel on May 2, 1957, the Government of Israel informed the United States Government that:

Israel reaffirms that, in the conduct of its international relations, it is guided by the principles and purposes of the Charter of the United Nations, to strengthen universal peace, to foster friendly relations among nations, to settle international disputes by peaceful means

---

19. James P. Richards, former Chairman of the Foreign Affairs Committee of the U.S. House of Representatives, was Special Assistant to President Eisenhower on Middle East affairs.

and to achieve international cooperation in the economic, social and humanitarian spheres.

In conformity with her obligations under the Charter, Israel is opposed to aggression from any quarter against the territorial integrity and political independence of any country. Israel entertains no aggressive intent against any other people or nation anywhere, and is agreed on the importance of preserving the political independence and territorial integrity of the countries of the Middle East.

Israel recognizes that every effort must be made to achieve lasting peace both in the Middle East and throughout the world and will cooperate with the United States and other friendly Governments to this end.

The Government of Israel herewith expresses its desire for cooperation with the Government of the Soviet Union and with all other friendly Governments for the purpose of achieving the above aims.

As a small nation dwelling on the Mediterranean as well as on the Red Sea shores at the western end of the Middle East [region], and as a people which only ten years ago was privileged to renew its independence, with the assistance of the Soviet Union, the United States and the great majority of the members of the United Nations at the time, Israel regards as its chief task the development of its small country for the benefit of all its inhabitants and the rooting of the Jewish immigrants, coming to the country from various parts of the world, in productive and creative endeavors. To achieve these purposes, Israel is all the more in need of peace in its region and in the world.

The note then outlined the history of hostile Arab acts against Israel since May 1948, stressing in particular the closure of the Suez Canal to peaceful Israeli navigation, the Arab economic boycott of Israel and the refusal of the Arab States to negotiate the establishment of peaceful relations. It continued:

Israel demands nothing from the neighboring countries except peaceful coexistence on the basis of the principles so forcefully put forward in the note of the Soviet Government, that is, abstention from the disturbance of the *status quo* and from the imposition of territorial changes upon anybody.

It is Israel's desire to base its relations with the neighboring Arab countries on the proposal put forward by the Government of the Soviet Union at the Twelfth Session of the General Assembly of the United Nations, namely, on respect for the territorial integrity and sovereignty of Israel and its neighbors, on abstention from attacks and from interference in its internal affairs as well as in theirs, and the maintenance of coexistence on the basis of amicable cooperation with the purpose of the fruitful development of the entire region as well as the strengthening of world peace.

The Government of Israel feels certain that the Government of the Soviet Union could greatly assist in the promotion of peace in the Middle East if it were to call upon all nations in the region to maintain peaceful and cooperative coexistence and to respect the territorial integrity and sovereignty of all nations in the Middle East, as expressed in the Soviet Government's note to the Government of Israel, and if, toward this end, the Government of the Soviet Union were to advise Israel and the Arab States in the Middle East to enter into direct negotiations for the conclusion of a treaty of peace and the establishment of cooperation.

Having stated its position, the Government of Israel tried to use the opportunity to stress its hope for an improvement of bilateral relations, and concluded the note by stating:

Finally, the Government of Israel wishes to declare its strong desire to establish closer economic and cultural relations between Israel and the Soviet Union and, with an improvement of the international climate in view, to improve relations between Israel and the Soviet Union. The Government of Israel is convinced that such an improvement in relations would strengthen peace in the Middle East and would perhaps contribute, in a modest measure, to the reduction of world tension.

More than once during the decade of 1957–1967, hopes were raised of the possibility of an improvement in relations between Moscow and Jerusalem, only to be speedily shattered. The Soviet note of December 10, 1957, was one example. It was followed by the fact that in 1958, for the first time, there were Security Council debates in which one Arab State spoke against another Arab State—Lebanon's complaint against Egypt, and Jordan's complaint against Egypt. On both occasions, the Soviet representative, while adopting Egypt's position, did not make any attempt to involve Israel even indirectly. The Russians also remained silent when (on January 22, 1958) reciprocal complaints of Israel and Jordan were discussed. For optimists, these were hopeful signs. With very few exceptions, even the attacks against Israel in the Soviet press disappeared temporarily.

In this "cease-fire" atmosphere, Ben Gurion invited the new Soviet Ambassador, Mikhail Bodrov, to discuss (on July 17, 1958) the possibilities of improving relations between Israel and the Soviet Union. Bodrov, as will be remembered, had been instrumental, as Ambassador to Sofia, in negotiations about renewal of diplomatic relations after the break in 1953; and the fact that he was now appointed Ambassador to Israel was interpreted by some in Jerusalem as another promising sign. Ben Gurion made some concrete suggestions on this occasion. Israel wanted friendship with the Soviet Union. To refute the accusations that it was receiving arms from the West to serve the West's interests, Israel was ready to apply for arms from the Soviet Union. Iraq was receiving arms from the United States, Jordan from Britain, Egypt from the Soviet Union. Why could the Soviet Union not supply arms also to Israel? However, Israel was more interested in peace than in arms; and if the Soviet Union could persuade the Arabs to negotiate peace with Israel, Israel was ready to forego the application for weapons. This was the tenor of Ben Gurion's suggestions. Bodrov promised to inform his Government and added only that what was most important for the Soviet Union was that Israel should not play the colonialists' game.

There was no answer from Moscow to Ben Gurion's suggestions. Instead, a month afterward (August 20), in the Special Emergency Session of the General Assembly, Gromyko introduced another variation on his old theme:

> We must also draw attention to . . . the frequent and mysterious hints which have been dropped to the effect that the United Kingdom is allegedly prevented from carrying out an early withdrawal of its troops from Jordan by the threat of an attack on Jordan by Israel. . . . Can this attempt at intimidation by raising the specter of a campaign by Israel against Jordan be interpreted otherwise than as a part of a preconceived plan? While all this is going on, the representatives of Israel are occupying their places among us, listening to all our statements and, of course, keeping themselves fully informed of what is going on behind the scenes. The Israeli delegation listens to all this, it has so far remained enigmatically silent, it is hedging to sell itself dear. . . . We must frankly state that unless Israel has the support of other countries, there can be no danger that it will attack Jordan. If, on the other hand, it is anticipated that Israel will nevertheless do so, then obviously someone has laid plans along these lines in advance. . . . If there are no such plans, there is no need to arouse fear of Israel among the Arabs. In that case, the delegation of Israel should make a statement to that effect and put an end to speculation on the matter. If it does not, it will only strengthen our conviction that the General Assembly is witnessing a stage performance in which roles have been assigned in advance.

Abba Eban answered Gromyko's challenge the same day, in the evening session of the General Assembly:

> The Foreign Minister of the Soviet Union referred to what he calls talk in the lobbies about Israel's policy. The policy of the Government of Israel on the integrity and independence of all States in the Middle East has been set forth in numerous statements. . . . Speculations and conjectures made by other parties or by organs of the press cannot commit us in any way. The only way to understand the

policy of the Israeli Government is to read what the Government says. Our policy . . . has been, and is, based on mutual respect of all the Middle East States for the integrity and political independence of States; and, under strict observance, on integral implementation of existing agreements on the basis of reciprocity. . . . The agenda does contain a complaint by Jordan about a threat to her independence and integrity. That complaint is not against us. Indeed, there is no change in our constant policy of readiness to conclude here and now mutual pacts of nonaggression with each or all of our neighbors. So nobody who wants to find out what Israel's policy is need go into the anterooms, the corridors or the lobbies. The question at issue, I respectfully suggest, is not Israel's policy toward her neighbors. The question is, what their policy is toward us. . . .

Apparently, this clear and prompt reply did not register, because, less than a fortnight later (October 2), Gromyko, when pressing in the General Assembly for American and British compliance with the Special Emergency Session's resolution on withdrawal of troops from Lebanon and Jordan, found it necessary to repeat:

We are told now and then that, in the event of a United Kingdom withdrawal from Jordan, the latter will be liable to attack by Israel. We consider that this story has already been sufficiently discredited, since everyone knows that an attack by Israel on Jordan would, in actual fact, be an attack by the United States and the United Kingdom. Israel would obviously not lift a finger without their sanction and encouragment. . . . If the United States and the United Kingdom continue to intimidate Jordan by speaking of a possible attack by Israel, they will clearly be doing so deliberately, to hinder the withdrawal of their forces, and if so, they will bear the responsibility for the performance which they stage from time to time, in which they assign the leading part to Israel.

This time it was Foreign Minister Golda Meir who replied to Gromyko. Her answer, on October 7, was very brief:

I can assure the Foreign Minister [of the Soviet Union] that despite his innuendoes, Israel's policy is neither a dictated one nor a subservient one. The policy of Israel, small State though it be, will continue, as in the past, to be determined by the Government of Israel and that Government alone.

Once more the hopes for a chance to improve relations with Moscow were fading rapidly. The anti-Israeli attacks in the Soviet press were resumed,[20] and when, in December, Israel found itself forced to turn to the Security Council with a complaint against Syria, Soviet intervention on Syria's behalf was an unmistakable return to familiar Russian performances. Calling Israel the "instigator of the incident" about which Israel had complained, Sobolev (on December 15) said:

Israel, instead of using the existing machinery (established by the Armistice Agreement), is infringing on the established procedure and has appealed to the Security Council, obviously to divert possible blame from itself, whereas the actual victim is the one which is entitled to lodge a complaint that the Armistice Agreement has been violated. It may also be that Israel is influenced by the fact that, in the past years, it has frequently been blamed by the Security Council for having provoked serious incidents which have led to major violations of the Armistice Agreement and to a state of tension in the area. Apparently, in the present case, Israel is anxious for the records of the Council to include some mention of its complaint, although that complaint is completely unfounded.

To avoid another Soviet veto, the Council suspended discussion. The President expressed the hope that the incidents about which Israel complained were of an isolated nature and that the parties concerned would do everything to prevent similar occurrences.

In Israel, the frustrated hopes led to an atmosphere of fatal-

---

20. The Red Navy organ *Sovietski Flot*, for instance, wrote, on October 27, 1958: "With the Nuri Said bulwark of the colonizers in the Arab East having been destroyed by the revolution in Iraq, the imperialists pitch an even larger stake on Israel."

ism. It was plain that the character of relations was dictated in Moscow by considerations differing completely from those in Jerusalem. The general feeling was that no matter what Israel did or did not do, it would be wrong in Russian eyes.[21] Moscow was not going so far as to identify itself with Arab claims for the liquidation of Israel, but neither was it ready to use its influence to convince the Arabs to negotiate peace with Israel, or at least to adopt a less hostile attitude. This gave the Arabs confidence that the Soviet Union would, in fact, support them even in extremist actions against Israel.

Such was the Israeli appraisal of the situation at the end of 1958. The conviction of its soundness was strengthened by a series of conversations with Soviet diplomats during the next two years. Israel was to be blamed for the bad state of relations with Moscow; so the Israeli Ambassador in Paris was told by his Soviet colleague, Ambassador Sergei Vinogradov on June 1, 1959; so was Ambassador Elath informed, while on a visit to Moscow, by the Acting Head of the Middle East Department in the Foreign Ministry, Ambassador Solod, on July 7, 1959; so was Ambassador Aryeh Harel told by the Deputy Foreign Minister, Semyonov, on February 29, 1960; and so on.

In the same year, however, in these and other conversations the Russians tried to rekindle the last sparks of Israel's hope. Thus, for instance, Vinogradov told Ambassador Yankov Tsur that the Soviet Union was, in fact, helping Israel more than Israel knew. For example, it did not let Nasser occupy Iraq after the revolution there. He said that the Soviet Union was for freedom of navigation through the Suez Canal just as through the Dardanelles. He even allowed himself to admit:

We are not blind to the fact that anti-Semitism exists in Soviet Russia. The Government does everything to suppress it. But do not forget that we have been in power only forty years and that before

---

21. The year 1958 also saw the publication of the book by Ivanov and Sheinis, *Gosudarstvo Izrail, yevo polozheniye i politika*, which long remained the Soviet standard work on Israel. Its tenor: Anti-Semitism and reactionary Zionism are two sides of the same coin.

that, there was a period of more than three hundred years of education in hooliganism. Patience. Do not get desperate over every undesirable occurrence. We shall overcome all this, if we know that the intentions on your side are basically good.

Solod reminded Elath that Moscow had made a conciliatory gesture toward Israel when Ambassador Bodrov went to Jerusalem to greet the President on the occasion of the Jewish New Year. It was now up to Israel to make some gesture in the right direction. A change of tone in the Israeli press, for one, could help considerably. Bodrov informed Tsur—who at the time (January 26, 1960) was Acting Director General of the Foreign Ministry—that Gromyko had told the Arabs clearly that Israel was a fact which they would have to accept and that they should stop talking about Israel's liquidation. Finally, Gromyko promised Ambassador Harel (on December 26, 1960) to see what could be done about improving trade and cultural relations. Even Khruschev himself took part in this pacifying game. "You think we do not like Jews," he said to Ambassador Harel at a Kremlin reception for Czechoslovak President Novotny (May 3, 1960). "I have more Jewish friends than you have. They are excellent people."

But nothing transpired that could be described as positive. On the contrary. In 1960, the Head of the Israeli Mission in Moscow was called three times within seven months (January 1, June 6, July 29) to the Foreign Ministry to be handed protests against allegedly illegal behavior of his staff regarding contacts with Soviet Jews. A member of the Embassy, the son of former Prime Minister Sharett, was declared *persona non grata.* Nothing emerged from Gromyko's promise of expanding trade and cultural relations. In a conversation with Ambassador Harel (June 9, 1960), Gromyko expressed the hope that Eichmann would be punished.[22] Yet there was no cooperation from the

---

22. Mentioning Bormann on the same occasion, Gromyko said: "If he is alive, he has to be caught. And if he can be caught at all, you will succeed in doing it."

Soviet side in gathering material for the trial.[23] During a press conference in Paris (April 4, 1960), Khruschev was asked if it were true that he had received Ben Gurion's request for a meeting. He answered in the negative. When further questioned as to what would have been his answer had he received such a request, Khruschev replied. "Ah! If! I would have to answer with an if."[24] And when Ambassador Bodrov was reminded, in November 1959, that at his first meeting with Ben Gurion, the Prime Minister had made concrete suggestions regarding the improvement of relations between Israel and the Soviet Union to which he had never got an answer, Bodrov did not reply.

---

23. The editor of *Pravda*, to whom Ambassador Harel spoke about the lack of Soviet cooperation in the Eichmann trial, said openly: "We are not interested in strengthening the impression that Israel is the main defender of the Jewish people. The Red Army saved thousands of Jews."

24. During Khrushchev's visit to Paris, Ambassador Vinogradov gave a reception. Among the guests was Baron Edmond de Rothschild. Khrushchev said to him on that occasion: "Once you were richer than we, today we are richer than you."

XV

1960–1963
Moscow's difficulties in the Arab world
Furtseva's explanation of Soviet attitude to Israel
Soviet veto against condemnation of Syria for murders at Almagor
Eshkol's conversation with Bodrov on September 23, 1963, and Golda
Meir's talk with Gromyko on October 2, 1963
Some positive results and a certain change of style in Moscow

Disappointed by the suspension of debate on its complaint against Syria in December 1958, Israel lodged another complaint on January 26, 1959. This time the Russians kept silent. They could afford to, knowing well that the fear of their veto would bring about an inconclusive meeting. In the General Assembly, Khrushchev recalled (September 23, 1960) that "the United Nations helped to rebuff the aggressors who encroached on the freedom and rights of Egypt, and helped to call to order those who were intervening in Lebanon and Jordan." That was all. Israel was not mentioned by name. And the next two years the Middle East was not discussed in the Security Council at all.

By 1961, the Russians had maneuvered themselves into a somewhat difficult position in the Arab world. This did not come out in the General Assembly; Gromyko made no allusion to the Middle East during the general debate. In the Security Council, however, the Russians were forced to reveal their preference for one Arab State against another. In the discussion of April 6, 1961, on Jordan's complaint against Israel for holding its Independence Day parade in Jerusalem, the Soviet delegation remained silent. Jordan was obviously not important enough to be supported. But in July there was a further case of one Arab State's complaining against another. This time it was Kuwait complaining against Iraq (and Iraq, not recognizing Kuwait's independence, parrying—with a complaint against the United Kingdom). Zorin (on July 2) tried to prevent a Kuwait representative from being invited to attend the Security Council debate on the ground that Kuwait was "occupied by Britain" and therefore unable to express an independent opinion. Attacking Britain on behalf of Iraq, Zorin (on July 5) found it necessary to recall that "somewhat earlier, the United Kingdom, this time together with France and Israel, made a direct attack on the U.A.R. [United Arab Republic] and again claimed to be doing this for the sake of the well-being of the peoples of the U.A.R. and peace in the Near East." The Soviet delegate, Platon Morozov, who took over from Zorin, continued to defend Iraq, and in the end (July 7) vetoed a British draft resolution, casting the only vote against it, while even the Egyptian delegation abstained. Later in the year (November 30), when the admission of Kuwait to the United Nations was discussed, Zorin again objected, claiming that "the available information about the situation in Kuwait does not enable us to consider Kuwait an independent State." When the Egyptian delegate voiced disagreement with Zorin and while the Iraqi delegate was also against admission, Zorin declared: "Kuwait's admission to the United Nations in present circumstances could only cause a widening of the division between the Arab countries." He suggested that discussion be postponed, and when the suggestion was defeated, he used the veto against an Egyptian draft resolution that had been adopted by all other members of the Security Council. It was the first and only time in the history of the Council that the Soviets went so far as to use the veto in opposition to Egypt. If we exclude the Machiavellian idea of a collusion between Moscow and Cairo, meaning that the Egyptian delegation was in fact only putting up a show for the benefit of rich Kuwait—and it can be argued that Cairo, badly in need of Kuwait's financial assistance, was interested in demonstrating it had done all in its power for that country—we must conclude that, at this particular moment, the support of the postrevolution regime in Iraq was more important to Moscow than a possible temporary displeasure in Cairo.

On the whole, 1961 was a comparatively quiet year in Soviet-Israeli relations. There were no constructive developments, but neither was the anti-Israeli attitude of Moscow unduly conspicuous. The press continued being unfriendly, but not to the extent of certain past years. The efforts to renew trade relations yielded no fruits but were not written off with a final *no*. In the field of cultural exchange there was no real progress, but at least there were promises. Again a glimmer of hope flickered. For instance, the Soviet Ambassador in Warsaw, who was a member of the Party's Central Committee, suggested to his Israeli colleague (November 20) that they work out together a proposal for the resumption of trade relations; and the Soviet Ambassador in Oslo, returning from a leave in Moscow, told the current Israeli Ambassador, Barkatt, that he saw himself "authorized to state that the relations with Israel are moving in the direction of normalization."

In the light of previous experience, these and similar hopeful words were not taken too seriously in Israel. But those who were inclined even then to pay them some attention could easily be brought to a more realistic evaluation by authoritative statements made by high Soviet dignitaries the same year. Probably the most outspoken was the Soviet Minister of Culture, Mme. Ekaterina Furtseva, who, in a conversation with Ambassador Harel (April 24), admitted that the nonexistence of cultural relations between Israel and the Soviet Union was due to political reasons, and then volunteered a few more remarks. It was impossible, she said, to separate cultural affairs from general policy, and Israel found itself invariably in the camp opposing the Soviet Union; sometimes she was even more extremely anti-Soviet than the Americans. "We have to take into account those States which are supporting us all the time in the United Nations and are following a policy of positive neutrality, but we have always backed the existence of Israel, and not only in 1948. Naturally, if you could come to peace with the neighboring States, the relations with the Soviet Union would also develop much more quickly."

Early the next year, Gromyko told Ambassador Harel in a friendly talk (January 3), "lately we have not been quarrelling. There is no dispute between us." However, Mme. Furtseva, somewhat less of a diplomat, proved to be nearer the truth. On January 19, a five-column article appeared in *Trud*, the Soviet trade union organ, accusing Israel of recruiting the employees of its Embassy in Moscow as spies. When the Director General of the Foreign Ministry, Chaim Yakhil, called in Ambassador Bodrov and protested against the article, Bodrov parried with an attack on the Israeli press. And when, in March, the Security Council was discussing reciprocal complaints by Syria and Israel (March 28), there was no doubt in the mind of the Soviet delegate, Morozov, that "the Government of Israel should be condemned for the new acts of aggression committed by it against Syria." In border incidents, in his opinion the Syrians acted under provocation and "the guilty party is not Syria but Israel." He went on:

> Israel did not draw the appropriate conclusions from the warnings given by the Security Council in 1956, it did not cease violating the Armistice Agreement and the obligations undertaken under the United Nations Charter. It did not refrain from aggressive action, as it was specifically called upon to do by the Security Council. . . . In disregarding the numerous Security Council resolutions which condemned military actions by Israel—not only against Syria . . . but also against Jordan . . . and against Egypt—Israel went so far that, as we know, in October 1956 it undertook, together with the United Kingdom and France, an armed intervention against Egypt in which tens of thousands of Israeli soldiers took part.

Morozov enumerated all the complaints against Israel in the history of the Security Council and then continued:

> The Security Council is now once more faced with an arbitrary breach by Israel of the Armistice Agreement. . . . The Council should address a quite unequivocal warning and admonition to the

Government of Israel concerning the utter inadmissibility of actions
like those which took place on March 16 and 17 . . . [and] should
consider what further specific measures are required . . . to make
Israel comply with the obligations under the Charter and the Armistice Agreement.

Israel was the aggressor, Syria the victim. Therefore, argued
Morozov, warning should not be addressed to both sides. Later
(April 6), he tried to show that Israel's action was "a well-
prepared and organized military operation planned in advance,
in fact an aggressive attack," and added:

Attempts to arouse our sympathy, as the Israeli representative tried
to do . . . are bound to fail, since nearly 20 percent, or one-fifth, of
the entire work of the Security Council throughout the existence of
the United Nations has been devoted to violations by Israel against
the Arab States.

In spite of all this, Israel persevered in its attempts to improve
its relations with the Soviet Union. On May 14, 1962, the
Director General of the Foreign Ministry, Yakhil, visited Moscow and spoke to Deputy Foreign Minister Sergei Lapin. Again
he heard what Ambassador Harel had been told by Mme. Furtseva, namely, that "Israel in the United Nations is almost always in the camp hostile to the Soviet Union." Lapin had at
least one suggestion ready: If, for instance, Israel should vote for
an atom-free zone in Africa, it would bring the two countries
closer together. The rest of the conversation comprised complaints against the Israeli press which, according to Lapin, was
the main cause of the nonexistence of cultural exchanges. In
August, David Hacohen, Chairman of the Foreign Affairs and
Defense Committee of the Knesset, who had attended the Moscow meeting of the Inter-Parliamentary Union (IPU), wrote to
the President of its Soviet branch, Aleksandr Volkov, reminding
him that during his stay in Moscow, all members of the Soviet
delegation with whom he spoke kept assuring him that trade
relations with Israel would be resumed and that even Kosygin
himself gave that promise, but there were still no signs of reali-

zation. Finally, on September 2, Ambassador Tekoah spent a whole day with the head of the Middle East Department of the Soviet Foreign Ministry, Aleksandr Shchiborin, in his dacha and discussed Israeli-Soviet relations and prospects for their improvement. At the end, Shchiborin confessed that, for the Soviet Government, the main obstacle to good relations was Zionism. It could not accept the idea that the place for Russian Jews was outside the Soviet Union.

In short, there was hardly any development. At the same time, the Middle East was not standing still, but moving in a direction which caused justifiable worry in Israel. On April 17, 1963, Egypt, Syria and Iraq signed a pact of unity, expressly declaring its aim was to create a military partnership that "will be able to free the Palestine Arab homeland from the Zionist danger." On May 5, Ben Gurion sent a note to Khrushchev— similar notes were dispatched to President Kennedy, President de Gaulle and Prime Minister Nehru—in which, drawing attention to this step taken by the three Arab States, he pointed out:

> The Soviet Union has always advocated peaceful coexistence and we are sure that this is the supreme, sincere will of the Russian people. Peaceful coexistence must be brought also to the Middle East. All nations of the Middle East must honor the national independence and territorial integrity of all other nations in the Middle East and arrive at a peaceful settlement on a basis agreed by both sides. A nation which refuses this should not enjoy any international support, and above all, not the support of the Great Powers. I am sure that if the Soviet Union will help to realize these principles, it will be contributing to the stability and peace in the Middle East.

> The peace in the Middle East depends above all on one Middle East country—Egypt. This State needs the help of the Soviet Union as well as the help of the United States. A joint request of this kind, coming from these two Powers, would undoubtedly bring about the desirable results.

There was no reply from Khrushchev, for other things besides the tripartite Arab pact to which Ben Gurion's note was drawing attention were happening in the Middle East. On May 7, two days before Ben Gurion's note was sent, the Security Council again discussed Kuwait's application for United Nations membership. This time, Ambassador Fedorenko, head of the Soviet United Nations delegation, voted for Kuwait's admission in spite of the fact that Iraq continued to object, having, in 1962, even broken off diplomatic relations with the United States and several other countries that established relations with Kuwait.

The change in Soviet attitude could be explained by the trend in relations between Moscow and Baghdad since the Iraqi revolution of 1958. Immediately after coming to power, President Kassem resumed diplomatic relations with the Soviet Union, which had been severed by Nuri es-Said in January 1955. Three weeks later (August 4, 1958), Soviet Ambassador Grigori Zaitsev, who had been the Head of the Middle East Department in the Soviet Foreign Ministry, arrived in Baghdad. The future looked bright for Moscow. In January 1959, Iraq withdrew from the Baghdad Pact. In March of the same year, an agreement for economic and technical cooperation was signed between the Soviet Union and Iraq, followed in May by a cultural agreement. Moscow expected that the granting of a long-term credit of £50 million sterling to cover the construction of a number of industrial plants, including those for heavy industry, a geological survey and other programs involving the presence of hundreds of Soviet experts would turn Iraq into another Egypt for it. Kassem's refusal to give the Communists representation in his Government in April 1959 was not regarded as too serious an obstacle to Soviet designs on Iraq. Things began to look bad, however, when, after the Communist-inspired massacre of Kirkuk, many Communists were sentenced to death, and when, in February 1960, a "Titoist" Communist Party was legalized while a pro-Moscow Communist Party was refused a license. The Soviet press began to adopt an increasingly critical attitude toward the Kassem regime. When Kassem was finally removed and shot on February 8, 1963, Moscow immediately recognized Aref's Government. Though the coup was followed by arrests and executions of Kassem's supporters and of Communists, the

Soviet press abstained for a whole week from comment on the events. Only on February 16, the Soviet Communist Party—not the Soviet Government—issued a statement strongly condemning the "bloody terror" in Iraq, and not until a month later, on March 14, were demonstrations organized in front of the Iraqi Embassy in Moscow.

If the Kremlin still cherished hope of effecting changes by working through the Nasserite elements in the Aref Government, it was shattered at the beginning of May 1963, when those elements were eliminated. This was just about the time when Kuwait's application for membership in the United Nations was discussed in the Security Council.

For the moment, the Russians again found themselves with Egypt and Syria as their only footholds in the Middle East. It is, of course, difficult to say whether the Soviet delegation would have acted differently under different conditions, but the loss of ground in Iraq may at least have contributed to the fact that even in a case as clear as Israel's complaint against the Syrian murderous attack on Almagor,[25] the Soviets went all out to defend Syria.

On that occasion, (August 30), Fedorenko described the Syrian penetration into Israeli territory and the murder of the unarmed members of Kibbutz Almagor as an "unfortunate event," but added that, from the report of the Chief of Staff of the U.N. Observers Corps, "it does not follow that it was Syrian soldiers who perpetrated the attack." He continued:

We cannot pass over certain statements which are being made by leading Government officials of Israel, and which are clearly at variance with the decisions of the Security Council, with the United Nations Charter and with the spirit of the times. . . . Prime Minister Eshkol warned, in a statement to the special session of the Knesset

25. Almagor, a village on the northern shore of the Sea of Galilee, was the scene of an incident on August 19, 1963, in which two nineteen-year-old Israelis, working in the Huleh Valley fields, were ambushed and killed by Syrian soldiers who had crossed into Israeli territory. It was the climax of more than a hundred acts of aggression perpetrated by the Syrians since December 1962 in that sector of the border area.

on August 28, that if the Security Council limited itself to a routine appeal to the parties to keep the peace, Israel would take appropriate steps to defend itself. Such a bellicose statement can hardly be regarded as anything but an attempt to exert pressure on the Security Council, as an unequivocal threat to resort to arms. . . . As regards the draft resolution sponsored by the United Kingdom and the United States, the Soviet delegation feels that the provisions, which in effect contain a one-sided indictment of Syria in connection with the incident at Almagor, are not supported by the facts and therefore cannot be regarded as well-founded. Consequently, the draft is, in the view of the Soviet delegation, unacceptable in its present form.

When he failed to change the Council's mind, Fedorenko used the right of veto on September 3. In explanation he said:

The charges leveled against Syria are not based on proven, indisputable facts. . . . The Soviet delegation was guided by the principles . . . that a one-sided approach must be avoided, [and] that anti-Arab action for which there was no sound reason must be prevented.

The Israeli delegate, Michael Comay, declared in a statement after the vote:

The employment of the veto power to shield the Arab party in disputes with Israel has been regrettable in the past. It is even more regrettable now, when the same Great Power concerned has joined with others in an historic attempt to relax international tensions, and might have been expected to attend the same attitude to the task of peace-keeping in the Middle East.

It was this total lack of readiness on the part of the Russians to apply to Israel and the Middle East the same principles to which they were subscribing elsewhere that was so puzzling in Soviet policy. Soon after taking office, Prime Minister Levi Eshkol called in Ambassador Bodrov on September 23, 1963, in order to attempt to clarify the reasons for this situation and to ask what could be done to overcome it. Bodrov was outspoken though not very helpful. He thought that the relations between the Soviet Union and Israel were not bad, though admittedly not friendly. This was because of the East-West fight in the Middle East, in which the Soviet Union regarded Israel as a Western bastion. It would first be necessary to change Israel's policy. What change in Israel's policy would help? That the Prime Minister must know best. The Soviet Union did not advise other States what policy to pursue. When Nasser opened his campaign of incitement against Israel, Khrushchev wrote to him saying that it could hurt his relations with the Soviet Union: "We do criticize, but we do not try to direct. Israel, no doubt, has reasons for its policy, but I, as Ambassador, believe it hurts Soviet interests." In Moscow's view, there was no place for a change of Soviet policy at the moment. Asked why there could be no trade between the two countries, Bodrov answered that apparently the Ministry of Foreign Trade was afraid to take a step toward resuming trade relations, and there was no encouragement from above. Situations like that happened in centralized regimes, but trade would not change the political climate, anyway. Finally, the Ambassador remarked that the Israeli regime was not a step on the way to socialism as the Soviet Government understood it. Nasser, of course, was also bourgeois, but his regime was nearer to Moscow because it contained the element of struggle for national liberation.

When Golda Meir met Gromyko in New York shortly afterward (October 2), the conversation was equally inconclusive. Gromyko assured her that the Soviet Union wanted peace among all nations, but Israel and its neighbors must settle things among themselves. The Soviet Union would not interfere. When Mrs. Meir observed that the Soviet Union was in a unique position with regard to the possibility of influencing Nasser because it was from Moscow that he was being supplied with arms, Gromyko ignored the implied suggestion. On the arms issue, he replied that Arab countries were receiving arms from the Soviet Union because, in Moscow's opinion, their fear that they would otherwise be liable to become victims of imperialist forces was not unfounded. When Mrs. Meir mentioned Israel's readiness to sign nonaggression pacts with the Arab

States, he repeated that the two sides must come to an agreement between themselves. Finally, Gromyko told Mrs. Meir that he had read Bodrov's report on the Ambassador's talk with Prime Minister Eshkol, but did not understand what improvement in relations Eshkol had in mind. There were no conflicts or disputes between the two countries, Bodrov maintained. Israel was not threatening the Soviet Union and the Soviet Union was not threatening Israel. Except for some hostile statements in the Israeli press, relations were normal and correct, though not very warm.

It was "normal and correct," in Soviet opinion, to call Israel a tool of imperialist forces, to refuse to trade with it, to suppress every positive mention of it in the Soviet press, to insult its leaders on the pages of the State-controlled newspapers, to hurl insinuations against its political honesty in hostile propaganda campaigns, silently to accept that the principle of peaceful coexistence did not apply to Israel's relations with its neighbors, to abandon all objectivity and take the Arab side on every occasion, however blatant the Arab guilt might be, and to use the veto when all other attempts at saving their Arab friends and protégés had failed. All this was "normal and correct"; and having once adopted this line, Moscow saw no reason to change it.

Gromyko uttered not a word on the Middle East in the General Assembly. Golda Meir reminded him of the area when, in the general debate, she said:

> We agree with the appeal by the Foreign Minister of the Soviet Union, who said: "Let us develop the relations between States so that international disputes shall be settled at the conference table and not on the field of battle." President Kennedy, Foreign Minister Gromyko and other distinguished speakers have suggested that what happened in Moscow on the question of nuclear tests can and should happen in various parts of the world where local tension threatens the peace.

The hint was answered in the conversation with Gromyko recorded above, which took place on the same day.

When, at the end of 1963, Ambassador Tekoah reviewed the development of Soviet-Israeli relations in the past year, he was able to list a number of positive points. Two Israeli artists had given a series of concerts throughout the Soviet Union. The director of Israel's television authority was granted facilities to study educational television in Moscow. There was an exchange of delegations of diamond-industry experts. The Soviet Union took part in the International Book Fair in Israel. An Israeli passenger ship arrived for the first time in Odessa. In the negotiations about Russian property in Israel which had been going on for many years, the Russians at last suggested payment of part of the price in goods, and even sent an official to Israel with orders to study the possibilities of trade. All this was, no doubt, of some weight, but it had no political impact and did not influence the general atmosphere between Moscow and Jerusalem. There was no political content and the ambience could, at best, be summed up as a certain change of style. Even that was questionable. Khrushchev, who granted audiences to all other ambassadors, did not receive the Ambassador of Israel in spite of his repeated advances.

XVI

1964-1965
Eshkol's notes to Khruschev of January 3 and March 26, 1964
Khruschev in Egypt
Eshkol's Knesset speech of May 20, 1964
Another Soviet veto
Eban's meeting with Gromyko, December 18, 1964
Some positive signs in 1965
Golda Meir in the Knesset on March 28, 1965
The problem of Russian Jews presented as an obstacle to improvement of
relations

On January 3, 1964, Ambassador Bodrov handed to Prime
Minister Eshkol Khruschev's note of December 31, 1963 (similar notes were sent to all member-States of the United Nations),
with the Soviet suggestion that an international agreement be
signed renouncing the use of force as a means of settling outstanding disputes between nations. Eshkol's reply, dated January 16—it could be handed to Foreign Minister Gromyko only
on January 28—expressed the accord of the Government of
Israel with the basic principles of renouncing the use of force
for changing territorial situations and accepted the obligation to
settle international differences by peaceful means. It said further:

My Government has examined and considered the basic principles
set forth in your letter, and found them to be in accord with the
traditional declared policy of the State of Israel. . . . I would like to
add that in the opinion of my Government a global and general
declaration would not be sufficient, and that the principles in question should be equally applied to specific regions . . . , an action
which should be taken with the view of reducing tension in our

region, on the basis of an undertaking by all the States to respect mutually each other's territorial integrity as it exists today. We have subscribed, and we continue to do so, to the principles set forth in your letter, according to which territorial disputes should be settled without recourse to force. All the States of the region should, consequently, abstain from threats or use of force, put an end to their policy of belligerence and solve all their differences peacefully and by negotiations.

My Government is favorably inclined to the suggestion of the Soviet Government that an international treaty should be signed with the view of renouncing the use of force for the settlement of territorial differences and border disputes, and of settling international conflicts by peaceful means. . . . I am therefore happy to be in the position to inform you that the Government of Israel is ready in principle to associate itself with an agreement which will be based on the principles set out in this reply and which correspond with those you have pronounced in your letter.

On March 26, Eshkol found it necessary to address another letter to Khrushchev. He recalled his reply to Khrushchev's note of December 31, 1963, and stressed the hopes that it had raised in Israel. He felt the need, however, to point out that among all the answers Khrushchev had received from heads of other governments, one—Nasser's reply of February 13—was exceptional. Though he accepted the principle, Nasser went on to say that he was not prepared to act accordingly with respect to Israel. Nasser said, in effect, that he was not ready to settle any question with Israel, to respect its territorial integrity, to abstain from threats or use of force. He indicated that the Government of the Soviet Union supported this policy of his— which was clearly incompatible with the principles of peaceful coexistence. Nasser's words could not by any means be taken lightly.

Eshkol proceeded to give a brief account of Egyptian threats to Israel and to draw Khrushchev's attention to the fact that Nasser was trying to use Khrushchev's note to justify Egypt's belligerent stand against Israel. Eshkol suggested that a clear declaration, to the effect that governments resorting to ways and means different from those set forth in the note could not expect the support of the Soviet Union, would certainly contribute to the strengthening of peace.

Ambassador Tekoah was instructed to hand Eskhol's letter personally to Khrushchev, but again he was unable to obtain an audience. In the absence of Gromyko, he could only deliver the letter to Deputy Foreign Minister Lapin on April 22, almost a month after it had been written. By that time, Khrushchev was preparing for a sixteen day state visit to Egypt.

He arrived in Cairo on May 9 and was welcomed by Nasser who, in his airport speech, attacked Israel for being "an imperialist base in the heart of the Arab world," for "building a new Nazism in the Middle East," and for having infiltrated Africa and thus opening up new fields for imperialism. Two days later (May 11), the Egyptian National Assembly gave Khrushchev a standing ovation when he said:

> The Soviet Union supports the just demands of the Arab countries and all the Arab peoples concerning the necessity that Israel should carry out the United Nations resolutions. The Soviet Union also supports the just demands of the Arab countries concerning imperalist projects aiming at the diversion of the Jordan River. Those projects greatly harm the rights of the Arabs who use the water of this Arab river.

Golda Meir called in the Soviet Ambassador (on May 13), and expressed Israel's surprise and shock at this part of Khrushchev's speech, in which he demanded that only Israel implement United Nations decisions while the Arabs were left free to ignore them. She also expressed surprise at the complete lack of knowledge and understanding of Israel's water problem shown in Khrushchev's speech. She reminded Bodrov that the Foreign Ministry offered to arrange for him a visit to the national water source but that he was not interested. She then asked about another part of the speech. How could Khrushchev say that the Soviet Union was supplying arms only to countries which had to defend themselves, when Nasser, at the same time and in his presence, spoke of the liquidation of Israel? When, in the past, Israel had protested against tendentiously hostile articles in the Soviet press, Bodrov's answer had always been that the press was unimportant and that importance should be attached only to official pronouncements. Now Khrushchev identified himself with the Arab views. She asked the Ambassador to inform his Government of Israel's grave concern for its security, as a result of Khrushchev's pronouncements against Israel in front of Nasser and the Arab masses.

On May 18, in a banquet speech, Nasser declared, among other things: "We are in a sensitive place in the world. . . . Close to us is Israel, which is a base for imperialism. She gets $400 million in aid. This is in addition to military aid and this exceeds the needs of its two million people. We cannot trust Israel because it is a base for imperialism. In 1956, the first attack came from Israel, so we have to keep a strong army to repel Israel and those who back Israel." Khrushchev answered: "There will be no delay over arms, if they are needed. If there is a request for arms, we shall supply them. Of course, it is better that we should have the best types of arms and that the enemy should know we have them, so they don't force us to use them."

Two days later, Prime Minister Eshkol, when asked in the Knesset to comment on newspaper reports, particularly in *The Guardian*, on the development of nuclear weapons in Egypt and Israel, used the opportunity to express Israel's attitude to Khrushchev's promise to supply Nasser with arms. He repeated a previous statement by Ben Gurion that nuclear development in Israel was designed exclusively for peaceful purposes, and went on to redefine Israel's position in regard to the arms race in the Middle East. He condemned the policy of belligerence maintained by the Arab States, especially by Egypt; he described the arms race in the region as unnecessary and harmful to peace and social development; he expressed the readiness of Israel "to join in any effort to rid the area completely of all arms at present in the area, under reciprocal control, without posing total world disarmament as a prior condition"; he declared that

Israel had not taken the initiative in introducing new types of arms—conventional or unconventional—into the Middle East; but he also declared that "as long as our enemies are not prepared to cooperate in regional disarmament, it is our duty to take all necessary measures for the consolidation of the deterrent and defensive strength we require for the maintenance of peace." Finally he addressed the following words to Moscow:

> The Government regrets that in spite of the Egyptian ruler's aggressive declarations against Israel, he receives political support and supplies of arms from sources that generally advocate peace and coexistence. The world is composed of regions, and anyone who aspires to world peace must also support regional peace in theory and practice.

Eshkol then spoke of the feverish arms race in which Egypt, for many years, had been introducing the most modern weapons into the Middle East.

> It was Egypt that received from the Soviet Union, and was first to introduce into the Middle East, the supersonic jet planes, the missile craft and the heavy armor now in its possession. The arms in Egypt's possession are not designed for any anti-imperialist purpose or for any purpose of national liberation. These arms are dedicated, according to Egypt's declared policy, to war against Israel. They also serve Nasser's aims of winning domination over the neighboring Arab countries.

> All this is obviously and profoundly incompatible with the belief in peaceful coexistence, which is accepted by the Soviets and the West alike, and with the ban on efforts to solve border disputes by force of arms instead of by negotiation and agreement.

The joint communiqué published at the conclusion of Khrushchev's visit on May 24 announced not only that the Soviet Union would be granting Egypt a long-term credit of $227 million, but also that it "supports the Arab States' struggle against the aggressive intrigues of the imperialist forces that seek to hinder solution of the Palestine problem and the utilization of the Jordan River waters."

The day after Khrushchev's departure from Egypt (May 26), Nasser and Aref of Iraq, who was in Cairo during Khrushchev's visit and attended some of the conversations, signed an agreement which was heralded as a first step toward union between Egypt and Iraq. At a press conference in Moscow on May 27, Khrushchev denied rumors that there had been differences of opinion on the issue of Arab unity, though it was true that the Soviets believed in the unity of the working class regardless of racial, religious or geographical distinctions. He added on that occasion: "There was a time when Communists were persecuted in Egypt, but I was told this was no longer so."

Despite all this, the Russians seemed eager to assure Israel that it was in no serious danger. At the beginning of the year (January 21), Ambassador Bodrov stressed, in a conversation with Prime Minister Eshkol, that arms supplied to Egypt were not directed against Israel. At the end of the year (December 7), Ambassador Bodrov's successor, Dmitri Chuvakhin, again in a talk with Eshkol, assured the Prime Minister that, in Soviet opinion, it was inconceivable that the world would permit Nasser to liquidate Israel, which was not only a fact but also a member of the United Nations. Eshkol replied that President de Gaulle had also told him the same thing, but when asked if Israel, in his view, should rely on this comfortable evaluation, de Gaulle had answered: "No. You also have to be strong." Taking leave, the Ambassador made a point of emphasizing that the Government of the Soviet Union was interested in an improvement of relations with Israel.

The sincerity of this statement was densely clouded by doubts raised by another Soviet performance in the Security Council. Since November 16, the Council had been discussing reciprocal complaints of Syria and Israel. Just a few days before Chuvakhin's first meeting with Eshkol, the Soviet delegate, Fedorenko, fulminated in the Council (December 3):

The initial incident . . . had its origin in provocative actions from
the Israeli side. . . . What followed . . . was a gross violation of Syrian
air space by Israeli military aircraft, which bombed a whole series
of points on Syrian territory. . . . This, obviously, was nothing other
than a deliberately planned and executed large-scale attack, occur-
ring after both sides had agreed to a cease-fire.

Provocative acts and direct aggression by Israel against the Arab
countries cannot be tolerated. . . . This act of aggression must be
resolutely condemned by the Security Council. . . . This time the
condemnation must be of such a nature as to make it clear to the
Israeli side that the Security Council has firmly and inflexibly decided to put an end to such actions.

On December 21, Fedorenko voted for a Moroccan draft resolution condemning Israel. When the draft was defeated, and
when an Anglo-American draft resolution received the majority
of eight votes, Fedorenko once again used the veto to save
Syrian face. This was hardly proof that Moscow was really
interested in an improvement of relations and ready to take
steps in that direction.

Nor did Abba Eban's meeting with Gromyko in New York
at about the same time (December 18) bring about any change.
Gromyko was, of course, not speaking to the gallery and was
more diplomatic than Fedorenko; but nothing emerged from
the talk. Eban informed Gromyko that Israel would support the
Soviet item on the Assembly agenda suggesting that territorial
disputes be settled by peaceful means, but it was important, in
Israel's opinion, that the Soviet Union make clear that this
principle was to be applied also to the Middle East. Gromyko
evaded a direct answer. The basic objectives of the Soviet Union, he said, were peace and a lessening of tension. This applied
also to the Middle East. His Government wanted relations between Israel and the Arab States to become normal, peaceful
and "good neighborly." A lessening of local tension in the Middle East would lessen the danger of interference by imperialist
powers. Eban expressed the hope that the Soviet Union would

take a similar attitude in talks with Arab Governments. The Soviet Union could play a decisive role in promoting peace in the Middle East by championing the principles of respect for sovereignty, territorial integrity and peaceful settlement of disputes in the area. Gromyko's answer was that the more trouble there was in the Middle East, the more room for intervention by imperialist powers. The important thing was that the peoples of the area provide no pretext for such outside intervention. Eban tried once more. General principles, he said, were tested by application to particular cases. It served little purpose if countries endorsed general principles but claimed exception for a particular conflict which concerned them, as the Arabs did with regard to Israel. Gromyko did not react. As for relations between Israel and the Soviet Union, when told by Eban that the two States might be influenced by certain dialectic necessities, yet, in Israel's view, within that framework there was room for increasing friendly relations, Gromyko repeated that the relations were "normal and correct, though not warm or friendly." For this he blamed the unfriendly and critical attitude expressed in the Israeli press and official statements on Soviet foreign policy, which were seldom objective.

Similarly inconclusive was Foreign Minister Golda Meir's first conversation with Ambassador Chuvakhin early the next year (on January 14, 1965). She spoke of the great reservoir of sympathy for the Soviet Union existing in Israel but completely ignored by Moscow, which, instead, was actually encouraging the Arabs in their hostile attitude to Israel. She tried to show the weakness of Soviet argumentation that Israel was a tool of imperialism, acting under American pressure and dependent on American capital. She assured Chuvakhin that no American pressure was being exerted on Israel and that when there had been such pressure in the past—for instance, Eisenhower's stand in 1956—it was not always favorable to Israel. As for American financial aid, it began with a loan of $100 million in 1949. At the same time, Israel asked for credit also from the Soviet Union. No answer to the request was received. To all this —and more—Chuvakhin could reply only by complaining

about the unfriendly attitude of the Israeli press and the activities of the Committee for Help to Russian Jewry, a subject
which was subsequently to be often raised.

However, there were a number of events in 1965 that could
be interpreted as possible signs of a slight change in the Soviet
attitude. Some examples:

> At the end of August, Nasser visited the Soviet Union. Needless to
> say, he used every opportunity to speak against Israel. Soviet repre-
> sentatives who were on the platform and answered his speeches on
> these occasions, never devoted a single word to the anti-Israeli parts
> of his declarations. Only once did Khrushchev speak of the "trian-
> gular aggression of 1956," but even then he did not mention Israel
> explicitly.

> During this same visit, Nasser severely censured Israel while ad-
> dressing Egyptian students. While much of the speech was pub-
> lished in the Soviet press, the anti-Israeli parts were not. The
> Director of the Middle East Department of the Soviet For-
> eign Minstry drew the attention of the Ambassador of Israel to
> this fact.

> On September 13 Kosygin cabled greetings to the Casablanca Con-
> ference.[26] He spoke about "freeing the Arab East from all forms of
> colonial aggression." Nasser, in his reply, spoke of "colonialism and
> Zionism." The Soviet press did not publish the anti-Israeli para-
> graph in the final communiqué of the conference.

> The same happened in November in respect to Nasser's speech to
> the Egyptian Parliament (November 27), from which all references
> to Israel and to the Israeli-Arab conflict were omitted.

---

26. The Casablanca Conference of the Heads of Arab States, held in September 1965, adopted a "Solidarity Pact" with the primary aim of ending the
inter-Arab propaganda strife. It was generally regarded as a manifestation of
Arab unity. Only a few months later, inter-Arab relations again deteriorated,
however, and an open split between the "revolutionary" bloc (Egypt, Syria,
Iraq, Algeria, Yemen) and a "conservative" one (Saudi Arabia, Jordan,
Morocco, Tunisia) wiped out the results of Casablanca.

Novoye Vremya, of the same month published an article by the Moscow correspondent of *Kol Haam* on the Jordan water question which was surprisingly objective and in no way pro-Arab.

The 1965 yearbook of the *Bol'shaya Sovietskaya Entsiklopediya* left out a number of anti-Israeli statements that had appeared in previous editions. In comparison with the edition of 1964, for instance, it did not mention unemployment or the previous "facts and figures" showing two-thirds of Israeli workers as earning less than the minimum necessary for subsistence. In the chapter on Israel's internal affairs, a paragraph on "militarist psychosis" and hostile attitudes to the Arab and Christian minorities was excised. So were a paragraph about Israel's not complying with the United Nations resolution on repatriation of Arab refugees and another saying that, in the past year, the Government of Israel had shown a hostile attitude toward the Soviet Union and the Socialist camp.

This may have seemed minor, yet in the context of Soviet-Israeli relations, it could have been regarded as significant had it not been accompanied by other occurrences which definitely swung the pendulum to the other side.

Foreign Minister Golda Meir, reviewing the situation before the Knesset (March 28), summarized it as follows:

Israel continues in its efforts to arrive at an improvement and deepening of its relations with the Soviet Union and other East European States. Here and there, lately, there were signs of a widening of cooperation with the Soviet Union. In the field of cultural relations, there was an increase in exchanges of artists, and Soviet ensembles appearing in Israel and Israelis appearing in the Soviet Union were received with great success and appreciation in both countries. In October [1964] an agreement was signed in Jerusalem for the purchase of Russian property to the value of $4.5 million, one-third of which will be paid in cash and two-thirds in goods. Even if the Soviet Union had not yet begun to use the sum at her disposal, we trust she will do so soon. We would all like to hope that these signs constitute the first evidence of a more positive attitude in the relations between the two countries. To our regret, however, it is impossible to ignore some other happenings. Lately, the Soviet Union used the veto twice against draft resolutions accepted by the majority in the Security Council, in the case of the murders in Almagor and in the case of the Syrian attacks in the region of Dan. In May 1964, Mr. Khrushchev visited Egypt, in December of the same year Mr. Shelepin went there as the head of a Soviet delegation.[27] On both occasions the Soviet representatives made statements supporting the Arab point of view, especially in the question of Jordanian waters, and the Egyptian ruler made, in their presence, a declaration on his aggressive program against Israel. These clear declarations by the Egyptian ruler did not stop the Soviet Union from continuing to supply Egypt with offensive weapons in large quantities and even at an accelerated tempo. We say again that we do not understand how supplying weapons to those who openly declare that these weapons are needed for attacking another State is compatible with the policy of peace declared by the Soviet Union. It is particularly incompatible with the proposal tabled by the Soviet Union in the last United Nations Assembly—which we are supporting—calling for a settlement of disputes by peaceful means and for refraining from the use of force, and with the words of the Soviet Minister of Foreign Affairs. On the same occasion Mr. Gromyko, speaking of this proposal, said that territorial disputes and all other disputes between sovereign States are to be settled not by the force of arms but solely by peaceful means. We would like to hope that these principles will guide the policy of the Soviet Union in our region also, for we are convinced that the Soviet Union is in a position, by using these principles, to contribute to the lessening of tension and to bring peace nearer.

Shortly afterwards, on April 12, at a meeting with Ambassador Chuvakhin the Foreign Minister asked him, as she had his predecessor, what Israel could do to bring about an improvement in relations with the Soviet Union. Once again the answer was that he was not there to advise the Government of Israel. After the meeting, however, Chuvakhin told the Director of the East European Department of the Foreign Ministry, who had

---

27. Speaking before the Egyptian National Assembly, Deputy Premier Shelepin declared on December 27, 1964: "Imperialism exploits the Palestine issue to increase tension in your area. We believe this issue should be solved by restoring the rights of Arabs in Palestine."

been present at the conversation: "You know well what stands in the way of an improvement of our relations with you. It is the problem of Soviet Jews and of your activities on this subject, especially in international forums. If you change your policy on this point and if you stop provoking us, an improvement in relations will follow."

This was not the first time the subject had been raised by the Russians that year. They had become sensitive to world opinion on this point. It had been mentioned by Ambassador Chuvakhin in his first meeting with Foreign Minister Golda Meir on January 14. On February 5, there was a violent attack in *Vechernaya Leningrad* on Israeli tourists who, during their stay in the Soviet Union, were contacting Soviet Jews, and spreading lies and arousing hatred against Russia upon their return. Mrs. Meir touched upon the subject in the previously quoted Knesset speech of March 28. As the result of the Nazi holocaust, she said, one of the largest concentrations of Jews today was in the Soviet Union. Israel was asking that Soviet Jews be given the right to live their national life and be allowed to join their families living outside the Soviet Union. She stressed: "In these demands there is not a shadow of an anti-Soviet policy." In May, the Ambassadors of certain Soviet bloc countries in some European capitals tried to convince their Israeli colleagues that to improve relations with Moscow, Israel should stop being interested in Soviet Jews. (Instead, Israel should use its "fantastic" influence with the world press to eliminate anti-Soviet criticism and to influence Jewish organizations throughout the world to be favorable to the Soviets.) The same month (May 21), *Izvestia* published an article sharply criticizing Ambassador Tekoah for alleged contacts with Russian Jews during his visits to several towns in the Soviet Union. On May 25, Tekoah was invited to the Foreign Ministry, where the Director of the Middle East Department warned him against the activities of members of his staff (he did not repeat *Izvestia's* accusations against the Ambassador himself) among Soviet Jews. A month later (June 25), Shchiborin repeated the warning to the Israeli chargé d'affaires, Avraham Agmon. "So long as you continue your

activities among the Jews," he said on this occasion, "there will
be no improvement in our relations. Stop it, because this question is the main obstacle to an improvement of relations." On
July 7, President Shazar wrote a personal letter to Mikoyan
regarding the question of the reunion of Jewish families. It was
never answered. On October 3, newly appointed Ambassador
Katz met the head of the Middle East Department, Shchiborin,
for the first time, only to be told that relations could be better,
as both sides wished, but the blame for lack of progress did not
lie on the Soviet side. Jews in the United States and other
countries, under the leadership of Zionist organizations, were
inciting hostility against the Soviet Union, and there was also
such a campaign in Israel. Finally, on December 7, Mrs. Meir
again received Ambassador Chuvakhin. Once more she asked
what Israel could do to improve relations with Moscow and this
time she got an answer. The Government of Israel could use its
influence on the Israeli press and, above all, stop interfering in
questions concerning Russian Jews. When the Foreign Minister
replied that the press in Israel was free and the Government
could not force it to refrain from reporting negative Soviet
steps, and that no word favorable to Israel could be found in
Soviet publications or official declarations, the Ambassador retorted that he, for instance, was unable to find in the Yad
Washem Memorial[28] any mention of the part the Red Army
had played in the liberation of thousands of Jews. He added that
President Shazar's letter had been discussed by the highest
authorities, and that he was authorized to assure the Government of Israel that the Soviet Union would continue its positive
attitude toward the humanitarian principle of the reunion of
families.

There were yet other talks about the possibilities of improving
relations, but in none did the Russians show any signs of willingness to take a constructive step. On May 9, Ambassador Tekoah

---

28. Yad Washem is the Martyrs and Heroes Memorial in Jerusalem, established in memory of the six million Jewish victims of Nazism. It is a center
of documentation and research on the holocaust.

used the opportunity of a brief encounter with Kosygin at a Kremlin reception (his efforts to be received for a longer conversation with Khrushchev had been as unavailing as previously) to bring up the question of the necessity to improve relations, but he was told only: "We have to think about it. This is a very complicated and very delicate problem." In June, Eliezer Doron, Director of the East European Department of the Israeli Foreign Ministry, visited Moscow and was received by Deputy Foreign Minister Semyonov, who attacked "Israel's aggressiveness against Jordan," spoke of a repetition of the situation of 1956 in the sense that Israel was once more acting as a tool of the Western Powers, and at the end said: "Our relations with Israel are normal, but the shadow of Suez is still falling on them." At the end of that month (June 28) Ambassador Tekoah, upon taking leave of Gromyko at the termination of his assignment, was told by the Foreign Minister that Israeli-Soviet relations were "normal and more or less correct." The Soviet Union, Gromyko said, had nothing against Israel. He agreed that relations with substance encourage mutual understanding and friendship. There were already some fields in which cooperation existed, and there were quite a number of strings, though admittedly weak ones, which were binding the two countries together. However, he would not like to discuss Israel's relations with its neighbors, or other events like those of 1956, or the unfriendly attitude of the Israeli press.

The previous February, a visiting foreign statesman, a friend of Israel, asked Khrushchev how he could explain the Soviet Union's attitude to Israel, the most progressive country in the Middle East. Khrushchev answered very frankly: Communism was always against Zionism. Zionism was always bound to the West, and especially to the United States, and since the establishment of Israel, the Jewish State was being spoiled by American support.

Nothing in the conversations held in 1965 indicated any change in this basic posture.

XVII

1966
Israeli Government's policy declaration in January
Abba Eban's meeting with Ambassador Chuvakhin a week later
Eshkol's talk with the Soviet Ambassador in April
Kosygin in Egypt
Soviet statement of May 25
Eshkol's Paris press conference in May
Israel's reply to the Soviet statement

On January 12, 1966, Prime Minister Eshkol, presenting the new Cabinet to the Knesset, outlined the Government program, certain passages of which were obviously addressed to Moscow. He said:

Israel's central aim in the Middle East is the advancement of peace. We aspire toward relations founded on respect for the independence and integrity of all the States in the area. The time has come for Arab statesmen to show a wise sense of reality and abandon their declared purpose of changing the map of this area in the delusion that Israel's existence may be ignored. . . . Insofar as there exist in the Arab world tendencies—even if weak and hesitant—toward moderate and positive thinking about Israeli-Arab relations, we shall try to encourage and foster them to the best of our ability. But the tendency that is proclaimed in the Arab world today is opposed to peace and coexistence. . . .

Countries outside our area have their influence, for better or worse, on the fate of peace within it. If it is their desire to advance and stimulate positive measures, they should contribute to the strengthening of Israel's economy and security and help to convince the Arab world that the State of Israel is a permanent fact in the international fabric. . . . We demand that peace-loving States should put an end to the arms race in our area. . . . There is no doubt that the prospects of peace and stability would be strengthened if the Western Powers and the Soviet Union arrived at an agreed policy founded on support, in theory and practice, of the independence and integrity of all the existing States in the Middle East.

It was this prospect that I had in mind when I expressed hope, two years ago, that parallel with the improvement of our ties with the United States, France and Britain, there should also be more understanding between the Soviet Union and Israel. True, there has not been much progress in this direction, but we should not despair of the aim itself. And indeed, reason dictates that there should be better understanding between Moscow and Jerusalem because, for one thing, Israel plays no part in what is called "the cold war"; on the contrary, it aspires to see it ended.

The basic principles of the new Government's policy concerning foreign affairs affirmed these points:

The Government will persist in its readiness for unconditional negotiations with its neighbors, on the signing of peace and nonaggression pacts, and the cessation of political, economic or military hostility. . . .

Until such time as there is general disarmament in the world at large, the Government of Israel will propose to all its Arab neighbors an agreement leading to full disarmament and the disbandment of armies in Israel and the Arab countries, conditional on a guarantee of continuous mutual supervision over its execution, and the nonviolation of the frontiers and sovereignty of each of the countries concerned. . . .

Israel acknowledges the right of every nation, large as well as small, to a free national life and political independence. It abjures colonialism and will come to the assistance of peoples in their struggle for liberation from the foreign yoke and the building of an independent national existence.

The Government of Israel will demand that Nazi criminals be brought to justice and punishment; their crimes shall not be subject to any statute of limitations.

So far, the declaration was either in complete harmony with the Soviet Union's official policy, or at least difficult for Moscow to reject openly. But there was also this paragraph on Soviet Jewry which could hardly have been expected to be to Moscow's liking:

Soviet Jewry has been cut off for almost fifty years from the body of the nation and our work in this country by the power of an external force which, to our regret, ignores the great, universal, human significance of the Zionist enterprise. We hope and long for the day when the Jews in the Soviet Union will be able to make their contribution to the building of the nation in its homeland.

Let us hope that, following the failure of forced assimilation, in the wake of the new winds that are blowing in the Soviet Union itself, and as a result of the pressure of the Jewish people and enlightened world public opinion, the Soviet authorities will change their attitude to the Jewish problem.

On January 19, 1966, Foreign Minister Eban summoned Ambassador Chuvakhin and conveyed to him the contents of Prime Minister Eshkol's Knesset speech. Chuvakhin answered that he had studied the "constructive basis" of the Prime Minister's pronouncement in detail. He hoped for an improvement of relations between Israel and the Soviet Union, but he also hoped that Israel's policy would not be limited to declarations. At the same time, he sharply criticized what the Prime Minister had found necessary to add on the subject of Soviet Jewry. This was a defamation of the Soviet Union and an invitation to foreign pressure. The expression "forced assimilation," which the Prime Minister had used, was offensive. Nahum Goldmann, for instance, held a different opinion on the subject. This part of the Prime Minister's speech was not only an interference in the internal affairs of a Great Power, but, in fact, annulled the effect of the positive passages of his statement.

Chuvakhin then informed Eban (with whom he was meeting for the first time as Foreign Minister) that he had reported to his Government on his conversation with Mrs. Meir, on December 7, 1965, and that he was now authorized to read the following reply from his Government to Israel's Foreign Minister:

> The announcement by the Government of Israel, expressing its desire to normalize relations, was received in Moscow with great interest. The Government of the Soviet Union welcomes the declaration of Mrs. Meir regarding Israel's desire for disarmament, liquidation of colonialism, opposition to aggression and the desire to live in peace with the neighboring countries. Actual steps which will be taken by the Government of Israel to implement this policy will be received with understanding and support by the Soviet Union and by all peace-loving nations. To the regret of the Government of the Soviet Union, for the time being Israel's policy is not in line with these declarations, and especially not with the aim of keeping peace and lessening tension in the Middle East. Israel's attempts to use force and its policy of preventive war, which stand in the way of the solution of conflicts with its neighbors, prove that Israel does not understand that it is exactly this policy of power which endangers its security.

The Soviet reply added that, for the improvement of relations, it was necessary first to create a suitable atmosphere. The worsening of relations was not the fault of Moscow. The Soviet Union always wanted cooperation with Israel. Israel's behavior on the international scene, its support of reactionary and imperialist forces, pronouncements by its leaders against the Soviet Union, and the hostile attitude of its press did not encourage good relations. Despite all that, however, Moscow "appreciates very much Mrs. Meir's words about Israel's desire for an improvement of relations" between the two States.

Eban answered the Soviet communication on the spot. He told the Ambassador that Israel had no policy of preventive war, but a policy of preventing war. Nasser's declarations about the liquidation of Israel and the Soviet Union's supply of arms to Egypt determined Israel's policy for safeguarding its independence. The Soviet Union followed the same line. He rejected as groundless the accusations that Israel was supporting imperialist forces, and he assured Chuvakhin that Israel's desire to arrive at an improvement of relations with the Soviet Union was sincere.

This was followed by a note from Prime Minister Eshkol to Kosygin, congratulating the Soviet Premier on the Tashkent agreement between India and Pakistan reached through his intervention, and expressing the hope for a similar settlement between Israel and the Arab States. (The note was handed to the Director of the Middle East Department of the Soviet Foreign Ministry, Shchiborin, by Ambassador Katz on February 4.)

On March 9, Ambassador Chuvakhin met with Aryeh Levavi, Director General of the Israeli Foreign Ministry, and expressed the opinion that as long as there was no settlement in Vietnam, there was no possibility of an agreement between Moscow and Washington on any other problem, including the Middle East. Washington was interested in keeping up tension in the area, not in solving its conflicts. As for Israel, it was continuing, in spite of all denials, to follow the policy of the anti-Soviet imperialists. He quoted, as examples of Israel's pro-Western orientation, its recognition of the regime in Ghana after the fall of Nkhruma and the Berlin visit of the Israeli Ambassador to Bonn which in effect, amounted to an anti-Soviet demonstration.

At the same time (March 11) in Moscow, Ambassador Katz was received by the President of the Supreme Soviet, Nikolai Podgorny, who tried to avoid political themes in their conversation. But when Katz suggested that an exchange of visits by political personalities would certainly speed up the improvement of relations, he replied: "Declarations about the desire to improve relations are not sufficient if, at the same time, in your Parliament and from members of your Government, we also hear declarations harmful to the Soviet Union, for instance, regarding the so-called Jewish problem." In such circumstances, he added, it was no wonder that cultural relations were limited and trade relations nonexistent.

At the end of the month (on March 30), Chuvakhin repeated to Foreign Minister Eban the complaint about Israel's continued pro-Western orientation, which was not in line with the declarations of Israel's desire to improve relations with Moscow. Eban replied that Israel had no preferences, but a small country naturally must look for security and material assistance, and this Israel was able to receive only from the West.

On April 20, Prime Minister Eshkol called in the Soviet Ambassador. He had been told about the Ambassador's objections to that part of his last Knesset speech in which he had dealt with the question of Soviet Jewry, and he would therefore like to give him a detailed explanation of Israel's stand. Lenin's attitude to Zionism, the Prime Minister said, was not that of Stalin—Zionism was a revolutionary movement. It turned Jews into workers and peasants. It was an insult, Eshkol went on, to call Zionism a reactionary and bourgeois movement and even compare it with Nazism. He told the Ambassador that he had a personal ambition to improve economic and cultural relations with the Soviet Union. The economic assistance that Israel was receiving from the West should not be regarded as an obstacle. Israel was ready to receive economic assistance from the Soviet Union, as well, and if credit was difficult, it should at least be possible to establish normal trade relations between the two countries. And he concluded by saying that if it had not been for Nasser, there would already have been peace between Israel, Lebanon and Jordan. The Soviet Union should help this tendency and it was able to do so. The Soviet Union was a Great Power with influence in the area and should use that influence. The Arabs depended on Moscow. The meeting was really a monologue; Chuvakhin hardly reacted. He listened and promised to inform his Government.

A number of things happened in May. At the beginning of the

month, there was a meeting between Kosygin and the Syrian Prime Minister, Zeayen. In the subsequent joint communiqué, the Soviet Premier pledged his Government's support in the "struggle against Zionism." The Director General of the Israeli Foreign Ministry called in Ambassador Chuvakhin on May 4 and expressed regret at this part of the communiqué, stressing that the Arabs as a matter of course identified Zionism with Israel and therefore saw in such pronouncements an encouragement of their aggressive policy. Chuvakhin rejected the complaint by claiming that Zionism was an ideology which he would not discuss on an intergovernmental level. When Levavi accused him of formalism and reminded him of the Fascists' using the term "Communist bands" when referring to the Soviet Union, Chuvakhin answered, "Arab interpretation does not interest us." However, the Russians seemed to have been very receptive to Arab interpretation, for on May 7 *Izvestia* published an article accusing Israel of creating "armed provocations" against Syria in an attempt to hasten the overthrow of the pro-Moscow Government in Damascus. The article added that "the expansion of the anti-Syrian campaign coincided with the stay in Israel of United States Assistant Secretary of State Raymond Hare and other American representatives."

On May 10, Kosygin arrived in Egypt for an eight-day state visit. (A prominent member of his party, this time, was Admiral Korshkov, Commander in Chief of the Soviet Navy.) For an entire week, Kosygin refrained from making any anti-Israeli statements, a fact which was appreciated and which raised hopes in Jerusalem. On the eve of his departure on May 17, however, in an address to the Egyptian National Assembly, Kosygin made his first reference to Israel: "In the Middle East, it could be that a certain country dreams of obtaining such [nuclear] weapons. The U.A.R. is contributing to checking the atomic arms race.[29] . . . We know the Arab interest in the

---

29. On February 4, 1966, the United Press reported from Cairo that the Soviet Defense Minister, Marshal Grechko, had pledged, during his visit to Egypt, the use of Soviet nuclear forces to safeguard Egypt should Israel develop an atom bomb.

Palestine case and believe it should be settled on a just basis. The Soviet Union has all sympathy for the struggle to regain legal rights for Palestine's refugees."And the joint communiqué of May 18 expressed Soviet support for the "legitimate, inalienable rights of the Palestinian people."

Jerusalem saw nothing significantly new in this, and Kosygin's statement was even regarded as hardly likely to have satisfied his Egyptian hosts. But Prime Minister Eshkol deemed it necessary to reply, on May 18, to at least that part of Kosygin's speech that dealt with nuclear weapons in the Middle East. "Israel has no atomic arms," he said, "and will not be the first to introduce such arms into our area." He tried to explain that Nasser was attempting to deceive the world by seeking to divert attention from the existing arms race by speaking of a threat of nuclear weapons which did not exist in the area. Eshkol used the opportunity to repeat Israel's desire to establish more friendly relations with the Soviet Union, relations similar to those which had existed at the time of the establishment of the State. He termed the recent Soviet-Syrian communiqué "regrettable" but refrained from criticizing Kosygin's visit to Egypt.

The same day, there was another article in *Izvestia*, describing Israel as a "dangerous bridgehead of imperialism in the Middle East." The West, according to the paper, was investing more and more in Israel, was supplying it with arms and pressuring it into perpetrating provocations and frontier incidents. Israel was represented as one of the three main instruments against progressive forces in the Arab world. The other two were the Arab monarchies and the reaction inside Egypt, which was supported by the West. On May 23, *Izvestia*, commenting on the agreement on the supply of arms provided by the United States to Israel, wrote:

> The United States is supplying strictly offensive weapons. The deal . . . cannot be regarded as isolated from other subversive U.S. activities in the Middle East. We have in mind pronouncements by American statesmen on resolute and immediate aid to an Arab State

[Saudi Arabia] on three conditions. . . . One of these conditions is
not to use these weapons against Israel. Against whom can these
weapons be used, then? It is clear, only against Arab peoples.

The entire Soviet press was highly critical of Israel during the
month of May for having invited Adenauer to visit the country.

On May 25, Deputy Foreign Minister Semyonov called in
Ambassador Katz and read him an official Government statement warning Israel against troop concentration on its frontiers
with Arab States, which was the more dangerous because it
coincided with a hostile campaign by Israel against Syria. The
statement mentioned border incidents with Syria and Jordan
and linked them with the "war spirit of Israel's military leaders." It quoted as an example a speech by General Rabin in
which he allegedly threatened "taking military steps against
Syria." All this, the statement asserted, was the result of increased activities of imperialist forces in the Middle East, directed against the independence of the Arab States and
interfering with their internal affairs. The Government of the
Soviet Union also knew, of course, of the peace-loving declarations by Israeli Government representatives; however, these
were not in line with actual facts. Those Israeli extremist circles,
which were following a policy of hostility to their Arab neighbors, were leading Israel into the role of a blind pawn of imperialism and neocolonialism in the Near East. "The Government
of the Soviet Union hopes that the Government of Israel will
realistically recognize the possible consequences of its dangerous plans directed against independent Arab States, including
the Syrian Arab Republic. The Government of the Soviet Union
expresses its hope that the Government of Israel will not permit
outside forces to play with the fate of its nation and State." The
statement concluded by emphasizing the interest of the Soviet
Union that peace should prevail in a region which was in the
immediate vicinity of its borders. While the text of the Government statement was not published—and the press did not even
mention that it had been made—two days later (May 27), TASS
issued a statement, very similar in content but even more vehe-

ment in form, bluntly accusing Israel of preparing a war against Syria.

The TASS statement was emphatically rejected by Prime Minister Eshkol at a press conference held in Paris on May 29:

> Israel denies most energetically all insinuations of the TASS declaration that it is acting in its relations with other States as someone else's agent. The talk about concentration of forces on the Syrian border, cancelation of leave in the army and so on, are complete lies. The sincere desire of Israel as a sovereign State in the Middle East to live in peace with its neighbors, has been expressed many times from the Knesset rostrum and in many international forums. It is Syria that is active in provocations on the Israeli border all the time, from Syria came the murderers of Israeli workmen tilling Israeli soil, as was the case these days in Almagor, and Syria repeatedly makes declarations about its intention of attacking Israel. We suppose it will not be difficult for the Soviet Union to find out about the aggressive activities of Syria on the Israeli border, activities which are expressed both by the kind of weapons and by concentrations forbidden by the Armistice Agreement.

The Prime Minister then quoted from his Knesset speech of May 18 and added: "I also suggested in my speech that, if Moscow would refrain from declarations, she could make a contribution to peace in the area. Unfortunately, the TASS statement and parallel articles in the Soviet press during recent days do not contribute in this direction."

In Jerusalem on the same day, after a Government meeting, Foreign Minister Abba Eban issued a statement to the press, rejecting all the accusations in the TASS statement and in the note sent by the Syrian Government to the Security Council regarding alleged Israeli army concentrations on the border. Even before that, on May 26, the day after Deputy Foreign Minister Semyonov read the Soviet Government statement to Ambassador Katz, Eban called in the Soviet Ambassador and expressed astonishment at the Soviet declaration. "We are not the accused, but the accuser," he told Chuvakhin. There was no truth in the accusation that Israel was concentrating troops on the Syrian border. The nervousness in Syria was caused by the regime's lack of stability. The Soviet statement was based on completely wrong information. General Rabin never made the statement the Soviets had quoted. Israel did not represent any other power and was concerned solely with its own interests. The Soviet Union could and should influence Damascus. It was free to inform the Government of Syria that Israel would honor Syria's independence and integrity; and it would be all to the good if the Soviet Union were to receive a similar declaration from Damascus.

On May 30, TASS published a reaction which completely ignored Israel's reply. "The timeliness of the exposure," it said, "in the TASS statement of May 27 on an imperialist complot against Syria and of the warning to the plotters is proved, among other things, by the stormy reaction . . . of the world press. This statement was received with great satisfaction in Arab political quarters. It was assessed as evidence of the Soviet Union's solidarity with the Arab countries in their struggle against the intrigues of foreign powers and domestic reaction." Although every accusation in the statement had by then been rejected thrice by the Prime Minister and the Foreign Minister of Israel, TASS continued: "It is significant that in the capitals of the imperialist States and Israel, no attempts were made to deny the facts contained in the statement. . . ."

On May 31, Levavi, Director General of the Ministry for Foreign Affairs, summoned Chuvakhin again and read to him a statement in answer to that which Semyonov had read to Ambassador Katz in Moscow. The main points of the reply were:

1. An emphatic rejection of Soviet accusations regarding Israeli troop concentrations on the Syrian border. In fact, the very opposite was true: There were Syrian concentrations on the Israeli frontiers.
2. An equally emphatic démenti of the accusations regarding the alleged pronouncements by General Rabin, which he had, in fact, never made.
3. Rejection of the accusation that Israel's policy was controlled by

foreign powers. Israel acted solely in its own natural interest, which was determined by its desire for peace on its borders and the preservation of sovereignty and integrity of all Middle East States.

4. A categorical rejection of the contention that Israel was responsible for border incidents. The border situation resulted from acts of murder and sabotage carried out by attackers from Syria. The Government of Syria not only aided the terrorists, but even boasted of their activities, which were climaxed by the Almagor murders.

5. The Government of Israel regretted to state that neither the Soviet Government statement, the TASS statement nor the Soviet press made any mention of these attacks and of the Almagor murders, or expressed regret at the loss of life. This attitude might be construed by Arab extremists as encouragement of their bellicose tendencies.

6. Syria's proclaimed policy, threatening to wage a war of extermination against Israel, was reaffirmed by the President of Syria on May 17 and 22. Israel's policy, on the other hand, was based on respect for the integrity and sovereignty of all Middle East States, peaceful settlement of disputes, cessation of the arms race and observance of the United Nations Charter and of the Armistice Agreement. Syria's readiness to implement these principles in regard to Israel would facilitate a détente; and the Government of Israel considered that the Soviet Union, which had often declared that these principles guided its policy, could bring its influence to bear on Syria.

7. The Government of Israel noted with satisfaction the Soviet assertion that the policy of the Soviet Union was guided by the desire to support peace in the Middle East; a desire which was in complete harmony with the policy and interests of Israel, and for whose realization Israel was ready to cooperate with the Soviet Union.

Again there was no response. Chuvakhin listened and promised to report to his Government. But, whatever the reason, a quiet month followed. There was a feeling in Jerusalem that the Russians may have realized they had gone too far in their effort to prop up the regime in Syria at Israel's expense.

XVIII

In May 1966, the heads of Israel's diplomatic missions in Eastern Europe met in Warsaw for consultations with Foreign Minister Eban. Not only did the Polish Government agree, in spite of Arab protests, that the meeting could take place in Warsaw, but Eban was given the opportunity for two "very friendly" talks with Polish Foreign Minister Adam Rapacki. If the Polish authorities made the necessary technical arrangements to be able to follow the proceedings—a possibility which could not be excluded since, not long before, planted listening devices had been discovered at other embassies in Warsaw— they could hear the Foreign Minister stress Israel's interest in improving its relations with Moscow, Warsaw, Belgrade, Prague, Budapest, Bucharest and Sofia. Eban expressed the belief that the understanding regarding Israel that had existed between Moscow and Washington in 1947 could be revived. He also emphasized that East European Governments would come to comprehend that whoever wanted to be a factor in the Arab world had to be a factor also in Israel, and that acceptance of the principle of parallel friendships would not entail loss of prestige or of confidence in the Arab world. Israel itself was interested in good relations with the West, but would also continue to work with great patience in the direction of improving relations with the Soviet Union and the Communist countries of Eastern Europe. On his return from Warsaw on May 18 Eban told the press that Israel's policy toward these countries might be affected by the results of the Warsaw talks.

It cannot be excluded that, by the beginning of June, information on the Warsaw meeting had reached Moscow and made an impression there. In any case, there were signs during that month to warrant a certain optimism and to suggest that, at least temporarily, the Russians had decided to put a brake on their anti-Israeli drive. For instance, during the Supreme Soviet "election campaign" held during June, not a single candidate spoke about Israel and the Middle East. Another reason for this toning down of the anti-Israeli campaign may have been de Gaulle's visit to Moscow in June. The Middle East was discussed in general terms only. The Russians dwelt on the need for stability in the area and stressed their close ties with Egypt. De Gaulle answered that the first condition of stability was maintenance of the *status quo*, and added that Israel was an existing fact and that France had excellent ties with it. The Russians were satisfied to leave it at that. On June 28, Ambassador Chuvakhin informed Tekoah[30] that the Soviet Ambassador in Damascus was working to preserve peace and tranquillity on the borders. He also tried to justify the Soviet statement of May 25 by saying he believed that, in fact, it "helped to save Israel from a dangerous involvement." On June 30, Chuvakhin told Levavi that the Soviet Union was now ready to receive a delegation of Israeli agriculturists.

All these were good signs. Yet the hopes which they raised were once again short-lived. Foreign observers in Moscow were not taking the Soviet campaign against Israel too seriously; they explained it as simply a by-product of Moscow's efforts to

---

30. Yosef Tekoah became Deputy Director General of the Foreign Ministry after his tour of duty as Ambassador to the Soviet Union. Later, he was appointed Israel's Permanent Delegate to the United Nations.

strengthen the weak and unstable Syrian regime. In Jerusalem, the groundless charge of Israeli troop concentrations on the Syrian border was being interpreted as a Soviet tactical trick designed to convince the Syrians that Moscow had succeeded in stopping Israel from allegedly planned steps against Damascus and to show that Soviet political pressure was strong enough to defend Syria and give it security. While all this may have been correct, it did not alter the fact that, the next month, the Soviet press renewed its attacks on Israel. *Pravda,* for instance, wrote on July 20:

> Israel's provocations are directed against tranquillity and peace in the Middle East and against the Arab national liberation movement. But Tel Aviv should not forget that international lawlessness and the effort of finding approval in the eyes of American imperialists will always meet with energetic rejection on the part of all who are interested in the strengthening of peace and security in this area of the world.

The same month saw the Soviet delegation in the Security Council repeating its stereotyped anti-Israeli performance.

On July 25, Syria brought a complaint against Israel to the Security Council and Israel retorted with one against Syria. Fedorenko objected to Israel's complaint being put on the agenda, claiming that the Israeli countermove was a "procedure maneuver" and arguing that "we cannot allow those responsible for acts of provocation to divert our attention from the substance of the matter before us." He then spoke of "the creation of ever increasing tension and armed conflict in the Middle East —a situation brought about by Israeli extremist circles," and went on:

> Israel has pushed matters to such a point that it has made international disregard for law part and parcel of the normal conduct of the Government of Israel toward the Syrian Arab Republic and other Arab States. . . . We are confronted with open aggression by Israel, an act which is in direct contradiction with principles and terms of the United Nations Charter, with the elementary and universally

recognized rules of international law, and with the Armistice Agreement between Syria and Israel. . . . Israel's activities are an obvious reflection of the strengthening of the imperialistic policies of the Western Powers and of their reactionary agents in the Middle East. . . . Since February of the present year, tension in the Middle East has not ceased to increase. At Ankara, an urgent meeting of the military-colonialist CENTO bloc[31] was held. At Beirut, the thirteen American ambassadors to the countries of the Middle East held a meeting. At Beirut also, an imposing squadron of the American Sixth Fleet appeared, while a British squadron dropped anchor in the Israeli port of Haifa. Israel prepares for combat an army of a quarter of a million men and concentrates its armed forces on the frontier with Syria. Israel concludes an agreement with the United States for the purchase of jet bombers . . . and finally carries out a provocative raid on the Syrian Republic. . . . The Soviet Union cannot and will not watch with indifference all these attempts to disturb peace in a region which is in the immediate proximity of its frontiers. All these provocations of Arab countries and the overt aggression against Syria are intolerable. The Security Council . . . must condemn Israel as an aggressor.

The Israeli delegate, Michael Comay, said in answer to Fedorenko's attack:

I regretted very much the tone and the one-sided nature of the statement made . . . by the representative of the Soviet Union. The Soviet Union is a World Power with a position of influence in the affairs of the Middle East. It could exercise that influence in a very constructive manner if it were to call upon all the States in that area, without exception, to respect each other's territorial integrity and political independence, and to settle all outstanding disputes between them by pacific means. The representative of the Soviet Union has seen fit to link the situation on the Israeli-Syrian frontier with other situations elsewhere and with the allegedly sinister plans and policies of other Governments. All I wish to say on this score

---

31. CENTO is the acronym for the Central Treaty Organization, established in 1959 as successor to the Baghdad Pact. With economic and military cooperation as its goal, its members include Great Britain, Iran, Pakistan and Turkey. The United States has affiliate status.

is that the Government of Israel acts as the Government of an independent and sovereign State, that it is concerned only with the national security of Israel and that it is accountable for its actions only to the people it represents.

On August 1, Fedorenko pursued his attack, this time asking for a "radical solution": "The Soviet Union decisively condemns the provocative actions of Israel against the Syrian Arab Republic." He then went on to reject the charge of the Israeli representative, who went so far as to say that the Soviet veto had become a kind of foreign aid used as a device to further the interests of the Soviet Union in the Middle East." The Soviet Union," Fedorenko stated, "does hold dear the interests of peace and security in the Middle East. . . . without any doubt it will continue to support the strengthening of the political and economic independence of Arab countries." And on August 3 he added that "the Security Council is duty-bound . . . to protect a small Arab country, the Syrian Arab Republic."

A day later, Fedorenko was defending another Arab client, this time not against Israel but against Britain's complaint of Egyptian-manned MIG's based in Yemen bombing the South Arabian town of Nuqub. He called the British complaint "a page pulled at random from a lurid detective novel" and "a groundless act of pettifoggery," and asked the Security Council to "cease consideration immediately of this fallacious and unfounded claim." There was nothing the Russians would not do to bolster Arab interests. It was clear that nothing had changed.

In Moscow, the Foreign Ministry informed Ambassador Katz, on August 11, that one of the members of his staff had been declared *persona non grata*. He had been accused of spying and expelled. After TASS had published an announcement about the expulsion, the spokesman of the Foreign Ministry in Jerusalem emphatically rejected the accusation which "can be interpreted only as part of a propaganda campaign intended to suppress natural proofs of sympathies shown for Israel." The spokesman added that "these tactics certainly do not strengthen mutual understanding and goodwill between the nations." The press campaign against Israel was again escalated.[32] On August 22, the wife of a member of the Israeli Embassy staff was physically assaulted at the airport in Kiev by two men who tried to grab her handbag. On September 5, *Izvestia* published an attack on another member of the Embassy staff. In New York, Fedorenko stayed away from a luncheon given by U Thant in honor of President Shazar, and in Jerusalem, Ambassador Chuvakhin failed to attend the festive opening of the new Knesset building. Deputy Foreign Minister Malik would not receive Tekoah, the visiting Deputy Director General of the Israeli Foreign Ministry and former Ambassador to the Soviet Union, or even reply to Ambassador Katz's invitation to attend a luncheon in Tekoah's honor. Tekoah, together with Katz, met twice with the Director of the Middle East Department of the Soviet Foreign Ministry, who assured him that the chances of increasing cultural exchanges between the Soviet Union and Israel were good and that prospects for trade also existed, but that activities like the "Week of Soviet Jewry," were impairing the development of relations. A few weeks later (September 22), however, the Soviet Embassy informed the Foreign Ministry in Jerusalem of the decision of the Soviet authorities to withdraw their approval for a series of concerts by the Israeli Philharmonic Orchestra in Moscow and other cities in the Soviet Union, which had been planned for November of that year. The Embassy gave "the anti-Soviet campaign organized in Israel" as the reason for the decision. The Foreign Office spokesman, informing the press about the Embassy's decision, rebutted the Soviet argument. It was true that a serious concern for the future of Soviet Jewry existed in Israel, but this concern was shared by many non-Jewish groups in many other countries, including the Communist parties in Italy, Britain, France, Sweden, Canada and elsewhere. It was impossible to accuse those elements of organizing an anti-Soviet campaign. In fact, for many months an anti-Israeli campaign had been conducted in the Soviet Union. Political circles in Israel received the news

---

32. See, for instance, *Izvestia* of August 11 and 16, 1966.

of the decision of the Soviet authorities with regret, but were not giving up hope that the day of better understanding would come.

This was the atmosphere in which the Foreign Ministers of the two countries met on September 30 in New York. A few weeks earlier, on August 10, Prime Minister Eshkol received Soviet chargé d'affaires Yakushev, who handed him a copy of the declaration on the security of Europe, which had been adopted at the Bucharest meeting of the East European bloc. Eshkol used the opportunity to emphasize that many points of the declaration coincided with the views held by the Government of Israel. He mentioned especially Israel's stand on the question of the Oder-Neisse border and on arming Germany with nuclear weapons, but admitted that Israel was more worried about peace in the Middle East. Finally, he reminded Yakushev of Israel's positive answer to Khrushchev's note of December 1963. When Nasser, in his reply to an identical note, refused to apply the principle of peaceful settlement of disputes to Egypt's relations with Israel, the Prime Minister wrote once more to Khrushchev, but he never got a reply. Eshkol asked the chargé d'affaires to convey to his Government Israel's disappointment on that score. The Bucharest declaration on the security of Europe and the applicability of its principles to the Middle East were the points with which Abba Eban (who was accompanied by Gideon Rafael and Michael Comay) opened his talk with Gromyko.

Eban pointed out that territorial *status quo* was as important in the Middle East as in Europe. Similarly, the principle of peaceful coexistence must also apply to the Middle East. He then explained that coexistence did not mean only refraining from war. Israel was cooperating with many countries, and that served as example and proof that small countries could help each other without being dependent on big powers. Israel was against colonialism, for peace in Vietnam, for the *status quo*, for peaceful coexistence, for economic cooperation between countries and for assistance to developing countries. The area of understanding and agreement with the Soviet Union was, therefore, much wider than that of disagreement between the two States. Eban further enumerated the points around which the disagreement between Moscow and Jerusalem revolved:

1. The Soviet Union's incorrect contention that Israel was acting against Syria as an instrument of foreign forces with a view to bringing about a change of regime in Damascus. Israel was, in fact, not interested in what kind of regime there was in Syria, as long as the obligations of the United Nations Charter and the Armistice Agreement were observed. Israel was acting solely to defend its own, and no other country's, interests.
2. The nonexistence of trade and the highly limited cultural exchange, which resulted in a lack of contact and emptied diplomatic relations between the two countries of all practical content.
3. The erroneous idea in Moscow, also held by Ambassador Chuvakhin, that there was no suitable atmosphere in Israel for closer relations with the Soviet Union.
4. The complicated problem of Soviet Jews which the Soviet Union did not really try to understand.

Gromyko admitted the existence of positive elements in Israel's definition of its stand regarding some international problems (for instance, its refraining from the use of force to settle territorial conflicts) and especially the European security question. He lauded the stand Israel had taken on the question of the Oder-Neisse frontier. He repeated that he regarded relations between the Soviet Union and Israel as more or less normal, even if not warm. He said there was a "perspective" for trade relations. As for political relations, he regretted to have to point out that since the proclamation of the State of Israel, there had been circles in Israel "with too high a norm of unfriendliness" toward the Soviet Union. Soviet friendly relations with some of the Arab States, in his opinion, did not eliminate the possibility of good relations with Israel. There was no conflict between the Soviet Union and Israel. Even if Zionist ideology was, for the Soviets, too conservative and sometimes even reactionary, there was no conflict with the State of Israel.

Israel had no intention of "surrounding and crushing" the Soviet Union, neither was the Soviet Union looking for new enemies. The Soviet Union advocated the creation of Israel as a just solution, and was not supporting the slogans clamoring for its liquidation.

One or two new points could be found in Gromyko's answer. Gromyko had admitted for the first time the possibility of parallel friendly relations with the Arab States and Israel. He also underlined the existence of differences between the Arab States. After years of embarrassed silence about the Soviet role in 1947, he now spoke with pride of the part the Soviet Union had played in establishing the State of Israel. Finally, while not reacting to Eban's remarks on Soviet Jewry, he did not explode as on some previous occasions.

All this was positive. The conversation was regarded as favorable and important. Its significance, however, was soon neutralized when, only three days later (on October 3), an article in *Pravda*, under the heading "General Rabin Sharpens the Swords," returned to the old charges of Israeli troop concentrations on the Syrian border. "It seems," the newspaper stated, "that reactionary militarist circles in Israel do not limit themselves any longer to provocations . . . but are considering and deciding on preparations for a deep penetration of Syrian territory with the aim of overthrowing the present Government there." On October 4, the Foreign Ministry spokesman in Jerusalem refuted it by quoting Prime Minister Eshkol's statement of September 18 that Israel had no intention of interfering with Syria's internal affairs, but wanted peace. The charge was, nevertheless, reiterated the next day in a TASS statement which added: "In the event of unprovoked aggression against them, the Syrian people will not be alone." On October 8, *Izvestia* reported preparations for combined action against Syria, planned by Israel and by reactionary forces in the Arab world." The newspaper, like TASS, added: "Syria is not alone in its just struggle." All during October, the same canard was spread in public meetings organized by the Communist Party throughout the Soviet Union.

Prime Minister Eshkol decided to talk with the Soviet Ambassador once more—on October 11. The purpose was to afford Eshkol an opportunity to protest against the lying Soviet press reports and charges, but principally to ask Chuvakhin to inform his Government that the Soviet Union could foster peace by using its influence with the Syrian Government to bring an end to Syrian infiltrations. Chuvakhin answered that while the Soviet Union was interested in peace, there were foreign forces in the area that were concerned with keeping the Middle East tension alive. It was up to Israel to make these forces stop their activities in the area. The Soviet Union had normal relations with Syria but could not use influence which might be interpreted as interference in Syria's internal affairs. Eshkol expressed disappointment with the Ambassador's reply and assured him repeatedly that it was not true that foreign forces were responsible for Syrian policy or that Israel was acting as an agent of these forces. However, there was no on-the-spot reaction.

The reply came the next day when Chuvakhin asked for an urgent meeting with the Prime Minister and handed him the following note:

According to information in our hands, there are at present renewed serious concentrations of the Israeli Army on the Syrian border, and preparations are in progress for an air attack on the border areas in Syria, with the aim of enabling Israeli forces subsequently to penetrate deeply into Syria. The Chief of Staff of Israel's Armed Forces recently declared publicly that Israel's military preparations will be directed first of all against the existing political regime in Syria. Actions of this kind bear witness to the existence of unceasing efforts on the part of extremist circles in Israel to step up activity against those neighboring Arab States that are following a line of political independence, and above all against the Arab Republic of Syria. These Israeli actions create threats to peace and tranquillity in the Middle East and are not in harmony with the promises of the Government of Israel that it will work for peace and tranquillity on the borders and for the safeguarding of the independence, sovereignty and territorial integrity of the States in the Middle East, and

they are also in contradiction to the declaration, made by the Director General of the Israeli Foreign Ministry to the Soviet Ambassador, that Israel has no pretensions against Syria and does not intend
to interfere in the internal affairs of that State.

Eshkol answered instantly that the statement was neither true
nor just. In fact, it was an insult. He asked on what ground the
Government of the Soviet Union based its information and
suggested that the Ambassador should accompany him on a
visit to the border area to see for himself if there were any truth
in the Soviet allegation on Israeli troop concentrations. Chuvakhin promptly rejected the offer. Levavi, Director General of the
Foreign Ministry, who attended the meeting, said it was clear
from the statement that the Soviet Union was intervening on
behalf of one side only, namely, on behalf of the "aggressors
who are murdering our people." Chuvakhin did not react but
merely pointed out that the note was not a reply to yesterday's
request for the use of Soviet influence in Damascus.

Israel's Permanent Delegate to the United Nations, Michael
Comay, addressed a letter to the President of the Security
Council, which was at once defined by TASS (on October 12)
as "another hostile move against the Syrian Arab Republic."
The comment of the TASS New York correspondent was:

Comay claims that the acts of sabotage committed, as he says, on
Israeli territory by members of the Al Fatah organization, consisting
of Palestinian Arab refugees, have assumed the character of guerrilla activities. Despite repeated Syrian denials, the representative
of Israel holds Syria responsible for the activities of this organization and alleges that the attacks on Israeli territory are planned,
organized and directed by the Syrian authorities and armed forces.
Comay threatens that the Government of Israel considers it its duty
to "take measures which might be necessary to protect the integrity
of its borders." Comay's letter appears to be an attempt to justify
Israel's participation in the campaign against the Syrian Arab
Republic, instigated by the imperialist circles and their yes-men.

On October 14, the Israeli complaint against Syria reached the Security Council. Israel's position was psychologically weakened by a raid the same day on the Syrian delegation's office by undisciplined non-Israeli elements, which the Arabs and their defenders turned to a propaganda advantage. In the Security Council discussion itself, Fedorenko was once more Syria's main advocate, saying:

> We are more convinced than ever that the hasty recourse by Israel to the Security Council is nothing but a tactical maneuver, the objective of which is to divert attention from the true sources of tension in the Middle East and to camouflage the military preparations of Israeli extremist circles against the Syrian Arab Republic.

> It is common knowledge that of late the forces of reaction in the Middle East have expanded their activities, because the number of Arab countries pursuing an independent policy is constantly increasing. The Syrian Arab Republic is one such State. . . . The ruling circles of Tel Aviv must understand correctly the serious consequences which flow from serious violations of the Armistice on the borders with Arab States. The Security Council is duty-bound to address a solemn warning to those who nurture aggressive designs against an independent and sovereign State—the Syrian Arab Republic.

At a later stage in the debate, Fedorenko, on October 28, tried to gain time by asking for a detailed report on what was happening in the demilitarized zone between Israel and Syria, and by attempting to prevent the Israeli delegate, Comay, from speaking. Still later, on November 4, he declared: "The Syrian Government is in no way responsible for the incidents which took place on the territory of Israel. . . . It is not Syria but Israel that is violating the statutes of the demilitarized zone by generating constant tension in the area." When these tactics failed and Syria was facing condemnation by the Security Council, Fedorenko used the veto, this time without even bothering to explain his action.

At this stage the Foreign Ministry in Jerusalem reassessed Soviet Middle East policy. It was estimated, now as before, that Moscow was not interested in an armed conflict that would bring with it Western intervention in the Middle East. The Russians probably did not even consider such a possibility. Much more likely, they thought Israel could be provoked into a short thrust into Syria, which the Soviet Union would stop not by military intervention but by an immediate convoking of the Security Council, where the Western Powers would find themselves in an embarrassing position while the Soviet Union would act as Syria's main protector, its savior, in fact. Thus, it would strengthen the stability of the pro-Soviet Syrian regime while gaining further ground in the Arab world.

If this were really Moscow's plan, the fact that Israel did not take any retaliatory action against Syria but instead went to the Security Council, where Fedorenko found himself in the unpleasant situation of having again to use the unpopular veto, may have convinced the Russians that, at least for the time being, the plan was not easy to realize. This may be the explanation of the fact that, while the Soviet press continued to charge that Israel was preparing war against Syria, Ambassador Katz was called on November 9 to the Soviet Foreign Ministry, where Deputy Foreign Minister Semyonov handed him an *aide-mémoire*. It read as follows:

> The Soviet Government has taken attentive note of the statement delivered by the Israeli Ambassador to the Soviet Foreign Minister, containing the views expressed by Prime Minister Eshkol in conversation with the Soviet Ambassador in Tel Aviv on October 12 regarding descriptions of the situation that is developing at the moment in the border zone between Israel and the Syrian Arab Republic.
>
> The Soviet Government takes cognizance of the statement of Prime Minister Eshkol concerning the absence of aggressive intentions on the part of the Government of Israel with respect to the neighboring Arab States, including the Syrian Arab Republic, and with respect to the aspiration of the Government of Israel to do everything possible for the preservation of peace in that zone. The Soviet

Government, must, however, affirm with regret that the policy which—to judge from all information—is pursued in Israel conflicts with these claims of the Prime Minister. More than once in the past, the Soviet Government has drawn the attention of the Government of Israel to the danger of an increase of tension in the Middle East, to which the policy of the Imperialist Powers is leading—Powers which for a long time now have been endeavoring to use Israel in their designs for war against the independent Arab States. It is the strong conviction of the Government of the Soviet Union that preservation of peace in the Middle East and disallowance of interference in internal affairs of the States in that region are in accordance first and foremost with the basic interests of the State of Israel and also with the interests of the neighboring Arab States. Prime Minister Eshkol in his talk endeavored to place responsibility for the worsening of the situation on the Syrian side. But how can one speak of Syrian responsibility when in Israel there continues actively, against the background of persuasive peace-loving statements, a build-up of public opinion in favor of preparations for warlike assault upon Syria, when the present deterioration of the situation is synchronized with the mounting activity of external imperialist forces that are striving to interfere in the internal affairs of Syria and that are organizing plots against it and are not ashamed to proclaim openly that they are not satisfied with the present regime in Syria and that it would suit their interests better if elements linked with Western oil monopolies and certain Imperialist Powers were to take over authority in Syria? It is impossible not to be disturbed by the fact that the rising tension on the Israeli-Syrian border manifests itself just when the great Western Powers openly admit that they are not content with the progress of the discussions that are being held between their oil companies and the Syrian Government about payments for the pipeline across Syrian territory. The coincidence in time between the incidents which, as is clear from the memorandum of the Government of Israel, occurred on Israeli territory, resulting in loss of life, and the aforementioned maneuvers of the Western Powers cannot but induce misgivings as to the extent to which it is possible that incidents of that kind were organized in a special way by certain services or by an agency of those services for the purpose of provocation. History knows an abundance of examples of that kind of provocation, and can nations be expected to remain indifferent? The Soviet Government would

like to believe that the Government of Israel will not find itself again
exploited as a tool by the policy of foreign Imperialist Powers, a
policy alien to the basic interests of Israel, and that the Government
of Israel will display the necessary caution, steadfastness and far-
sightedness in the present situation. We regard it as imperative to
say this openly to the Government of Israel, inasmuch as the Soviet
Union maintains diplomatic relations with Israel and the Middle
Eastern region is situated in the immediate vicinity of the frontiers
of Russia. The Government of the Soviet Union would like, on its
part, to state that, as always, it takes, and will continue to take, the
necessary measures to prevent any breach of peace and security in
the Middle East and to contribute to the avoidance of any outbreak
of friction in that region.

Semyonov had just returned from a trip to the Middle East. In
conversation with Ambassador Katz he said that his Government was acquainted with all the hostile declarations of Arab
statesmen but was not taking them seriously, and that Israel
should not take them seriously either. The purpose of the *aide-
mémoire*, he said, was to tell the Government of Israel that it
should act with wisdom and caution. It was sometimes wise to
refrain from immediate reaction for the sake of long-term interests. The Arabs, in spite of all their declarations, understood
well that it was not in their interest to push the area into war.
As for Shukairy, he did not represent anybody. It was not true
that the Soviet Government had invited him to Moscow.

This was certainly a new tone. The *aide-mémoire* presented
the Arab-Israeli conflict as part of "the cold war." It did not
even say that Israel was acting as a tool of the opposite side in
that confrontation, but only drew Israel's attention to the fact
that the Western Powers might try to exploit it. In fact, a certain
apologetic undertone could be discerned. The document was
perhaps even more important for what it did not contain. There
was no mention of Israeli troop concentrations on the Syrian
border. There was not a word about Israel's plans to penetrate
into Syria or about certain Israeli declarations to which the
Russians had found it necessary to object in the past. Finally,
the last paragraph of the *aide-mémoire*, in which the Soviet

Union stated that it would "continue to take necessary measures to prevent any breach of peace and security in the Middle
East," could be interpreted as an answer to Eshkol's request
that Moscow use its influence in Damascus.

True, a week later when, on November 16, the Security
Council was discussing a complaint by Jordan against an Israeli
retaliatory action, Fedorenko spoke with his old accents:

> We are confronted with an open act of aggression perpetrated by
> Israel against the Arab nation, a State member of the United Na-
> tions, Jordan. What we are dealing with here is not only military
> preparations on the part of Israel that are dangerous to the world
> and to peace, but a flagrant violation of peace and security on the
> part of the extremist circles in Tel Aviv, intrigues by Israeli armed
> forces in the form of open military aggression against the territory
> of a neighboring Arab country.... Israel has flagrantly and brutally
> violated the most important provisions of the United Nations, and
> this alone deserves condemnation. . . . The new act of aggression
> . . . which we are forced to describe as lawlessness and brigandage,
> is an open and arrogant challenge to the Security Council. . . . The
> causes of the constant and permanent tension in that area boil down
> to the extremist policy of Israel and of those who are behind it . . .
> and to the desire of the Imperialist Powers to restrain the national
> liberation movements of peoples by force. . . . The Security Council
> . . . must severely condemn Israel as an aggressor [and] take effective
> measures to ensure the cessation, once and for all, of aggressive
> actions on the part of Tel Aviv against Arab countries.

In other words, Fedorenko was his familiar self. This time,
however, the impact of his intervention was considerably weakened by the fact that Israel, on this occasion, was censured
unanimously (with only New Zealand abstaining), and above all
by the impression of change resulting from the Semyonov statement. As late as December 6, Ambassador Chuvakhin told
Foreign Minister Abba Eban; "You do not realize to what extent Semyonov's statement was positive."

There were, of course, also some doubts as to how far Semyonov's statement should be taken as an important first step in the

right direction, and to what extent it was merely a temporary, tactical abandonment of a specific line of attack. These doubts were somewhat reinforced when, only two days after the Semyonov-Katz meeting, Gromyko, during the General Assembly debate, on November 11, in "strict observance of the prohibition of the threat of use of force in international relations," found it necessary to say:

> There are continuing acts of aggression and use of force by the United Kingdom against Yemen, and the extremist circles in Israel, encouraged by Washington and London, are threatening to use force against Arab States and are engaging in acts of provocation.

Optimism was further dampened by Kosygin's statement at a press conference during his visit to Paris (December 3). He was asked by a French journalist (representing *l'Aurore*): "In January 1965 you successfully chaired the Tashkent Conference which put an end to the conflict between India and Pakistan. Don't you envisage a similar initiative for the establishment of an atmosphere of peaceful coexistence in the Middle East?" He answered:

> It seems to us that no question of any conference on the Middle East arises now. You will yourself understand that a conference can be called only if the parties concerned agree to resort to it as a means of settling some other disputable question. Now, I believe, there are no conditions for calling such a conference.

The answer could, of course, have been worded differently, but it was realized that to expect Moscow to take any grand-scale initiative at this stage was unrealistic. Attacks on Israel could still be found in the Soviet press. *Novoye Vremya* on December 16, for instance, went on speaking of the danger of war in the Middle East, primarily because of "Israel, the main spearhead of imperialism in the Arab East"; and *Pravda* (December 18) repeated that "behind the tension in the Middle East are Israeli military circles, the reaction in Jordan and Syria, and Anglo-American oil monopolies." But the Semyonov statement still existed; it was not revoked and remained as a potential bridge to better understanding. It made the total situation look somewhat brighter.

It was principally to discuss the Semyonov *aide-mémoire* that Foreign Minister Eban called in the Soviet Ambassador on December 21. He explained to Chuvakhin that, in 1965 the Arabs had accepted the policy of a "People's War" through armed intruders. Israel had made various technical arrangements to prevent infiltration; it had built fences along parts of the frontiers and additional roads for patrolling the border areas; but this had proved and would continue to prove insufficient as long as the Arabs did not understand that, for political reasons, they must abandon that policy. Therefore, Israel tried to persuade the Big Powers to use their influence with the Arab Governments. Egypt was keeping her borders with Israel quiet; so was Lebanon; but not Syria or Jordan. The use of influence by the Great Powers, especially by the Soviet Union in Damascus, could bring about a lessening of tension. Eban welcomed Semyonov's statement that the Soviet Union opposed military conflicts in the Middle East and interference in internal affairs of sovereign States in the area. But he rejected the assertion that the tension was caused by foreign elements or that Israel was acting in their interests. In reply to Chuvakhin's claim that it was impossible not to take into account the activities of Anglo-American oil companies, Eban drew his attention to the fact that these companies had, in fact, always been opposed to the existence of Israel and had tried to prevent the establishment of the State in 1948. Eban also welcomed the Soviet Union's negative attitude toward Shukairy. Finally, he expressed regret that, in spite of these positive points, the Semyonov statement had not so far led to any sign of improvement in the bilateral relations between the Soviet Union and Israel. He hoped that closer ties would follow.

Eban's approach was meant as a first step across the bridge. Early the next year it became clear that, in Moscow's plans, there was no bridge to be crossed.

XIX

January–April 1967
Eban's Knesset speech of February 14
Continuation of the dialogue in Moscow
Israel's retaliation against Syria in April
Moscow's renewed accusations about alleged Israeli troop concentrations
Malik's communication of April 4 and Semyonov's statement of April 25
Gideon Rafael's visit to Moscow

That the value of the Semyonov statement was questionable could not be recognized immediately. True, there were many new points of tension between Moscow and Jerusalem at the beginning of 1967, but they all concerned the Jewish problem —some directly, some indirectly—and were not discernibly connected with the Arab-Israeli conflict or the situation in the Middle East.

On January 3, Tekoah, as Assistant Director General of the Foreign Ministry, summoned the Soviet Ambassador and informed him that it was known in Israel that, in the case of the member of the Israeli Embassy's staff in Moscow who had been declared *persona non grata*, an attempt had been made by Soviet authorities to enlist him as a spy against a friendly country, and that he was expelled after refusing the offer. On January 5, the Israeli chargé d'affaires was invited to the Foreign Ministry, where the Director of the Middle East Department read him a complaint about the illegal and anti-Soviet behavior of Israeli tourists in the Soviet Union. On January 12, TASS published an interview with the Soviet Yiddish writer Vergelis, who claimed that "representatives of the Israeli Ministry for Foreign Affairs hinder contacts and exchange of objective information between Jews of the Soviet Union and other countries" because they allegedly had tried to prevent a meeting between him and the Israeli Nobel Prize winner, Shmuel Yosef Agnon, in New York. On January 27, Ambassador Chuvakhin complained to Tekoah about the decision to hold a "Week of Soviet Jewry." Tekoah assured him that the Government of Israel was not involved. On February 15, the Israeli Embassy in Moscow received (by messenger) a note to the effect that, in the course of court proceedings against a Soviet citizen, it was established that the accused, who was charged and sentenced for anti-State activities, was in contact with several former employees of the Israeli Embassy, including the present First Secretary. The note expressed hope that the Embassy would immediately take the necessary steps to stop such behavior, which was incompatible with the code of conduct prescribed for the personnel of diplomatic missions. On February 23, *Izvestia* discussed the case in a long article, giving the names of the Embassy staff members allegedly involved. In reply to Israel's repudiation of the charge, the Soviet Ministry of Foreign Affairs, in a note dated March 3, repeated the allegations.

The Syrian issue was not dead. On January 9, *Pravda* published an anti-Israeli report concerning the situation on the Syrian border, accusing Israel of doing the imperialists' dirty work. This was repeated by Radio Moscow on January 12. In an article on visits to Israel by senior officials of the U.S. State Department, published in the Red Army newspaper *Krasnaya Zvezda* of March 19, the accusation that Israel was making military preparations to overthrow the progressive Syrian regime was aired once more. But the attacks were still rather sporadic and, above all, the political dialogue which was made possible by the Semyonov statement was still continuing.

On February 1, Ambassador Chuvakhin handed Foreign Minister Eban a note regarding the emergence of neo-Nazism in West Germany. Eban expressed concern over the results of elections to the Land Parliaments in Bavaria and Hessen. He reminded Chuvakhin that, in the 1966 General Assembly, Israel was the only country outside the Eastern bloc that had

spoken in favor of the Oder-Neisse line as a permanent frontier.
On the other hand, East Germany did nothing for the victims
of Nazism. It did not even confirm the receipt of the 1956 Israeli
note on the matter, and all its statements on the Middle East
were clearly directed against Israel. Israel's attitude was critical
toward both German States. Certainly Israel was against revanchism. But one thing must be clear: It was impossible to be
against revanchism in one part of the world and not oppose it
in another.

A fortnight later (February 14), the Foreign Minister, in his
Knesset speech during the Foreign Ministry's budget debate,
developed this theme further:

> In the course of the last year, we have been conducting a dialogue
> with the Government of the Soviet Union in Jerusalem, Moscow
> and the United Nations. We explained openly the great importance
> that we attach to the attitude of the Soviet Union, . . . its influence
> on stability today and on the chances of peace in the future. . . . The
> Soviet Union stands for abstaining from the use of force in settling
> territorial disputes. This is the basis of Israel's position on the Mid-
> dle East, Europe, East Asia and the whole world. The Soviet Union
> has also initiated a resolution on noninterference in the internal
> affairs of States. We have no reservations on this important princi-
> ple. It would not occur to us to support any proposal which is not
> in harmony with the sovereignty of a State. We do not support any
> domination, interference or protectorate imposed on any State
> whatsoever from outside. In several official declarations, the Soviet
> Union explains the importance of free and normal trade and cultural
> relations between States, regardless of differences of regimes and
> social ideologies, and a few days ago the Soviet Ambassador to
> Israel delivered to me a note which, among other things, says that
> "a constructive approach to the matter of achieving peace and
> security in Europe and in the entire world is possible only on the
> basis of existing realities." Security in the entire world is indeed
> possible only on the basis of a realistic policy. The State of Israel
> certainly regards itself to be covered by the term "entire world."

But the question is whether these clearly formulated principles do
or do not apply to Israeli-Arab relations, for a principle is worthless

if it is scrupulously applied to one part of the world, only to be turned into a fraud in another part of the world.

Yet, when we turn our attention from agreed theoretical principles to practical policy, the logic turns upside down. Unlimited support is being given to States that do not accept the very principles that the Soviet Union describes as vital. Do Arab Governments agree that the use of force in settling territorial disputes between States is forbidden? Is it, in their opinion, forbidden to interfere in the internal affairs of States by limiting their sovereignty? Do they believe that a flow of trade and cultural exchanges should be moving with ever growing freedom beyond the frontiers of States with different regimes and ideologies? Do all the Arab States in our region agree that "a constructive approach to the matter of achieving peace and security in the entire world is possible only on the basis of existing realities"? Is it clear to all of them that the many weapons they are receiving are destined to defend the "existing reality" and not to disturb it?

The contradiction that has not yet been straightened out in the relations between the Soviet Union and Israel and its neighbors lies in the wide gap between the declared principles and the policy actually pursued. The influence of this contradiction is not limited to the Middle East. Masses of peace-loving people and many Governments would have greater confidence in the principles of Soviet international policy if they saw convincing proof that these principles are being consequentially and clearly applied with regard to the tension in the Middle East.

Naturally, the clarifying talks we are conducting with the Soviet Union about international subjects must go on. There is hope in the very existence of these talks. In the sensitive political and security balance in the Middle East, there is importance in the Soviet Union's reservations on acts of terrorist sabotage perpetrated on Israeli territory. We do not deprecate any expression of regret over the loss of life as a consequence of these acts. I admit that I cannot remain indifferent, when an official representative of the Soviet Union reminds me, in 1966, of the fateful contribution of his Government to the establishment of the State of Israel in 1948. . . .

The Government and people of Israel sincerely wish that relations may be established between Israel and the Soviet Union like the relations that existed in the first years of our independence. This, however, does not depend on us alone. There is room for the assumption that, since the spring of 1966, the desire to come nearer to certain Arab States began to influence exceedingly the Soviet Union's views of our region and of our policy.

I admit: Israel is unable to adopt the division of Arab States into "revolutionary" and "reactionary" States. We divide the States of the world into those that are peace-loving and those that are plotting aggression. This is the only polarization with an international significance. . . . The truly decisive criterion in our relations with any State in the area or in the world is that State's attitude to peace and its adherence to the principles of international coexistence. Every State in the area, regardless of its regime or ideology, which will honor our rights to security of life and the safeguarding of our sovereignty will enjoy a reciprocal attitude on Israel's side.

There is nothing wrong with a serious discussion of differences of opinion and views, but logic is being silenced and truth is being given a false face at the moment, when Israel is presented as an instrument in the hands of oil companies and other foreign factors that are interested in bringing about a change in the regime of Syria. We are only interested in changing, in Syria, its aggressive policy toward Israel. The kind of regime and the character of Syria's society are not our business. We do not dogmatically reject every pronouncement of the Syrian Government. For instance, when President Atassi declares that Syria is responsible for encouraging and permitting the acts of sabotage against Israel, we believe him.

But it is just here that the emphasized Syrian declaration meets with strange doubts. . . .

I am unable to say how Soviet policy in the Middle East regarding our problem will develop in this discussion a year from now. . . . What existed once cannot be regarded as impossible to be reclaimed. If, as we hope, the tendency of cooperation between the Great Powers becomes stronger, it may bring about a limitation of competition between the blocs and a greater readiness to apply the objective principles of coexistence. . . .

The dialogue continued in Moscow. As late as March 21, 1967, the Director of the Middle East Department of the Soviet Foreign Ministry gave the following picture of Soviet views to Ambassador Katz: Soviet public opinion was currently worried about three things: the situation in Vietnam, the German revanchism and the situation in the Middle East. In that region, Syria had gained an important victory over the oil companies, a victory important not only for Syria but for all Arab nations. The situation in Yemen, however, was still causing concern and the Soviet Union was therefore against the evacuation of Egyptian troops from Yemen. The Ambassador's remark that it was not consistent to oppose German but not Arab revanchism elicited the answer that not everything in Syria depended on Moscow's wishes. The Soviet Union was doing its best to convince the Arabs that to talk about the liquidation of Israel was one thing, but to realize these threats would be another. Moscow was against Arab propaganda and against Shukairy but could not dictate to the Arabs how to behave. As for bilateral relations between the Soviet Union and Israel, they had, in the opinion of the Soviet Foreign Ministry, become normal and could be developed even further, especially in the field of cultural exchanges.

The situation took a turn for the worse sometime in April. Whether or not the Russians could dictate to the Syrians on how to behave and whether or not they tried, the fact remained that acts of organized sabotage committed by Syria against Israeli territory had continued throughout the month of March with a dangerously increasing impetus. On April 7, Israel saw itself forced to put an end to these acts by retaliating in force. A fortnight later—a fortnight during which discussions probably took place in the Kremlin which resulted in a final decision to follow the line adopted before Semyonov's statement—Ambassador Katz, on April 21, was called in by Deputy Foreign Minister Malik, who delivered to him the following oral communication:

On various occasions in the past, the Government of the Soviet Union drew the attention of the Government of Israel to the worsening of the situation in the Middle East as a result of the policy of imperialist forces and of extremist and militarist circles in Israel. The forces responsible for the situation in Vietnam are responsible also for provocations in the Middle East and for bringing the situation there to the brink of war in order to secure larger profits for the oil monopolies. They do not take into account that this is a threat to these countries, and to the territory of Israel among them. On various occasions, the Government of the Soviet Union declared its views on the developments in the Middle East and expressed due warning. The Soviet Government does not deem it necessary to repeat itself. However, it cannot but pay attention to the incidents with Syria on April 7, in the course of which the Israeli side unleashed overt military actions against Syria, using planes, tanks and artillery. This dangerous playing with fire on the part of Israel in an area near to the borders of the Soviet Union was accompanied by declarations confirming Israel's will to settle its disputes with Arabs from a position of strength and by military means. The Chief of Staff declared that this Israeli attack was not the last and that the way, form and date of similar actions will be decided by Israel alone. The impression is necessarily gained that the military actions of April 7 are a part of those acts of retribution which are being directed against the Syrian people by imperialist forces, disappointed by the courageous fight against the oil monopolies. It must be clear to the Government of Israel that a policy of aggression against its neighbors is bound to result in serious consequences. . . . The Soviet Government hopes that the Government of Israel will consider well the existing situation and will avoid following groups which, by demonstrating political impatience, are ready to turn their country into an instrument in the hands of hostile foreign forces and thus to endanger the vital interests of their people and the fate of their State.

This was the gist of the communication. Coming after the Semyonov statement, it was a staggering change of tone and attitude. There was still a glimmer of hope in the possible explanation that it might have been just a gesture to an Iraqi delegation which was concluding its visit to Moscow the same day that Malik delivered the statement to the Ambassador of Israel. Another spark of hope was seen in the fact that the statement had been made orally. Malik refused to give a written copy to the Ambassador and there was no immediate publication.

However, on April 25, 1967, the Ambassador was called again to the Foreign Ministry, this time by Semyonov, who handed him the following written statement:

The Soviet Government is in possession of information about Israeli troop concentrations on the Israeli-Arab borders at the present time. These concentrations are assuming a dangerous character, coinciding as they do with the hostile campaign in Israel against Syria. It is also known that incidents have lately become frequent on the borders of Israel with Syria and Jordan.

In this context it is impossible not to draw attention to the bellicose statements by Israeli military personalities against Arab countries.

After quoting General Rabin's speech, the note went on:

All these actions combine with the intensification of the mobilization of activites of the imperialist forces in the Middle East, which aim at interfering with the independent position of the Arab States and at creating conditions for intervention in their domestic affairs.

It is quite clear that these actions constitute a flagrant violation of the declaration prohibiting intervention in the domestic affairs of States and assuring their independence and sovereignty, which was adopted at the Twentieth Session of the General Assembly of the United Nations. These imperialist designs and the threat of the use of force create an atmosphere of tension in the region of the Middle East.

The Soviet Government is also aware of the peace-seeking statements made by the leading personalities of Israel. However, these statements are in contradiction with the facts cited above and are open to doubt. The question arises as to whether these circles, which are adopting an extremely hostile attitude toward the Arab countries, will be capable of again imposing on the State and people of Israel the role of the blind weapon of imperialism and neocolonialism in the Middle East.

The Soviet Government would like to hope that a realistic attitude will be manifested by the Government of Israel in appraising the possible outcome of the implementation of these dangerous plans directed against the independent Arab countries, including the Syrian Arab Republic. The Soviet Government expresses its hope that the Government of Israel will not allow external forces to play with the fate of its people and State. In expressing these thoughts, the Soviet Government is entirely guided by the aspiration to support peace and tranquillity in the region of the Middle East which lies in the immediate proximity of the Soviet borders.

By chance, this happened during a visit to Moscow by Gideon Rafael, the newly appointed Permanent Representative of Israel to the United Nations. At the request of the Foreign Minister, Rafael stopped in Moscow on his way to New York to gain a firsthand impression from meetings with Soviet diplomats.[33] The day after the Deputy Foreign Minister Semyonov handed his statement to Ambassador Katz, Rafael, accompanied by Katz, was received by Semyonov. On the same day, TASS published the text of the note, stressing that the Soviet Government had warned Israel not to exasperate its Arab neighbors and that Israel's policy was fraught with danger for which it alone bore full responsibility. The Soviet press gave prominence to the text.

Nevertheless, the meeting between Rafael and Semyonov began as if it were a continuation of a previous dialogue. Rafael opened by speaking of the large reservoir of sympathy, gratitude and admiration for the Soviet Union in Israel, of which no use was being made. The reason might be lack of contact. "To see once is better than to hear a thousand times." Gromyko, Semyonov and others should come and see for themselves. This would also make it easier for them to understand how Israel's attitude must necessarily be influenced by the fact that the margin of its safety was so narrow and that the boiling point in the Middle East was much lower than elsewhere. He then stressed the many points of agreement between the Soviet Union and Israel on questions of world policy, especially the common attitude to revanchism, neo-Nazism and the atomic armament of Germany. He pointed out that not only past memories, but also concern for the future, made Israel and the Soviet Union natural allies; and, therefore, in Israel's opinion, the time had come to review relations and strengthen contacts between the two States.

Semyonov answered that he appreciated what Rafael had said about Israel's views on Germany, but he then turned immediately to the Middle East. Soviet policy, he said, was directed toward strengthening peace and security in that area. The Soviet Union believed it would not be to Israel's advantage

33. Chance played another trick and Rafael arrived in Moscow on the same plane that brought the Foreign Minister of Iraq. Rafael's talks at the Soviet Foreign Ministry were delayed until after the Iraqi delegation's departure.

to become involved in the game of the oil monopolists, who
were ready to enter into dangerous activities and to jeopardize
the national interests of the Arabs and Israel for a gain of a
single cent per gallon of oil. In the course of the last year, there
had been an intensification of these activities, which had increased tension in the Middle East. He referred to the statement
he had read to Ambassador Katz the day before regarding the
Israeli retaliatory action of April 7. Such moves put Israel in a
bad light and might have results different from those Israel
expected. "I do not think that you are interested in such results." American generals who were planning the war in Vietnam did not expect either that it would lead to the destruction
of the territory they were trying to defend. In times of tension,
it was particularly important that small nations should not let
themselves be provoked into action by imperialist forces, because the results might be very serious for their peoples and
countries. There was no need to exercise caution and wisdom
if they did not become involved in the furtherance of foreign
interests. He expressed the hope that the leaders of Israel would
understand this well and would keep in mind the historical
developments and perspectives of the Middle East and its envi-
ronment. Local conflicts could easily get out of control. Therefore, the Soviet Union could not remain indifferent should they
occur near its frontiers. Those who invited a conflict close to the
Soviet borders might pay a very high price. As for Soviet help
to the Arabs, the economic strengthening of Arab countries was
certainly good for peace. The Aswan Dam was serving peace.
When Rafael agreed that economic aid would definitely further
peace more than would the supply of arms, Semyonov said that
countries which had gained independence must be able to stand
up against colonialism, for which they also needed a certain
amount of arms. There was a difference between arms supplied
by imperialists and arms supplied by anti-imperialist States.
There was a difference between handing a knife to a robber and
passing it to someone who is a potential victim of the robber.

Again Rafael agreed. Israel understood that very well and
was giving military assistance to some countries in Africa to

enable them to strengthen their security against the threat of neocolonialism. But in the Middle East, Israel, with no aggressive designs against any of its neighbors, was exactly in the position of a potential victim. What the Soviet Union regarded as pinpricks, Israel felt as stabs in its heart. Semyonov had spoken of the need for a responsible Government to guard tranquillity on its borders. That was precisely what Israel was doing. As for the accusation that Israel was serving the interests of oil monopolies, Rafael pointed out that these monopolies were, in fact, Israel's enemies. Israel was the first Middle East State to nationalize the property of a foreign oil company. He assured Semyonov that Israel was not interested in serving foreign interests and was concerned solely with its own independence and territorial integrity. Concluding, Rafael expressed satisfaction with the Soviet statement that the Soviet Union continued to support all countries of the Middle East desiring peace. He suggested that it would be useful to proceed from academic declarations to discussions of practical steps for securing peace, "from a level of irritation to a level of clarification," and that the discussions should be held on a ministerial level.

Semyonov did not react to this suggestion. Instead, he returned once more to what he had said to Ambassador Katz the day before concerning discrepancy between Israel's peace-loving declarations and warlike actions like those of April 7. "I did not say," he added at the end of the conversation, "that Israel is a tool of the oil monopolies, but that I hope it will not serve as such a tool. It acted as their tool in the past. You cannot scratch 1956 out of history. You acted at the side of the [Suez] Canal shareholders. This was a factor that moved us apart. Do not make mistakes that are apt to bring results dangerous to your State and to your people."

The next day, Rafael visited Shchiborin. He expressed regret that the statement had been published, since, by its one-sided attitude, it would only encourage the Arab Governments in their aggressive tendencies. They would interpret it as Soviet sanction and support for their hostile policy. "We have heard,"

he said, "no Soviet reservations on Arab declarations against
the very existence of Israel; neither in the United Nations nor
elsewhere." Thus, the Soviet policy had not come out for peace.
Neither had the Soviet Union seemed concerned that the principle of peaceful coexistence was not being applied to the Middle East. This created doubts of the sincerity of Soviet policy
in the minds of many friends of Israel throughout the world. The
situation in the Middle East required more objectivity on the
part of the Soviet Union. Shchiborin answered that the Arabs
knew what Soviet policy was, and even if Israel thought that the
publication of the Soviet statement would encourage the Arabs,
the Soviet Government believed it served a good purpose.
Rafael kept to his point. Each time, he said, that the Soviet
Union censured Israel publicly without doing the same in regard
to the Arabs, Moscow's influence in the area was unsettling
rather than pacifying. He added, "We often have the impression
that, by criticizing us, you want to achieve gains with the
Arabs." There was no reaction. When Rafael vigorously refuted
the accusation that Israel was a tool of the interests of foreign
forces, Shchiborin commented, "There is the historic experience of 1956." Ambassador Katz, who was present at the meeting, interjected, "There is also an historic experience of 1948,
about which you are silent." But again there was no reaction.
Rafael met Shchiborin once more, the next day at a luncheon
given by the Israeli Ambassador, but this time no problems
directly connected with Israeli-Soviet relations were raised.
Deputy Foreign Minister Semyonov, who had also been invited, did not appear.

All in all, however, the Russians received Rafael well. They
arranged excursions for him, invited him to the First of May
parade, and he left Moscow convinced that the dialogue could
continue and that in some fields, even perhaps that of *aliyah*,
there were possibilities of development. The full meaning of the
fact that Moscow had decided to revert to its accusation of
Israeli troop concentrations on the Syrian border, and even to
publish it in the full knowledge that it was untrue, became clear
only in May.

XX

May–June 1967
The Soviet plan
Eban's conversation with the Soviet Ambassador on May 15
Nasser's closing of the Straits of Tiran
The Soviet statement of May 23
Security Council meeting
Kosygin's letter to Eshkol on May 26
Egypt's complaint to Security Council on May 29
Eshkol's answer to Kosygin on June 1
Moscow's avoidance of taking stand on closure of Straits of Tiran

The trumped-up charge of Israeli troop concentrations on the Syrian frontier was not to be abandoned a second time. It now became the main theme which, with little variation, the Soviet propaganda machinery repeated day after day. On May 16, *Izvestia* wrote, "In military and political circles in the Israeli capital, voices are being heard which increasingly talk about the necessity for demonstrating strength again." On May 18, the same paper, quoting "Egyptian sources," reported on Israeli army concentrations along the Syrian border. We know now, even from authoritative Egyptian sources—for instance, from the statements of some of the high-ranking officers accused at the Cairo trial—that the report originated in Moscow. However, this did not prevent the Russians from attributing it to Egyptian sources. *Pravda*, on May 19, spoke of further Israeli provocations. On May 20, reporting U Thant's assent to Nasser's request for the withdrawal of United Nations forces, it added: "Provocative declarations and actions by Israeli extremists prove that they are ready to turn the war of nerves into an open armed conflict with the Arab countries." In view of this situation, the paper commented, Arabs were taking justifiable steps to safeguard their security; on the Israeli side, there are "active preparations for military adventures" with the aim of bringing down the Syrian Government and then dealing a death blow to the Republicans in Yemen. On May 21, *Izvestia* featured a long article about continued Israeli troop concentrations on the Syrian border and Israel's threats to Egypt. A day later, it spoke of Israeli-United States collusion against Syria. The article linked the situation in the Middle East with that in Vietnam. And so on, and so on.

The pattern of Moscow's plans became clear. The charge of troop concentrations on the Syrian border was to serve a double purpose. First, since Israel would want to show that the accusation was false, it would take no action. Then the reports of the invented concentrations would be followed by reports of an equally invented withdrawal, which would be presented as a victory of Syria's resistance and of Moscow's support of the Damascus regime. This, on the one hand, would strengthen the pro-Soviet Government and, on the other, would bring Syria even closer to the Soviet Union by proving that political dependence on Moscow pays. Second, the Egyptians, who were told that Israel was concentrating its troops against Syria, would now see an opportunity to enter into war with Israel when that nation's capacity was severely diminished. By showing strength against Israel, Nasser was to regain his badly shattered prestige inside Egypt as well as in the Arab world. The "progressive" countries in the Arab camp, which had lately been showing some lack of unity, would be brought closer to one another. Above all, by making it clear that it was Soviet support that made the Arab "victory" possible, Moscow would gain additional ground in the Middle East. As for possible further developments, the Soviet plan had apparently two alternatives. If, as the Russians may have believed, Israel—this time without the West, for France was in the process of coming nearer to the Arabs and the United States could not be expected to add another worry to the one of Vietnam—made no move, the prestige of the Soviet Union in the Arab world would grow immensely by its ability to show that its mere political pressure was strong enough to stop Israel from fighting back. If, however,

Israel decided to take military counteraction, the subsequent hostilities could be stopped, at any moment chosen by Moscow and advantageous to the Soviet-supported Arabs, by a Security Council call for an immediate cease-fire. In the latter eventuality, the Russians would gain by appearing as saviors both of the Arabs and of peace.

Even after it became evident that this was the direction of Moscow's thoughts, the Israelis continued in their efforts to convince the Russians of their peaceful goals and to persuade them to use their influence in Damascus and Cairo. Minister of Labor Yigal Alon, who happened to be attending an international congress in Moscow at the time, met Deputy Foreign Minister Semyonov at the Independence Day party in the Israeli Embassy and used the opportunity to explain Israel's stand once more. Semyonov repeated the thesis that foreign forces were trying to bring down the Syrian Government and endeavoring to use Israel as their tool. There were circles in Israel who wanted war and the Government of Israel would do well to heed the Soviet warnings.

On May 19, Foreign Minister Abba Eban called in the Soviet Ambassador and drew his attention to the unprecedented concentrations of Egyptian troops on the Sinai border. According to Israel's information, they had already reached a total of four divisions and hundreds of tanks. Marshal Amer, Egypt's Minister of War,[34] had confirmed all this the same morning. Every government was, of course, free to move its army inside its territory, but the size of the concentrations and the fact that the troops were moved up to the very border of Israel were causing grave concern. The Egyptians explained their move by alleging that Israel was concentrating troops along the Syrian border. Such concentrations did not exist, either in the past or then. The Egyptians must have been aware of it, and a few days earlier

---

34. Marshal Abd el Hakim Amer, Minister of War and Commander-in-Chief of the Egyptian Army, Number 2 man in Egypt at the time of the Six-Day War, was arrested after the debacle of June 1967. According to the official Egyptian version he committed suicide, but there are many indications that he was, in fact, liquidated at Nasser's orders.

they had been officially informed by the United Nations Observer Corps that there were no such concentrations. Israel was now faced with:

1. Egyptian troop concentrations.
2. An Egyptian request for the withdrawal of the United Nations Emergency Force (UNEF).
3. Declarations by Syrian leaders that the "People's War" must continue.

All this was causing increased tension and anxiety. Israel did not think war was unavoidable, but it was vital:

1. To bring to an end sabotage and other hostile acts by Syria.
2. To effect the recall of the Egyptian troop concentrations in the south.

The concentrations had forced Israel to increase its forces on the Sinai borders, but it was ready for a reciprocal de-escalation. As for Nasser's request that the UNEF troops be withdrawn, Israel did not think that U Thant was authorized to act. The force was sent to the area by the General Assembly and U Thant could not decide on its withdrawal without prior consultation with all parties concerned. The initiative was now in Nasser's hands. "There will be no war if the Egyptians do not attack Israeli territory or do not interfere with Israel's freedom of navigation."

Ambassador Chuvakhin answered that in the opinion of the Soviet Union, the reason for tension was Israel's aggressive propaganda and its leaders' declarations against the Arab States, especially Syria. The latest developments had shown that the Soviet Government was right when it warned Israel that its policy might lead to serious consequences. Chuvakhin had no authority to discuss Egyptian army concentrations, but as for Egypt's request for the withdrawal of the UNEF, this demand, in the opinion of the Soviet Government, was legitimate because a State that agreed to placing United Nations forces on its territory was the only power entitled to ask for the ending of that situation.

The Foreign Minister rejected the contention that Israeli declarations caused the tension. There was never any statement by any responsible Israeli personage threatening the existence of Syria. All Israeli statements came only as reactions to actual attacks. On the other hand, Syrian statements were, in fact, unprecedented in the history of United Nations member-States. No Soviet warning to Syria was ever heard of in Israel, and the Government of Israel did not actually know the Soviet attitude to the Syrian threats. Israel had no doubt—as was true of the majority of the Security Council members—that the beginning of the tension could be traced back to Syria. When Eban added that the Government of Israel would also like to know the Soviet attitude toward the acts of sabotage perpetrated on Israeli territory, Chuvakhin answered, "We hear all the time about saboteurs, but we have no proof that those responsible are the Syrians and not the CIA" (U.S. Central Intelligence Agency). The Foreign Minister concluded by assuring the Ambassador that the Government of Israel had reason to be convinced that the responsibility lay with the Syrian High Command, and that Israel would like to receive Soviet suggestions on how to deal with the situation.

On May 22, Ambassador Katz called on Shchiborin to protest against the false information in the Soviet press regarding Israel's policy toward Syria. The answer he received was: What difference did it make if from time to time the Soviet press published reports "without stenographic precision"? All that mattered was the intention appearing in declarations made by Israeli leaders, and the Soviet Government warned Israel against exactly that intention. "We cannot be responsible for what is happening in the atmosphere which was poisoned by your leaders' statements." When Katz objected, saying that the Soviet Government well knew the Arab intentions against Israel but was doing nothing about them, Shchiborin did not react.

This was the day when Nasser declared the Straits of Tiran closed to Israeli ships and to non-Israeli vessels carrying strategic material to Israel. "If Israel threatens us with war," Nasser declared in the same statement, "we will answer thus: Go ahead then." While Nasser, by closing the Straits of Tiran, may have gone a step further than was bargained for in Soviet plans, the Russians apparently did not realize the full meaning of this miscalculation at once. They thought that the plans could still operate without a large-scale war actually breaking out. This seems to be the only explanation of Shchiborin's attitude of "we cannot be responsible for what is happening" and of the extensive coverage given by TASS the same day to demonstrations organized by Syrian students in Moscow.

Two things happened the next day, May 23. Prime Minister Eshkol declared in the Knesset that interference with Israeli shipping in the Straits of Tiran would be regarded as an act of war. And in Washington, President Johnson declared the Egyptian blockade to be illegal, adding that the United States was firmly committed to support the integrity of all States in the Middle East. Also on May 23, TASS published the following official Soviet statement:

> The Soviet Government warned the Government of Israel, as is known, following the provocative action of April 7, that the Government of Israel will bear all responsibility for the aggressive policy it is pursuing. The facts, however, show that wisdom did not yet prevail in Tel Aviv. Criminal Israel started again to create tension in the Middle East, which has reached a serious stage. From this arises the question about the kind of interests Israel is serving by its policy. If the Tel Aviv leaders believe that they are playing the role of a watchdog on behalf of imperialist States against the States of the Arab East . . . there should be no doubt that he who will try aggression in the Middle East will be met not only by the united forces of the Arab countries but also with energetic restraint from the Soviet Union and all peace-loving States.
>
> The Soviet Government is convinced that it is not in the interest of the peoples of the Middle East to start the fire of an armed conflict,

and that it is in the interest of no one but the masters of imperialist oil monopolies, and that it is only to the good of imperialist forces leading Israel in the direction suiting their own policy. The Soviet Union follows with great interest the development of events in the Middle East, with a view to preserving peace and security in the area bordering on the Soviet Union, keeping in mind the vital interests of the peoples of the Soviet Union. The Soviet Union takes cognizance of the existing situation and will not spare efforts to avoid a breach of peace and security in the Middle East and to defend the legitimate rights of the peoples.

While it is possible that the statement was issued before President Johnson's declaration had been received in Moscow, it was certainly published with full knowledge of Nasser's May 22 declaration on the closure of the Straits of Tiran. Yet it did not even mention Nasser's fatal step. The Soviet press carried the statement a day later and again did not mention the closing of the Straits. *Pravda's* comment was:

> The Israelis have planned a blitz attack on Syria, but they have clearly miscalculated, not taking into account the solidarity of the Arab countries.

Even Gromyko, replying to the American Ambassador, Llewelyn Thomson, who had handed him a copy of the American note to the Arab Governments, placed all responsibility for the tension on Israel. He pointed out that Syria denied supporting the terrorists and that it was the responsibility of the Big Powers to avoid any unnecessary war. He did not mention the closure of the Straits, although the matter was stressed in the American note.

On the same day (May 24), at an urgent meeting of the Security Council called at the request of Canada and Denmark because of the Secretary General's report describing the situation as "more disturbing . . . more menacing than at any time since the fall of 1956," Fedorenko declared:

> The Soviet delegation deems it necessary to stress that it does not see sufficient ground for such a hasty convening of the Security Council and the artificially dramatic climate fostered by the representatives of some Western Powers. . . . A considerable effort was made . . . to see to it that the NATO countries, which are far from being close neighbors to the Middle East, rather than any of the parties directly concerned, took the initiative in the urgent convening of the Security Council. . . . Is there not, here, more of a concealed desire to interfere in the affairs of someone else rather than a true concern for the peace and security of the Middle East?

During the afternoon session on the same day, he said:

> Having heard the statements of representatives of the Western Powers, we are even more convinced that certain forces are artificially heating up the climate for reasons that have nothing to do with a true concern for peace and security in the Middle East.

After this introduction, he read the Soviet Government's statement, issued on the previous day. Gideon Rafael reminded Fedorenko of the "unfounded nature" of the Soviet allegation about Israeli troop concentrations on the Syrian border, quoting the Secretary General's report. Fedorenko did not react. Instead, later in the meeting, he repeated that the Soviet Union "does not consider it appropriate at the present time to have any urgent or extra-urgent meetings of the Security Council." He also saw no need to engage in any consultations and announced that the Soviet delegation had no intention of taking part in such consultations if they were held.

A certain uneasiness could be discerned on the Soviet side only on May 26, when Kosygin decided to address a personal note to Prime Minister Eshkol. He wrote:

> Mr. Prime Minister, according to the latest news reaching the Government of the Soviet Union, the tension on Israel's borders with the United Arab Republic and Syria is growing more and more, with the two sides increasing their forces, and the situation in Israel is sharpening as if there were no way of avoiding war actions. It would be a tremendous mistake should war-loving circles, uninhibited by

serious political thought, gain the upper hand and should arms begin to speak. Guided by the interest of peace and eager to avoid a blood bath, the Soviet Government decided to send you this message.

We want you to use all means to avoid the outbreak of an armed conflict which would have serious consequences for international peace and security. We turn to you in order to avoid creating in the world another center of war, which would bring suffering without end. We are concerned that, however complicated the situation on Israel's borders with Syria and the United Arab Republic may be, it is necessary to find ways to settle the conflict by unwarlike means. It is easy to light a fire, but to put out a conflagration may not be at all as easy as those who are pushing Israel beyond the brink of war may be thinking.

We hope that, after serious consideration of the situation which was created and which continues to exist, and of the responsibility which will rest with the side that starts aggression, the Government of Israel will now do everything in order to avoid a war conflict in the Middle East.

Kosygin's letter was sent the day after the departure of British Foreign Secretary, George Brown, from Moscow. Brown told Kosygin that the British Government identified itself with President Johnson's statement regarding the Straits of Tiran as an international waterway that must be reopened. But again there was no mention of the Straits in Kosygin's note. After Brown's departure, the Soviet Foreign Ministry spokesman declared only that "it is clear that Britain actually supports the State of Israel, while it is known that the real responsibility lies just with Israel, which is following a hostile policy toward Arab countries. The United Arab Republic and the Syrian Arab Republic are, in these circumstances, forced to take defensive measures and secure their interests." When asked directly whether the Soviet Union regarded the Bay of Aqaba as territorial waters, the spokesman said, "No comment. Our position is determined by general policies in the area and in the world.

I would not like to discuss the matter here, now."

In the generally accepted view of diplomatic observers in Moscow, the closing of the Straits of Tiran came as a surprise to the Russians. Some ambassadors were told as much by senior officials of the Foreign Ministry. The impression received was that the Russians were now trying to gain time to make the Egyptian *fait accompli* permanent. This may have been the reason why, on May 29, an Egyptian complaint about "Israeli aggressive policy, its repeated aggression threatening peace and security in the Middle East and endangering international peace and security," was added to the Security Council agenda. Speaking that day in the Council, Fedorenko said:

> We must draw attention to the fact that the real culprit in the dangerous aggravation of tensions once more is Israel. . . . It is most regrettable that Washington should show such partiality and attempt to defend the forces of aggression, namely the extremist circles in Israel. . . . Despite serious warnings, Israel does not wish to abandon its policy of provocation and military adventures against the Arab States. . . . Measures taken by Arab States are a legitimate answer to threats and dangerous Israeli troop concentrations on the Syrian border.

The lie about Israeli concentrations against Syria was apparently, even at this stage, too important a part of the Soviet plan to be dropped in midstream. Fedorenko went on to say:

> The Soviet Union has often drawn the attention of the Government of Israel to the fact that this policy of Israel, pursued for many years against its neighbors, is risky, is pregnant with danger, and that the responsibility fully lies with Tel Aviv. And it would be a fatal miscalculation if extremist militaristic circles in Israel, not hampered by any sound political considerations, got the upper hand in the present situation. . . . Those who push Israel to the brink of the abyss do not realize that it is much easier to fan the flames of a military conflict than it is to put out those flames. . . .

After delivering this slightly altered transcription of Kosygin's note to Prime Minister Eshkol, he added:

The Arab countries, defending their lawful rights, show great moderation when confronted with new Israeli provocations. . . . The Soviet Union considers that the Security Council must, under present conditions, decisively condemn provocations and threats against Arab States.

When Gideon Rafael demolished Fedorenko's statement point by point,[35] the Soviet delegate retorted for the first time with clearly anti-Semitic remarks, which may have been another sign of Russian nervousness. Even when, later in the debate (May 31), he could not help breaking his silence on the question of freedom of navigation, Fedorenko contented himself with entering into a legalistic squabble with U.S. Ambassador Arthur Goldberg about the American blockade of Cuba,

---

35. In the course of his speech, Rafael said: "The representative of the Soviet Union deemed it fit to repeat his unfounded charges against my Government and country. He spoke of provocations, military concentrations and threatening statements by Israel's leaders. . . . He spoke of mobilization by Israel, but has carefully avoided mentioning the fact that Israel took precautionary measures only after Egypt advanced several divisions in Sinai and along the borders of Israel. The representative of the Soviet Union bases his evidence on President Nasser's fabrications. He prefers them to the objective report of the Secretary General. I wonder whether this is the kind of impartiality which the representative of the Soviet Union recommends. Were he to apply only a modest measure of impartiality to the affairs of the Middle East, I am convinced that his country would make a major contribution to the establishment of peaceful conditions in that tormented region." Speaking of Fedorenko's references to statements made by Israeli Government leaders, Rafael said: "I know that Ambassador Fedorenko is a famous scholar in Oriental literature. I am not aware of whether his wide erudition also includes a knowledge of Hebrew. It may be that his lack of knowledge of our Hebrew language is the reason for his misreading of statements made by Israeli Government leaders." That gave Fedorenko the opening for the following reply: "Our information came from a very definite source. We quoted from a U.S. publication, the *U.S. News and World Report* . . . which—at least so we think—gets its information first hand either in Hebrew—they probably have Hebrew experts—or otherwise from oral statements by official representatives of Tel Aviv who, as we very well know, are extremely well-versed in American dialect."

without taking any explicit stand on the question of the Straits of Tiran. He repeated the performance as late as June 3 when, trying again to defend the Egyptian action in the Straits by attacking American policy against Cuba, he said:

> It is the United States which deserves the most categorical condemnation for its policies and its actions, including the abetting of the extremist circles in Israel that are committing acts of aggression against neighboring Arab states.

In the meantime, on June 1, the Director General of the Israel Foreign Ministry, Levavi, called in Ambassador Chuvakhin and delivered to him the text of Prime Minister Eshkol's reply to Kosygin's letter of May 26. It read as follows:

> Mr. Prime Minister, I wish to confirm receipt of your note of May 26 which was handed to me by the Soviet Ambassador in Israel. We appreciate the will of the Soviet Government to make known to us its evaluations with regard to the present crisis in the area. We are very pleased that the Soviet Union is hopefully interested in peace.

> As you know, the present situation has developed since Syria started drastic, openly hostile actions against the territory of Israel and its citizens. These actions were repudiated by the majority of Security Council members in the discussion which took place last October, and also in the correct report by the Secretary General of the United Nations to the Security Council on May 19, 1967. A fortnight ago, Egypt, which is bound to Syria by a mutual assistance agreement, began concentrating troops on the Sinai Peninsula near Israel's borders. At the same time, Egypt eliminated the United Nations forces. The decisive point is not the elimination of UNEF, but the Egyptian explanation that accompanied this step, that it is Egypt's intention "to start a campaign" against Israel. These aggressive steps reached their height when the Straits of Tiran were closed to free navigation. That, of course, is a classic act of war, and there is no need to stress that it is also in absolute opposition to the rules of international law and to human rights. There can be no accep-

tance of this situation. It is these actions by the Egyptians which have forced the Government of Israel to take security measures, to mobilize its forces and to order them to keep watch for the security of Israel's borders.

Eshkol went on to describe the border situation and the unceasing Arab propaganda attacks, and quoted from Nasser's speech of May 26 in which the Egyptian President said that "the closing of Sharm-el-Sheikh means that we have entered a total campaign against Israel. This will be a total war. Our basic aim will be the liquidation of Israel." Eshkol continued:

I ask you, Mr. Prime Minister, to let the Government of Egypt and all the world know the opinion of the Soviet Union about this kind of proclamation. At a time when Egypt declares it is not ready to coexist peacefully with Israel and is preparing for a war of liquidation against Israel, only a considered and objective approach can contribute to peace. We regret very much that on various occasions, as for instance, in the appearance of the Soviet representative in the discussion now taking place in the Security Council and in Soviet publications, the Soviet Union adopted the complaints that Israel is allegedly concentrating troops for an attack against Syria. I invited your Ambassador in Israel to visit the border area and to find out personally that there is no truth in these allegations. To my regret, the Ambassador did not accept our invitation. The Chief of the United Nations Observers Corps in Israel checked these complaints and informed the Secretary General of the United Nations and the capitals of the area that there are no concentrations of troops on the Syrian border. The Secretary General also included this information in the report which he submitted on May 19 to the Security Council. In spite of all that, Soviet representatives and the Soviet press continued to spread these false accusations.

Everybody studying the declarations of Israeli statesmen will see that they are only answers to threats hurled against us by Arab States since May 19, and that even in the most difficult situations they contained calls for peace and hope that it can be kept. An objective approach cannot believe either in the accusation that Is-

rael is acting as a tool of outside forces. This accusation is void of
all basis and implies a crude and unjustified insult to a State which
in its actions is governed solely by its own independent interests.
Equally lacking all foundation is the accusation that Israel intends
or has intended to bring about a change of the regime in Syria. All
we are interested in is that the subversive activities of that State
should stop. We have stressed these facts more than once in conversations with Soviet representatives and in statements handed to the
Soviet Government. Israel is a small State and its people are peace-
loving. It is only twenty-five years since one-third of the Jewish
people was cruelly exterminated by the murderous forces of our
common Nazi enemy. Suffering was a lot common to the Jewish
people and to the Soviet Union. It is only nineteen years since we
gained independence and began to build again, on ruins, our national existence. The people of Israel remember the support of the
Soviet Union for the creation of the State. Now the Jewish people
in Israel face once again a serious danger. We turn to you, Mr. Prime
Minister, to the Soviet Government and the great Soviet people and
ask you to understand the most serious situation in which we find
ourselves. Nothing is dearer to us than peace.

Ever since seven neighboring States waged war against us in 1948
and the Soviet Union stood at our side and repudiated this aggression, we have remained steadfast in our desire to come to a final
agreement on permanent peace, but our outstretched hand has been
left in the air. To put an end to the danger of war in our area, it is
necessary that the Soviet Union should join the other Great Powers
and use all its influence for a permanent peace settlement in the
Middle East. The settling of the conflict must be based on the
principles accepted by the peace-loving world, namely:

1. Territorial integrity and independence of all the States of the
   area, repudiating revanchism and attempts to change the territorial *status quo* in the area.
2. Refraining from hostile acts, diversionary activities over the
   borders and closing of maritime waterways.
3. Nonintervention in internal affairs of States.

These principles are part of the declared policy of the Soviet Union and such agreement, based on them, will serve as foundation of an effective peace in our area. We hope that you, Mr. Prime Minister, and the Government of the Soviet Union will be ready to help with all your great political weight to reach such a peace settlement.

Handing the letter to the Soviet Ambassador, Levavi expressed the hope that its contents would influence Soviet policy in the Middle East. He added that it would help the interests of peace if the Soviet Union were to approach the problems of the area objectively. Chuvakhin answered that it all depended on Israel but hinted that there was ground for optimism. Did this mean that Moscow had decided it had gained sufficient ground with the Arabs, was not keen on risking further steps and had hopes that Nasser could be brought to reopen the Straits?

There was another enigmatic sentence in what Foreign Minister Gromyko said the next day when he summoned Ambassador Katz and read him an official statement. Quoting from Eban's speech at a press conference on May 30 to the effect that, if the Big Powers did not succeed in reopening the Straits of Tiran, Israel would reopen them itself, Gromyko defined the declaration as openly hostile toward the Arab States. It could be interpreted only as an official confirmation of the policy of adventurist militarist circles in Israel "which were trying to force on the Government and people of Israel a line apt to have irremediable consequences, above all for Israel itself." This, Gromyko said, was in contradiction to previous Israeli statements made to the Soviet Union. Various peace-loving Governments, including the Soviet Government, were making efforts to find a peaceful solution for the Middle East conflict. "Should the Government of Israel take upon itself the responsibility for starting a military conflict, it would have to pay fully for taking such a step." The Soviet Government hoped that Eban's statement did not express the intention of the Government of Israel. The Soviet Government strongly repudiated the statement and would like to receive a clarification of the attitude of the Gov-

ernment of Israel. So much for the Soviet statement. The somewhat puzzling part was in the conversation that followed. Here
Gromyko changed his tone from one of stern reproach to one
of advice. Israel should not be governed by emotions but by
thought of its future, and should therefore exercise restraint.
"We are working for peace."

On receipt of the report on Gromyko's statement, Foreign
Minister Eban immediately instructed Ambassador Katz to inform Gromyko that the words he had put into his mouth had
never been spoken. On June 4, Tekoah, Deputy Director General of the Foreign Ministry, called in the Soviet Ambassador
and gave him a verbal transcript of Eban's speech at the press
conference on May 30. He expressed surprise at Gromyko's
statement and the hope that Gromyko would find it necessary
to correct the misunderstanding. As for Israel's intentions,
which Gromyko had asked to be clarified, they were formulated
in Prime Minister Eshkol's note to Kosygin and in Eban's press
conference speech.

The only published indication of what Moscow meant by
"working for peace" came from Ankara. On June 3, the Soviet
Ambassador there visited the Turkish Foreign Minister. On
leaving the Ministry, he declared to the press:

> We have informed the Foreign Minister that Israel has perpetrated
> acts of aggression against the Arab States and that we are giving
> support to the Arabs. We explained that the Arabs were fighting to
> defend their independence and their rights against the imperialist
> States. In this matter we are supporting the Arab countries. . . . An
> agreement exists between us and the Turkish Government for the
> adoption of all possible measures with a view to reestablishing peace
> in the Middle East.

XXI

June 1967
Outbreak of the Six-Day War
Exchange of notes between Eshkol and Kosygin
Rupture of diplomatic relations

On June 5, 1967, the day the War broke out, the following note from Prime Minister Eshkol to the Chairman of the Council of Ministers, Kosygin, was handed to the Soviet Ambassador:

Dear Mr. Chairman,
I turn to you urgently to bring to your attention the grave developments of today. Since the early hours of the morning, fighting has broken out between Egyptian armored and air forces which moved against Israel and Israeli forces which went into action to contain them. After weeks in which our peril has grown day to day, we are now engaged in repelling the wicked aggression that Nasser has been building up against us.

I have discussed this fully in my letter to you of June 1, 1967. Israel's existence and integrity have been endangered. The provocative troop concentrations in Sinai, now amounting to five infantry and two armored divisions, the placing of more than 900 tanks against our southern frontier, the massing of 200 tanks opposite Eilat in an attempt to sunder the southern Negev from Israel, the lawless blockade in the Straits of Tiran, the insolent defiance of the international community, the policy of strangling encirclement in-

cluding the placing of Egyptian and Iraqi troops and aircraft in
Jordan, Nasser's announcement, in his speeches of May 26 and
June 4, of "total war against Israel" and of his basic aim to annihilate
Israel, yesterday's Order of the Day, by the Egyptian Commander,
General Murtagi, calling on his troops in Sinai to wage a war of
destruction against Israel, the acts of sabotage and terrorism by
Syria and Gaza, this morning's engagements and the bombardment
of the Israeli villages of Kisufim, Nahal Oz and Eyn Hashloshah in
Israeli territory—all of this amounts to an extraordinary catalogue
of aggression that must be abhorred and condemned by world opinion in all peace-loving countries.

This is a ruthless design to destroy the State of Israel, which embo-
dies the memories, sacrifices and hopes of an ancient people that,
in this generation, lost six million of its people, brutally murdered
in a tragedy without parallel in history. Surely this cannot be denied
by anybody, Mr. Chairman, when it is announced and confessed by
President Nasser himself. Throughout the weeks in which Egypt
was preparing itself for aggression against Israel, we have acted with
supreme restraint, hoping that the war machine mounted by President Nasser would not be put into action. Our hope proved to be
in vain.

We appeal to you again, Mr. Chairman, to understand the gravity
of the situation created by Egypt's warfare against Israel's existence.
We appeal to you in this hour, crucial to peace in the Middle East
and the entire world, to join in an effort to secure peace based on
the independence and territorial integrity of all nations. We claim
nothing except peaceful life in our territory and the exercise of our
international rights. Surrounded by enemy armies on all sides, we
are now engaged in a mortal struggle to defend our existence and
forestall Egypt's avowed intention to repeat against the Jewish people in Israel the inhuman crimes committed by Hitler.

We cannot but be confident that the Soviet Union's role in history
will be vindicated once more by an attitude of comprehension and
brotherhood toward the Jewish people in its hour of trial.

On the same day, late at night, Ambassador Chuvakhin asked
for an urgent meeting with Prime Minister Eshkol and handed
him the following message from Kosygin:

> The Government of the Soviet Union expresses its resolute con-
> demnation of the treacherous aggression by Israel against the neigh-
> boring Arab States, the United Arab Republic.

> This adventurist act is a direct and open violation of the United
> Nations Charter and its principles. The aggression perpetrated
> proves clearly the character of the policy of the ruling circles of
> Israel who are ready, for the sake of their own narrow interest, to
> play with the fate of peace. The attack which Israel executed has no
> connection whatsoever with the struggle of your country for the
> existence of the State of Israel. The future of Israel, as the future of
> other nations, is tied by unbreakable ties with peace. The Govern-
> ment of Israel knew that the conflict was avoidable.

> By putting the responsibility for the aggression perpetrated against
> the United Arab Republic on the shoulders of the Government of
> Israel, the Government of the Soviet Union insists on an immediate
> cease-fire and withdrawal of troops from the territories of neighbor-
> ing Arab States.

> Should the Government of Israel not follow the voice of reason and
> should it not stop the blood bath, it will bear the responsibility for
> the outbreak of war and for all its possible results.

Also on the same day, the Soviet Government issued the following statement, which was read to the Security Council on June
6:

> On 5 June 1967, Israel started military actions against the United
> Arab Republic, thus committing an aggression. The armed forces of
> the United Arab Republic are waging battle against Israeli troops
> which have invaded the territory of that State. Taking part in hostili-
> ties on both sides are tanks, artillery and aviation. The Arab Repub-

lic of Syria has taken the side of the United Arab Republic and is giving its armed assistance in repelling aggression. Jordan declared that it is in a state of war with Israel and that it will give military support to the United Arab Republic. Iraq, Algeria and other Arab States have also declared their support of the United Arab Republic with their armed forces and resources.

Thus, a military conflict has flared up in the Middle East because of the adventurism of the rulers of one country, Israel, which was encouraged by covert and overt actions of certain imperialist circles. The country was pushed to such dangerous actions by leaders who keep saying that they are waging a struggle for the existence of Israel as a State. But if there is anything that can most of all undermine the foundations of development and the very existence of the State of Israel, it is the course of recklessness and adventurism in policy which was chosen in Israel's ruling quarters today.

By launching aggression against neighboring States, the Government of Israel has trampled underfoot the United Nations Charter and elementary standards of international law. The Israeli Government cannot say that it was not aware of what course it was taking; nor can it say that it was not clear as to what position peace-loving States would take in the event of its launching a war of aggression. The Government of Israel knew that war could be avoided. That is what it was called to do by the Soviet Union and other peace-loving States. But it chose the road of war. There can be no doubt that the venture undertaken by Israel will rebound first of all upon Israel itself.

The Soviet Union, loyal as it is to its policy of helping peoples, victims of aggression, of helping States newly liberated from colonial oppression, declares its resolute support for the Governments and peoples of the United Arab Republic, Syria, Iraq, Algeria, Jordan and other Arab States and expresses confidence in the success of their just struggle for their independence and sovereign rights. Condemning Israeli aggression, the Soviet Government de- ·

mands that the Government of Israel should, as the first urgent stop to end the military conflict, stop immediately and unconditionally its military actions against the United Arab Republic, Syria, Jordan and other Arab countries and pull back its troops behind the truce line.

The Government of the U.S.S.R. expresses the hope that the Governments of other States, including the Great Powers, will, on their part, do everything in their power to extinguish the military conflagration in the Middle East and restore peace.

The United Nations must discharge its primary duty, condemn the actions of Israel, and take urgent measures to restore peace in the Middle East.

The Soviet Government reserves the right to take all steps that may be necessitated by the situation.

On June 6, the Security Council unanimously adopted a resolution calling "upon the Governments concerned as a first step to take forthwith all measures for an immediate cease-fire and for a cessation of all military activities in the area." Fedorenko voted for the resolution but made it clear, at the same time, that it did not satisfy the Soviet Union entirely and that "the Soviet delegation, decisively condemning the aggression of Israel, considers it to be the bounden duty of the Security Council to adopt without any further delay, a decision concerning the immediate withdrawal of the forces of the aggressor behind the Armistice lines."

On June 7, the following Soviet Government declaration was delivered to the Israeli Embassy in Moscow:

Reports are arriving from various sources to the effect that the Security Council decision on immediate cease-fire and cessation of all military activities is not being executed by the Israeli side. Israel tramples on this decision in a demonstrative and crude way, and continues its war against Arab countries. This attitude of the Government of Israel confirms once more the aggressive character of its policy, which does not take into account the elementary norms of international relations and openly reveals noncompliance with the principles and aims of the United Nations Charter.

The Government of the Soviet Union in all its statements had forewarned the Government of Israel against the pursuit of an aggressive and adventurist policy, but Israeli leaders did not lend their ear to the voice of reason. Should the Government of Israel now not fulfill immediately the general demand of the States in the matter of ceasing fire without delay, as adopted in the Security Council resolution, the Soviet Union will reconsider its relations with Israel and will adopt a decision regarding the continuation of diplomatic relations with Israel, which, by its action, has put itself against peace-loving States. The Soviet Government will, naturally, also consider and take other necessary steps as a consequence of the aggressive policy of Israel.

On June 8, Israel replied as follows to the Soviet Government statement of the previous day:

The Government of Israel desires to point out that the statement, transmitted on June 7, 1967, on behalf of the Government of the Soviet Union, can hardly be considered as contributing to the settlement of the crisis brought about by the aggression of the Arab States against Israel. It is regrettable that disregard of elementary facts known to all and groundless threats continue to characterize the Soviet Union's attitude toward Israel. The facts are:

1. The Arab States, not Israel, have maintained for nineteen years an illegal state of war, in flagrant violation of the United Nations Charter.
2. The Arab States, not Israel, have waged a campaign of active belligerency, including armed attacks, terrorist raids, acts of sabotage, maritime blockade and warlike declarations.
3. The Arab States, not Israel, have openly declared their intention

to destroy a neighbor State, a member of the United Nations, and
to annihilate its population.

4. It was Syria, not Israel, that defiantly announced to the world
that it will not end its guerrilla warfare against the territory and
citizens of a State to which it was bound by an Armistice Agreement prohibiting all hostile acts.

5. It was Egypt, not Israel, that concentrated its forces in offensive
array, evicted the UNEF, committed the warlike act of closing
the international waterway through the Straits of Tiran and
launched the attack on June 5, 1967.

If the Soviet Government has any doubts about the above facts, the
Government of Israel would like to draw its attention to the official
pronouncements by Arab statesmen, the records of the Security
Council debates and the recent report by the Secretary General of
the United Nations.

With regard to the question of the cease-fire in the present hostilities, it is public knowledge that the Government of Israel welcomed
the resolution adopted by the Security Council on June 6, 1967,
while none of the Arab States accepted it, and again accepted the
cease-fire set by the Security Council resolution of June 7, 1967,
while of all the Arab States only Jordan agreed to it. The cease-fire
can be implemented only on a reciprocal basis. It is surprising that
the Soviet Government's statement should express an approach
which is in fact tantamount to a request that Israel agree to a
cease-fire unilaterally.

Israel is a small country and the Jewish people has through its
age-long history been subjected to threats, pressures and violence.
Israel feels that it has the right, like all nations, to live in peace, free
of menace from any quarter.

In Prime Minister Eshkol's letter of June 5, 1967, to the Chairman
of the Council of Ministers of the U.S.S.R., Mr. A.N. Kosygin,
Israel appealed to the Soviet Union to play a constructive role in the

situation and to join in an effort to secure peace in the Middle East. Israel still looks forward to the Soviet Union's playing such a role.

The same day, Fedorenko tried to force the following draft resolution through the Security Council:

The Security Council, noting that Israel has disregarded the Security Council decisions calling for the cessation of military activities, considering that Israel not only has not halted military activities but has made use of the time elapsed since the adoption of the aforementioned Council resolutions in order to seize additional territory of the United Arab Republic and Jordan, and noting that, even now, Israel is continuing military activities instead of halting its aggression, thus defying the United Nations and all peace-loving States,

1. Vigorously condemns Israel's aggressive activities and its violations of the aforementioned Security Council resolutions, of the United Nations Charter and of United Nations principles, and
2. Demands that Israel should immediately halt its military activities against neighboring Arab States and should remove all its troops from the territory of those States and withdraw them behind the armistice lines.

By now Fedorenko had obviously forgotten all the rules of diplomatic language. He called Israel's army "military hordes," asserted that "the responsibility of the Israeli aggressors will not be wiped clean by any quibbles," and lashed out against Foreign Minister Eban in a manner not paralleled in the history of the Security Council except by certain Arab speakers. In another performance on June 9, he went so far as to say:

The forces of aggression do not even bother to look for justification. They take their arguments from the garbage heap of history and from the arsenal of the most famous criminals in history. They follow the bloody footsteps of Hitler's executioners who always accused the victims of their own aggression.

Gideon Rafael answered him the same day:

The representative of the Soviet Union has deemed it fit, in the course of the last few days . . . to hurl insult after insult and vituperation at my Government and its representatives with an ever increasing vehemence that is matched in the annals of the United Nations only by certain Arab spokesmen. Ambassador Fedorenko reached the heights of his crescendo today when he compared Israel's fight for its existence to Hitler's aggression. This is unheard of. It appears that Mr. Fedorenko believes that, representing a powerful country, he has the right to trample on the honor of a small State and a people which suffered more from Hitlerite aggression than any other nation, a people one-third of whom was exterminated by Hitler. I believe that the Soviet representative, in his rage, indeed has overstepped the limits of the permissible.

Neither Israel nor the Jewish people concluded a pact with Hitler's Germany, a pact which encouraged Nazi Germany to unleash its aggression against the world. It was not Israel which proclaimed that the victims of this aggression were imperialist aggressors. The people of Israel volunteered from the first minute of that war to take up arms against the enemy of mankind while others stood by watching the developments. We are dismayed but not astonished that the Soviet representative should also confuse the issue in the present conflict and present the victim of aggression as the aggressor. In advancing his allegations, he finds himself in singular isolation. . . .

Did Israel first concentrate forces along the Egyptian border? Did Israel impose a blockade, a warlike act, against any of the Arab States? Did Israel proclaim that it intended to destroy the Arab States? Did Israel prepare and organize a war of liberation against the Arab States? Where was the voice of the Soviet Union then? Did we ever hear the representative of the Soviet Union take the slightest exception to those threats and war preparations? On the con-

trary. The representative of the Soviet Union spoke of a war psychosis. . . . Who enflamed that war psychosis in the Arab countries?
Who excited the Arab passions? Who supplied them with the arms
to wage war against Israel? The record speaks for itself.

The Soviet representative has stated that the Council has proclaimed Israel to be an aggressor. That is as false as his other
statements. There has not been a single resolution adopted by the
United Nations which has labeled Israel as an aggressor. The first
and only time the Council applied Chapter VII[36] was in 1948, when
it referred to the Arab aggression against the new State of Israel.
The representative of the Soviet Union has done nothing in the past
to allay passions and to reduce tension. From his statement today
and from his statements made on previous days, it is clear that he
does not intend to do so in the future either.

While this discussion was in progress in New York, the Communist leaders and party heads of Poland, Czechoslovakia,
Hungary, Bulgaria, East Germany and Yugoslavia were hur-
riedly called in to Moscow. After their meeting, the following
statement was issued on June 10:

We met to study the situation created in the Middle East by Israel's
aggression, which is the result of collusion between certain imperialist foreign countries, first of all the United States of America, against
Arab countries. The participants in the meeting exchanged views on
the measures necessary to cut short the aggression and to avert its
consequences, which are dangerous to the cause of universal peace.
The participants in the meeting find it necessary to draw appropriate
conclusions from the fact that Israel did not comply with the decisions of the Security Council and did not stop military actions
against the Arab States.

The occupation of the territory of Arab States by Israeli troops
would be used for the restoration of the foreign colonial regime. On
9 June, despite the cease-fire statements made by the Government

---

36. Chapter VII of the Charter of the United Nation, to which Ambassador
Rafael was referring, relates to action with respect to threats to the peace,
breaches of the peace, and acts of aggression.

of Syria, Israeli troops are conducting a new offensive on Syria's borders, subjecting Syrian towns to barbarous bombings. Struggling against imperialism for their freedom and independence, for the integrity of their territories, for the inalienable sovereign right independently to decide all questions of their domestic life and foreign policy, the peoples of the Arab countries are upholding a just cause. The peoples of the Socialist countries are fully on their side.

The peoples of the United Arab Republic and several other Arab countries have scored historic victories in recent years in the field of winning national independence and freedom. Important social transformations have been made in the interests of the working masses. We express confidence that these gains will be preserved and that the progressive regimes will be consolidated, despite the difficulties which beset the road of the Arab peoples.

In these difficult hours for the States of the Arab East, the Socialist countries declare that they fully and completely make common cause with their just struggle and will render them assistance to repel the aggression and defend their national independence and territorial integrity.

The States participating in this meeting demand that Israel immediately halt its military activities against the neighboring Arab States and that it withdraw all its forces from their territories behind the Armistice Demarcation Line. It is, moreover, the duty of the United Nations to condemn the aggressor.

If the Security Council does not take the proper measures, great responsibility will rest on those States which fail to fulfill their duty as members of the Security Council.

Today, more than ever, it is indispensable to act in a resolute and concerted manner. It is necessary for all progressive forces, all those who treasure the cause of liberty and justice to act in this manner,

and if the Government of Israel does not stop its aggression and if
it does not withdraw its troops behind the Armistice Demarcation
Line, the Socialist States which have signed this statement will do
everything necessary to help the peoples of the Arab countries to
reject the aggressor resolutely, to preserve their lawful rights and to
extinguish the hotbed of war in the Middle East and restore peace
to that area.

The just struggle of the Arab people will triumph.

The Soviet Government obviously did not have much confidence in the effectiveness of the call to Israel, because on the
same day (June 10)—the day when the Six-Day War ended—
Ambassador Katz was called to the Foreign Ministry and un-
ceremoniously handed the following note:

Information was just received to the effect that Israeli troops, ignoring the Security Council decision about the cessation of all war
activities, continue these activities, execute the occupation of
Syrian territory and are proceeding in the direction of Damascus.

The Government of the Soviet Union warns the Government of
Israel that it will bear all the serious responsibility for the treachery
and for the flagrant violation of the Security Council decision.
Should Israel not immediately stop its war activities, the Soviet
Union, together with other peace-loving States, will apply sanc-
tions, with all resulting consequences.

The Government of the Soviet Union announces that, in view of the
continued aggression by Israel against Arab States in flagrant violation of the Security Council decision, the Government of the Soviet
Union has decided to break off diplomatic relations with Israel.

Between June 11 and 13, all States that had participated in
the June 9 meeting followed Moscow's lead. The rupture of
diplomatic relations with Israel was palpably the only immedi-

ate help Moscow and its satellites were able and ready to render the Arab States to prop up their shattered prestige and, incidentally, that of the Communist bloc.

On June 13, when they must have known that the war was over, the Russians, to show their concern for Syria, took the unusual step of sending a note to a Government with which they had broken off diplomatic relations three days earlier. The note was sent through the Finnish Embassy in Israel, which had taken over the task of representing Soviet interests. (The Netherlands Government agreed to represent Israel's interests in the Soviet Union.) The Soviet note said:

> According to information received, Israel continues the invasion of Syria. On the evening and night of June 11, Israeli troops occupied the settlements of Rafiq, Jawada and Dzhisr-Istabel. The original Arab population is driven away from Gaza, Jerusalem and other regions. For the regions taken by the Israeli troops an occupation administration has been established. Military governors have been appointed for towns and districts. All seems to indicate that the same practice as that adopted by the Hitlerite invaders in regions which were the victims of aggression during World War II is being applied. The Government of Israel should have no illusions. Israel will be made entirely responsible for the criminal acts it commits.

> By continually showing its contempt for the Security Council decisions regarding immediate termination of all war operations, the Government of Israel has, apparently, decided to test the patience of peace-loving countries. By acting in this way, it commits a fatal miscalculation. Israel takes upon itself the whole burden of responsibility and punishment for its treachery, for all the crimes it has committed against peace and the interest of the people.

The Government of Israel answered on June 16—through the Netherlands Embassy in Moscow—as follows:

The allegations contained in the message are unfounded. They are based entirely on statements made by Arab sources for propaganda purposes, and it is regrettable that these false, tendentious statements should be given further currency by the Government of the Soviet Union.

The Government of Israel expresses its profound revulsion at the accusations voiced by the Soviet Government charging Israel with practices similar to those adopted by Hitlerite invaders. The Hitlerite war was against the peoples of Europe, following the pact concluded between the Soviet Union and Nazi Germany in September 1939, and it led to the slaughter of six million Jews and millions of other people in Europe.

Having severed diplomatic relations with Israel, it is obviously difficult for Soviet representatives to verify at firsthand the truth of these Arab-inspired allegations. In fact, the Israeli Army has scrupulously observed the cease-fire on the Syrian front and on all other fronts. That this is so was confirmed again in the report presented by the Secretary General of the United Nations at the session of the Security Council held on June 13, 1967.

The Arab population in all the areas under Israel is resuming its normal life. All public services are already operating. A certain number of civilians and soldiers who have discarded their arms and uniforms have moved to the east bank, returning to their families. Others have moved in the opposite direction and crossed into Israeli-controlled territory. Israeli authorities have not prevented this movement.

During the last nineteen years, the Government of Israel has held out its hand in friendship to the Arab countries and expressed its readiness to meet with them and to discuss peace at any place, at any time and without prior conditions. This remains Israel's position and the Government of Israel greatly regrets that the Soviet Union, by identifying itself with the extreme and belligerent policy of the Arab States, is in fact actively encouraging the Arab countries to even further intransigence and the creation of an atmosphere in which it is more difficult to arrive at a just peace.

Israel's note, dated June 16, could only be delivered by the Netherlands Ambassador in Moscow to Deputy Foreign Minister Aleksandr Orlov on June 20. In the meantime, Kosygin, on June 17, arrived in New York to attend the General Assembly and to renew the Soviet demand for a condemnation of Israel and for acceptance of a resolution ordering Israel to withdraw its forces to the June 5 frontiers. He asked that the Security Council "undertake immediate effective measures in order to eliminate all consequences of the aggression committed by Israel." Orlov told the Netherlands Ambassador that Kosygin's statement in the United Nations was the best answer to Israel's note. He quoted reports from the American, British and French press to prove the Soviet note's contention that the situation in Israeli-occupied territories was bad. He was shocked by the fact that Israel's note had mentioned the Molotov-Ribbentrop pact. The Netherlands Ambassador gained the impression that the Russians were not interested in a further exchange of notes.

The documents quoted in this chapter speak for themselves and need no comment. What remains to be added is an evaluation of this last stage of Israeli-Soviet relations and an interpretation of the break in diplomatic relations as it was seen at the time in Jerusalem.

This last stage was characterized by Moscow's complete identification of its interests in the Middle East with those of Egypt and Syria, and by a tactical use of the instability in the area and the existence of the Israeli-Arab tension to reduce these Arab countries to an even larger measure of dependence on the Soviet Union. With this aim in mind, the Soviet Union created a war psychosis in the area by spreading false reports about alleged Israeli troop concentrations along the Syrian borders. Nasser, in his resignation speech of June 9, admitted openly that Soviet reports about Israeli concentrations in the north had encouraged him to take the steps he took. The Russians had apparently made a few miscalculations. They probably did not expect Nasser to take the fatal step of closing the Straits of Tiran. They certainly did not expect him to try to bring the Soviet Union actively into the war by lying about American and British air cover for Israel. And they could hardly have expected that the Egyptian army and air force would disintegrate so quickly and completely in spite of the most advanced military equipment worth many hundreds of millions of rubles supplied to them by the Soviets, nor that a large part of this matériel would fall intact into Israel's hands. The defeat must have angered Moscow even more because of its psychological effect on the attitude of the Arab peoples toward the Soviet Union. Having been led to believe that the Soviet Union would come to their aid in the hour of need, the Arabs felt they had been let down and consequently lost confidence in Moscow's promises. The severance of diplomatic relations was, therefore, both an act of wrath and an attempt to prove to the Arabs that the Soviet Union was fully behind them and was working for their good. The replenishment of the empty Egyptian arsenal, the continuation of badly needed economic assistance to the Arab countries and the sending of the Red fleet into the Mediterranean Sea were further proof. They were also steps taken to keep the Middle East in the ferment of tension necessary to further Soviet aims in the area.[37]

---

37. This account actually ends with the rupture of diplomatic relations between the Soviet Union and Israel on June 10, 1967. It does not deal, therefore, with the continuation of the Security Council discussions which were characterized by the Soviet delegate's vituperative attacks on Israel and his desperate and unsuccessful attempts to persuade the Council to condemn Israel as aggressor and force it to withdraw to the pre-June 5 line. (Between June 6 and 14, when the Council ended its deliberations, Fedorenko intervened not less than 45 times, and his Bulgarian assistant 28 times.) Neither does the account deal with the Special Session of the General Assembly that took place between June 17 and July 21, 1967, or with the Security Council meetings between October 24 and November 22, 1967, which proved equally unsuccessful for the Soviet Union.

XXII

The future of Soviet-Israeli relations

While there is no doubt that, ultimately, relations between Jerusalem and Moscow will be resumed, no one at this moment can predict with certainty when this will occur. The initiative is clearly with the side that decided to make the break in the first place, and, for the time being, that side seems too deeply involved to be able to extricate itself from the situation into which it has blundered—mainly because of a number of political miscalculations. However, Soviet policy was basically never one of petrified positions. On the contrary, it has always been characterized by a high degree of elasticity—the example of the Soviet retreat in the Cuban crisis is sufficiently eloquent—and it can be assumed that this quality will eventually enable Moscow to find the way to a renewal of diplomatic relations with Israel without too great a loss of face.

The important question is not when, nor by what face-saving gesture, this will happen, but rather what will be the content of the renewed relations. Will they constitute just a continuation of the unhealthy, frustrating, sterile and irritating situation which existed during most of the two decades—at least since the spring of 1954—described in this account? Or is there a good chance that things may take a turn for the better? Is there hope that Moscow's one-sided approach to the problems of the Middle East will be replaced by objectivity, that fruitful cooperation will develop in trade, cultural exchanges and other spheres, and that political relations between the two States will become as normal and correct as those that the Soviet Union maintains with other States that have different regimes and ideologies?

There are certainly many more reasons against than for a positive answer to these questions. Moscow's military and economic involvement on the Arab side is so deep that any change of its Middle East policy may result in a heavy loss of prestige not only in the Arab world but also far beyond it. The struggle for influence in the Middle East must be viewed not in isolation but as a part of the East-West "cold war," in which the Soviet Union is not likely to abandon any foothold once gained. The irrational element of Russian anti-Semitism was strengthened by the official anti-Israeli propaganda conducted before, during and after the Six-Day War and is likely to become even more deeply rooted during the period of absence of relations with Israel. Equating Jews with Nazis and branding them as perpetrators of the crime of genocide may prove too difficult even for the powerful Soviet propaganda machinery to explain away overnight, and the atmosphere created by these slanders will hardly be conducive to a change of attitude toward Israel. There are many other factors to be considered: the Soviet Union's interest in the Suez Canal, particularly as long as the conflict in Vietnam continues; its interest in depriving the Western Powers of their approach to Arab oil, or, at least, in making it more difficult; the chances of entering the Indian Ocean in strength after the British departure from Aden and southern Arabia; and so forth.

Yet, in spite of all this, the fatalistic attitude often met within Israel ("Whatever we do, it will always be wrong in Moscow's eyes") is basically wrong.

Czechoslovakia's late Foreign Minister, Jan Masaryk, who

knew the Russians well, once said, "Soviet policy is 90 percent tactics and only 10 percent ideology." The truth is that, while based on a clear-cut ideology, Soviet foreign policy was never hindered by ideological considerations. Communist parties in Arab countries were conveniently forgotten and the Russian reader was not even told that his Egyptian and other comrades were languishing in Nasser's jails and were being executed by firing squads under the orders of Fascist military juntas, equally conveniently presented as leaders of progressive national liberation movements. No other country in the world has ever left its foreign-policy planners so much freedom of maneuver. There is a general plan and no move to achieve its aim is barred. It is a catch-as-catch-can policy. When it suited Moscow's immediate interests, Molotov did not hesitate to sign a pact with Ribbentrop. There are no fixed rules, no lofty, inviolable principles, no ideological inhibitions. In other words, the static element in Soviet foreign policy is much more limited, and the field of flexibility much larger, than in the foreign policy of any other Great Power. This applies also to Soviet Middle East policy and the fact that for many years—at least since 1954—Moscow has been following a certain line does not exclude the possibility of an unheralded change of that line if and when the Russians find that it would serve their purpose better.

Hegemony in one form or another over the Middle East has always been one of the imperial interests of Russia, whether Czarist or Soviet. It should be remembered that, when signing the Ribbentrop-Molotov pact, the Russians insisted that the Middle East be recognized as their sphere of influence. Also noteworthy is the number of times the Russians have repeated and stressed, especially in notes addressed to Israel and Turkey, that the Middle East is an area "in the immediate vicinity of the Soviet borders." To eliminate the influence of other Big Powers in the area and supplant it with its own decisive influence has been and remains the Soviet Union's basic aim in the Middle East. To achieve it—as well as any other Soviet aim—all means, in Moscow's view, are permissible. For almost two decades, this has included the exploitation of the tragic conflict between

Arabs and Jews. Because they found the existence of this conflict useful, the Russians did not try to solve it by constructive
suggestions or by using their influence in the right quarters at
the right time. Instead, they did all in their power to keep the
tension near boiling point and, having staked everything on the
Arab card, kept encouraging their protégés in Cairo and Damascus in their hostility toward Israel.

There are, for the time being, no visible signs or indications
of a change of heart, and there is very little concrete ground for
optimism. Yet, several points should be remembered:

1. Soviet policy in relation to the Arab States and Israel was
a special version of the stick-and-carrot game. The Arabs were
given the carrot of military and economic assistance and unlimited political support, while the stick—in the form of arms supplies to the Arabs, no trade, hostile propaganda and the use of
the veto in the Security Council whenever the Arabs faced the
danger of being condemned—was Israel's lot. However, from
time to time Israel was also shown the carrot—how many times
in the course of the two decades were Israeli representatives
told that relations were, in fact, "normal and correct" and could
develop further, if . . . ? And occasionally the Arabs were made
aware of the existence of the stick. This game is too integral a
part of Soviet policy for it to be entirely abandoned if and when
relations with Israel are resumed. But the overriding element of
flexibility in Soviet policy does not exclude a reversed use of
both the stick and the carrot, under new conditions. This, of
course, is purely theoretical, but what can be expected is that
changed conditions may bring about a revision of the rules of
the game, possibly leading to a more impartial use of both stick
and carrot.

2. The Russians, as we have seen, have made several miscalculations. They overplayed their hand and became victims of
their own bluff. If we are right in the generally accepted assumption that the Soviet Union is not interested in an armed conflict
which could lead to a military confrontation with the West and
a global conflagration, its policy in the Middle East ever since
1955 has to be defined as at least hazardous. From then on, the
Soviet bloc has been pouring arms into Arab countries. It has

been established that even in 1961 Soviet experts had begun to tutor Egyptian army planners who were preparing to overrun Israel. We know from maps found at Kuneitra that Soviet military experts had a hand in preparing Syrian plans for an attack against Israel that was aimed at occupying Tel Aviv and Jerusalem. As late as May 28, 1967, the Soviet Defense Minister, Marshal Grechko, broadcast from Cairo:

> The Soviet Union, its army, people and Government will stand by the Arabs and will continue to encourage and support them. We are and we shall continue to be your true friends. We, as armed forces, will continue to assist you and this is also the policy of the Soviet people, Party and Government. In the name of the Ministry of Defense and on behalf of the Soviet people, we wish you success and victory against imperialism and Zionism. We are with you, ready to help you at any time.

The realization of the fact, only a week later, that the promised help did not go so far as they had been led to believe was certainly a deep shock to the Arabs. Of course, they received and accepted new arms and new economic aid from the Soviet Union and other Eastern bloc countries after the Six-Day War, but this was obviously help that came too late. It could hardly be expected to heal the acute crisis of confidence created by the awareness of the fact that it was Moscow's encouragement that led Nasser to his fatal decisions, and the realization that in spite of that encouragement, Moscow was not ready to enter the war actively on their side when those decisions led the Arabs into catastrophe.

It was known even before Nasser's resignation speech of June 9, 1967, that Moscow was the source of the "information" about Israeli troop concentrations along the Syrian border on which Nasser—and, after him, Hussein—had taken action. Nor did the Russians leave much room for doubt about the authorship of the rumor. Ambassador Chuvakhin refused Prime Minister Eshkol's offer to accompany him to the Syrian border area and to see for himself if there were any truth to the allegation, and Fedorenko, when offered facts by Gideon Rafael, answered cynically: "Who is looking for facts in the Security Council?" Nasser's reproach of June 9 was probably not the only one the Russians had heard.

All this must have resulted in a rather radical change in the psychological relations between Moscow and the Arab States. The credibility of Moscow's promises must have dropped so low in Arab eyes that, at least temporarily, the loss of trust seemed almost irreparable. At the same time, the Arabs were made aware of the limit beyond which the Russians were not ready to go in order not to risk an open conflict with the United States. As a result, Soviet prestige suffered. This was on one hand; on the other, the complete collapse of the Arab military machine after twelve years of massive Russian arms supplies and other forms of military assistance must have come as a shock to Moscow, and it is hardly conceivable that it did not lead to second thoughts in the Kremlin.

3. Finally, since June 10, 1967, the realities in the Middle East have been very different from those existing before June 5, and they will never be the same again. On the contrary, as time goes on the new realities become more and more stabilized. It would, of course, be pure speculation to try to predict what conclusions the Russians are likely to draw from the new situation. Outwardly, they do not seem to admit the necessity of any change in their Middle East policy. While the steps they have taken since the Six-Day War can, to quote Robert McNamara, the former U.S. Secretary of Defense, be characterized as "primarily diplomatic gestures to recoup political defeats," they have nevertheless been steps along the old line. Yet it is difficult to believe that after the lesson of June 1967, the Russians could continue their old policy without a basic reevaluation of their position in the area. It is more likely that the process of rethinking has already started inside the Kremlin.

In this reexamination, as in all other evaluations of its global policy, the Soviet Union must be taking into account its own changed position in the world. The rapid escalation of the growing danger of a conflagration with China—accompanied as it is by growing signs of Moscow's loss of ground inside the Communist camp—forces the Soviet Union to mend its fences with the

West and particularly with the United States. That means that Moscow must, today, be even more careful than before to avoid the slightest danger of a possible involvement in an armed conflict with Washington.

This should, logically, lead to greater Soviet interest in a higher level of stability in the Middle East, which can be achieved solely by deemphasizing the Arab-Israeli conflict. It can only be hoped that past experience has proved convincingly to the Soviets that their completely one-sided attitude, while giving them certain advantages in the Arab world, did not by any means give them, simultaneously, the ability to control events in this part of the world or even internal development inside most of the Arab countries. In some of the Communist countries, opposition to this one-sided Soviet policy has already been openly expressed. True, it was suppressed, but it is not dead. It exists in the Soviet Union also. It becomes more and more difficult to believe that Soviet leaders should, even in the present circumstances, fail to realize that a larger degree of objectivity would not only serve to bring nearer the pacification of the Middle East but would also, in fact, strengthen Soviet prestige and respectability in the world, would give Moscow a moral standing in international discussions of the Middle East problems, and would help to minimize the danger of an East West conflagration, an aim which should be more important to Moscow's leaders today than ever before.

But does the Soviet Union cherish logic? Does it really want peace? And will the United States show sufficient firmness in its stand to force the Russians' thinking in this direction? That, of course, remains the big question of our times, and the answer will determine much more than the future of the relations between Moscow and Jerusalem.

Oslo, March 1970

BIBLIOGRAPHY

Allen, Robert Loring. *Middle Eastern Economic Relations with the Soviet Union, Eastern Europe and Mainland China.* Charlottesville: University of Virginia Press, 1958.

Ben-Asher, A. *Yakhasei Khutz shel Israel 1948-1953* [Israel's Foreign Relations, 1948-1953]. Tel Aviv, 1956.

Bol'shaya Sovietskaya Entsiklopediya [Great Soviet Encyclopedia]. Union of Soviet Socialist Republics, 1958.

Bolton, A. *Soviet Middle East Studies.* London, 1959.

Demshenko, P. *Sirijskaya Respublika na Strazhe svoyei Nezavisimosti* [The Syrian Republic Guarding Her Independence]. Moscow, 1967.

Dokumenty Vneshnei Politiki SSSR [Documents of the Foreign Policy of the U.S.S.R.]. Moscow, 1957.

Eliav, Binyamin. "The Russian Drive into the Middle East." *Israel Magazine,* January 1969.

Eytan, Walter. *The First Ten Years.* New York: Simon & Schuster, 1958.

Hurewitz, Jacob C., ed. *Soviet Rivalry in the Middle East.* New York: Columbia University Press, 1969.

Ivanov and Sheinis. *Gosudarstvo Israil, yevo polozheniye i politika* [The State of Israel, Its Situation and Policy]. Moscow, 1958.

Krammer, A. "When the Soviet Bloc Supported Israel." *The Winer Library Bulletin*, Summer, 1968.

Lang, Nicolas. "Responsabilitiés Soviétiques au Proche-Orient." *Est & Ouest*, July 1969.

Laqueur, Walter Z. *The Arab Cold War*. London: George Waldenfeld & Nicolson, Ltd., 1965.

————. *Communism and Nationalism in the Middle East*. New York: Frederick A. Praeger, Inc., 1959.

————. *The Road to War*. London, 1968.

————. *The Soviet Union and the Middle East*. New York: Frederick A. Praeger, Inc., 1959.

————, ed. *The Middle East in Transition*. London: Routledge & Kegan Paul, Ltd., 1958. (Particularly contributions by A. Bennigsen, "The 'National Front' in Communist Strategy in the Middle East"; H. Carrère d'Encausse, "The Background of Soviet Policy in the Middle East"; I. Spector, "Soviet Cultural Propaganda in the Middle East"; L. N. Vatolina, "The Growth of National Consciousness among the Arab Peoples, 1945-1955"; and G. Wheeler, "Recent Soviet Attitudes towards Islam."

Lenczowski, George. *The Middle East in World Affairs*. Ithaca, N.Y.: Cornell University Press, 1956.

Lutski, V. B. *Anglijskij i Amerikanskij Imperializm na Blizhnem Vostoke* [British and American Imperialism in the Near East]. Moscow, 1948.

————. *Liga Arabskikh Gosudarstev* [League of Arab States]. Moscow, 1946.

————. *Palestinskaya Problema* [The Palestine Problem]. Moscow, 1946.

————. *Angliya i Egipet* [England and Egypt]. Moscow, 1947.

Meir, Golda. *This Is Our Strength*. New York: The Macmillan Company, 1962.

Milogradov, P. V. *Arabski Vostok v Mezhdunarodnykh Otnosheniakh* [The Arab East in International Relations]. Moscow, 1946.

Pennar, J. "Soviet Road to Damascus." *Mizan Newsletter,* January 1967.

Primakov, E. *Strany Arabii i Kolonializm* [Arab States and Colonialism]. Moscow, 1956.

Schwadron, B. "The Soviet Union in the Middle East." *Current Affairs,* February 1967.

Schweitzer, K. "Soviet Policy towards Israel 1946-1952." *Mizan Newsletter,* January 1967.

Shalev, Mordekhai. *A Study of Soviet-Israeli Relations.* Washington, D.C., 1954.

Spector, I. *The Soviet Union and the Muslim World.* Seattle: University of Washington, 1959.

Stevens, Georgiana G., ed. *The American Assembly: The United States and the Middle East.* Englewood Cliffs, N. J.: Prentice-Hall, Inc., 1964.

Teller, Judd. *The Kremlin, the Jews, and the Middle East.* New York: Thoman Yoseloff, Inc., 1957.

Vatolina, L. *Araby v Borbe za Nezavisimost* [Arabs in the Struggle for Independence]. Moscow, 1957.

———. *Borba Narodov Blizhnego Vostoka za Mir* [Struggle of the Nations of the Near East for Peace]. Moscow, 1953.

———. *Sovremennij Egipet* [Contemporary Egypt]. Moscow, 1949.

Wheeler, G. "Russia and the Middle East." *Political Quarterly,* April-June, 1957.

This list is, by necessity, only a selective bibliography. Russian and Hebrew newspapers and periodicals published in the period between 1947 and 1967—a rather wide range—were also used as sources. When these publications were quoted, their names and dates may be found in the text. Another invaluable aid were the published stenographic minutes of U.N. General Assembly and Security Council meetings, as well as certain documents in the archives of the Israel Ministry for Foreign Affairs, to which the author was kindly given access.

INDEX